Microsoft Azure

From Basics to Expert Proficiency

Contents

Introduction

Cloud computing has fundamentally transformed the way businesses and individuals approach computing infrastructure. Among the numerous cloud service providers, Microsoft Azure stands out with its comprehensive suite of cloud services that cater to a wide range of requirements, from computing and storage to networking and artificial intelligence.

Microsoft Azure, launched in 2010, has continually evolved to become one of the leading cloud platforms available today. It offers an extensive set of services that can empower organizations to build, deploy, and manage applications through Microsoft's global network of data centers. The platform not only supports a variety of tools and frameworks, but it is also designed to facilitate flexibility, scalability, and innovation.

This book, "Microsoft Azure: From Basics to Expert Proficiency," aims to provide a detailed guide to understanding and mastering Azure. It is structured to help readers build a solid foundation in Azure, develop advanced skills, and adopt best practices for effective cloud management. Each chapter is dedicated to a specific aspect of Azure, ensuring that readers can progressively enhance their knowledge and expertise.

We begin with an introductory chapter that covers the essential concepts of cloud computing and provides an overview of Microsoft Azure. Following this, we delve into the architecture and services offered by Azure, giving you insights into how you can leverage Azure regions, availability zones, and various architectural components to build resilient applications.

Subsequent chapters guide you through the deployment and management of Azure resources, providing practical advice and step-by-step instructions for using Azure's tools and services. Networking is another critical aspect covered in detail, discussing how to create and configure virtual networks, security groups, and other networking essentials.

Storage solutions in Azure are explored in depth, giving an understanding of different storage options and their appropriate use cases. Security and compliance are paramount concerns for any organization, and this book dedicates a chapter to these topics, explaining how to secure your data, comply with various regulations, and leverage Azure's built-in security features.

Identity and access management is another vital area, with a chapter devoted to Azure Active Directory, role-based access control, and other identity management features. This book also covers Azure DevOps and application lifecycle management, demonstrating how to implement CI/CD pipelines, manage artifacts, and ensure quality in your development process.

Monitoring and optimizing your Azure environment is crucial for maintaining performance and cost-efficiency. We provide detailed information on using Azure Monitor, Application Insights, and other tools to track and optimize your resources.

Lastly, we present real-world case studies and best practices that highlight successful Azure implementations and provide practical lessons learned from the field.

By the end of this book, readers will have a comprehensive understanding of Microsoft Azure and its capabilities. Whether you are an IT professional, a developer, or someone looking to expand your cloud computing knowledge, this book will equip you with the skills and knowledge necessary to excel in the Azure ecosystem.

Chapter 1

Introduction to Microsoft Azure

Cloud computing has revolutionized IT infrastructure, offering scalable, on-demand resources over the internet. Microsoft Azure is one of the leading cloud platforms, providing an extensive range of services that include computing, networking, databases, analytics, and artificial intelligence. This chapter introduces the fundamental concepts of cloud computing, explores Azure's global infrastructure, explains essential Azure terminology, and guides readers through setting up a free account and navigating the Azure Portal. Key services and basic command line tools are also covered, enabling readers to create and manage their first Azure resources effectively.

1.1 What is Cloud Computing?

Cloud computing is the delivery of computing services—including servers, storage, databases, networking, software, analytics, and intelligence—over the internet ("the cloud") to offer faster innovation, flexible resources, and economies of scale. These services are typically offered on a pay-as-you-go basis, helping organizations lower their operating costs, run their infrastructure more efficiently, and scale as their business needs change.

Key Characteristics of Cloud Computing:

- **On-Demand Self-Service:** Users can provision computing capabilities, such as server time and network storage, as needed automatically without requiring human intervention with each service provider.
- **Broad Network Access:** Capabilities are available over the network and accessed through standard mechanisms that promote use by heterogeneous thin or thick client platforms (e.g., mobile phones, tablets, laptops, and workstations).
- **Resource Pooling:** The provider's computing resources are pooled to serve multiple consumers using a multi-tenant model, with different physical and virtual resources dynamically assigned and reassigned according to consumer demand. There is a sense of location independence in that the customer generally has no control or knowledge over the exact location of the provided resources but may be able to specify location at a higher level of abstraction (e.g., country, state, or datacenter).
- **Rapid Elasticity:** Capabilities can be elastically provisioned and released, in some cases automatically, to scale rapidly outward and inward commensurate with demand. To the consumer, the capabilities available for provisioning often appear to be unlimited and can be appropriated in any quantity at any time.
- **Measured Service:** Cloud systems automatically control and optimize resource use by leveraging a metering capability at some level of abstraction appropriate to the type of service (e.g., storage, processing, bandwidth, and active user accounts). Resource usage can be monitored, controlled, and reported, providing transparency for both the provider and consumer of the utilized service.

Service Models of Cloud Computing:

- **Infrastructure as a Service (IaaS):** This is the most basic category of cloud computing services. With IaaS, you rent IT infrastructure—servers and virtual machines (VMs), storage, networks, and operating systems—from a cloud provider on a pay-as-you-go basis. Examples include Amazon Web Services (AWS) EC2, Microsoft Azure Virtual Machines, and Google Cloud Engine.

- **Platform as a Service (PaaS):** Platform as a service refers to cloud computing services that supply an on-demand environment for developing, testing, delivering, and managing software applications. PaaS is designed to make it easier for developers to create web or mobile apps without worrying about setting up or managing the underlying infrastructure of servers, storage, network, and databases needed for development. Examples include Microsoft Azure App Services, Google App Engine, and AWS Elastic Beanstalk.

- **Software as a Service (SaaS):** SaaS enables delivery of software applications over the internet, on-demand, and typically on a subscription basis. With SaaS, cloud providers host and manage the software application and underlying infrastructure, and handle any maintenance, such as software upgrades and security patching. Users connect to the application over the internet, usually with a web browser on their phone, tablet, or PC. Examples include Microsoft Office 365, Google Workspace (formerly G Suite), and Salesforce.

Deployment Models of Cloud Computing:

- **Public Cloud:** Public clouds are owned and operated by third-party cloud service providers, which deliver their computing resources, like servers and storage, over the Internet. Microsoft Azure is an example of a public cloud. With a public cloud, all hardware, software, and other supporting infrastructure are owned and managed by the cloud provider. You access these services and manage your account using a web browser.

- **Private Cloud:** A private cloud refers to cloud computing resources used exclusively by a single business or organization. A private cloud can be physically located on the company's on-site datacenter. Some companies also pay third-party service providers to host their private cloud. A private cloud is one in which the services and infrastructure are maintained on a private network.

- **Hybrid Cloud:** Hybrid clouds combine public and private clouds, bound together by technology that allows data and applications to be shared between them. By allowing data and applications to move between private and public clouds, a hybrid cloud gives your business greater flexibility, more deployment options, and helps optimize your existing infrastructure, security, and compliance.

Benefits of Cloud Computing:

- **Cost Efficiency:** Eliminates the capital expense of buying hardware and software and setting up and running on-site datacenters.
- **Speed:** Most cloud computing services are provided self-service and on demand, so even vast amounts of computing resources can be provisioned in minutes.
- **Global Scale:** The benefits include the ability to scale elastically. In cloud speak, that means delivering the right amount of IT resources—for example, more or less computing power, storage, bandwidth—right when it is needed and from the right geographic location.
- **Productivity:** On-site datacenters typically require a lot of "racking and stacking"—hardware setup, software patching, and other time-consuming IT management chores. Cloud computing removes the need for many of these tasks, so IT teams can spend time on achieving more important business goals.
- **Performance:** The major cloud services run on a worldwide network of secure datacenters, which are upgraded to the latest generation of fast and efficient computing hardware. This offers several benefits over a single corporate datacenter, including reduced network latency for applications and greater economies of scale.
- **Security:** Many cloud providers offer a set of policies, technologies, and controls that strengthen your security posture overall, helping protect your data, apps, and infrastructure from potential threats.

1.2 Introduction to Microsoft Azure

Microsoft Azure, commonly referred to as Azure, is a comprehensive and ever-expanding set of cloud services that enables organizations to build, deploy, and manage applications through Microsoft's global network of data centers. Azure offers a myriad of services ranging from basic virtual machines (VMs) to sophisticated tools for artificial intelligence (AI), Internet of Things (IoT), and advanced analytics.

Azure's architecture is built around a variety of components that are designed to provide scalable, reliable, and secure cloud computing solutions. The platform's core functionalities can be grouped into several categories:

1. Compute: Azure provides multiple computing options, including VMs, container orchestration with Kubernetes, and PaaS (Platform as a Service) elements like Azure App Services. VMs in Azure allow you to deploy Windows or Linux operating systems and scale vertically or horizontally as needed. Azure Kubernetes Service (AKS) simplifies deployment, management, and operations of Kubernetes. App Services enable you to build and host web apps, mobile backends, and RESTful APIs, with auto-scaling and high availability.

2. Storage: Azure offers scalable, redundant, and secure storage options. Core storage services include Blob Storage for unstructured data, File Storage for managed file shares, and Disk Storage for VM disks. Azure Storage is designed to be massively scalable and high-performing for a variety of data persistence needs.

3. Networking: To connect and secure your resources, Azure provides comprehensive networking capabilities. Azure Virtual Network (VNet) allows you to establish private networks within the Azure environment, similar to on-premises networks. Azure Load Balancer maximizes the availability and reliability of applications by distributing network traffic. Azure VPN Gateway and Azure ExpressRoute facilitate secure and scalable communication between on-premises infrastructure and Azure datacenters.

4. Databases: Azure supports several database technologies, including Azure SQL Database, Cosmos DB, and managed instances of popular databases like MySQL and PostgreSQL. Azure SQL Database is a fully managed relational database with built-in intelligence that learns and adapts with the usage pattern. Cosmos DB is a globally distributed, multi-model database service with low latency and high availability.

5. Analytics: Azure provides a range of services for data analytics and business intelligence, such as Azure Synapse Analytics, Azure Databricks, and Azure HDInsight. These tools allow for the processing and analysis of vast amounts of data, enabling advanced insights and data-driven decision-making. Azure Machine Learning, part of the analytics offerings, empowers data scientists to build, train, and deploy machine learning models at scale.

6. AI and Cognitive Services: Azure facilitates the integration of advanced AI functionalities with services like Azure Cognitive Services, Azure Bot Service, and Azure Machine Learning. Azure Cognitive Services offers pre-built APIs for vision, speech, language, knowledge, and search capabilities, enabling the development of intelligent applications.

7. Identity and Security: Authentication and security are critical in any cloud environment. Azure Active Directory (Azure AD) is a cloud-based identity and access management service that helps employees sign in and access resources. Multi-Factor Authentication (MFA) and Role-Based Access Control (RBAC) enhance security by ensuring that the right users have appropriate access to resources.

Understanding the underlying infrastructure and services is crucial for effectively leveraging Azure. A critical component of Azure's global architecture is its datacenter regions. Each region is a set of datacenters deployed within a latency-defined perimeter, interconnected through a dedicated regional low-latency network. Azure operates in over 60 regions globally, each providing multiple availability zones to ensure high availability.

Azure's platform is designed to be both developer-friendly and enterprise-ready. It supports a wide variety of programming languages, frameworks, and tools, streamlining the development and deployment processes for both new and existing applications. Developers can use their preferred tools such as Visual Studio, Visual Studio Code, or integrated development environments (IDEs) with Azure integrations to build applications.

To interact with Azure, users have multiple interfaces at their disposal:

- - **Azure Portal:** A web-based, unified console for managing Azure resources. It provides a graphical interface to create, configure, and manage Azure services and monitor resource health and performance.

- - **Azure CLI:** A command-line tool for managing Azure resources. It enables automation and scripting of repetitive tasks, making it useful for DevOps practices.

- - **Azure PowerShell:** A set of cmdlets for managing Azure resources directly from the Windows PowerShell or PowerShell

Core. It is particularly beneficial for those who are already familiar with PowerShell scripting.

- - **Azure REST API:** Allows integration of Azure services with external applications, providing fine-grained programmatic control over Azure resources.

Understanding the concept of *Resource Groups* is essential for efficient Azure management. A resource group is a container that holds related resources for an Azure solution. You typically place resources sharing the same lifecycle, permissions, and policies in a resource group to simplify resource management. The Azure Resource Manager (ARM) is the deployment and management service for Azure, which provides a consistent management layer for creating, updating, and deleting resources within your Azure subscription.

Azure implements a robust access and authentication framework through Role-Based Access Control (RBAC). RBAC allows you to segregate duties within your team and grant only the amount of access necessary for users to perform their jobs. By default, Azure includes several predefined roles such as Owner, Contributor, Reader, and User Access Administrator, which can be assigned to users, groups, and service principals.

Microsoft Azure stands as a leading cloud platform that provides a broad spectrum of services tailored to diverse business needs. Its global infrastructure, comprehensive service offerings, and versatile tools make it an essential component for modern IT environments. Through an understanding of its core capabilities and integration mechanisms, organizations can harness the full potential of Azure to build resilient, scalable, and innovative solutions.

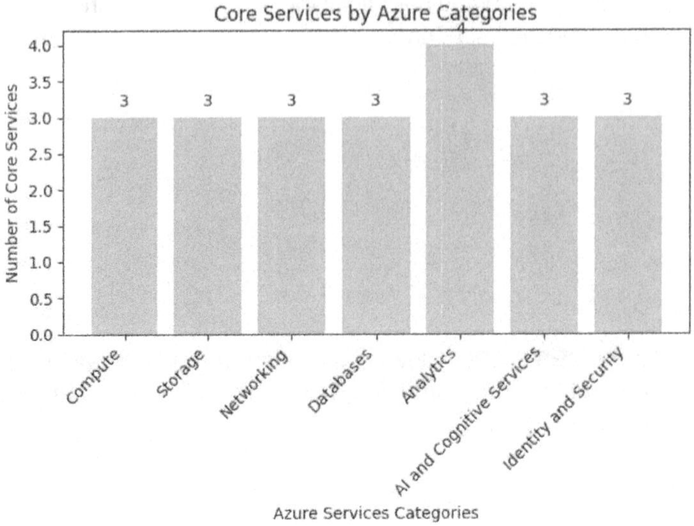

1.3 Azure Global Infrastructure

The global infrastructure of Microsoft Azure is meticulously designed to provide high availability, reliability, and scalability for a diverse range of cloud services. This infrastructure comprises datacenters, regions, availability zones, and geo-redundant storage, among other components. Understanding these elements is crucial for efficiently leveraging Azure's capabilities and ensuring optimal performance and resilience for applications.

Azure regions are geographically distinct locations where Microsoft has established multiple datacenters. As of the latest data, Azure operates over 60 regions worldwide, more than any other cloud provider. Each region is strategically positioned to support compliance, residency requirements, and to minimize latency by serving customers from a geographically proximate location.

The concept of **Azure regions** can be further dissected into several critical aspects:

- **Datacenters:** Each Azure region consists of one or more datacenters, which are highly secured buildings equipped with sophisticated power, cooling, and networking facilities. These datacenters are interconnected through a private high-speed fiber network, ensuring seamless data transfer and replication.

- **Paired Regions:** Azure regions are typically paired within the same geography, which allows for disaster recovery and data residency. For example, if a service or data needs to be replicated within the United States, it may be paired between the Eastern US and Western US regions. This pairing helps organizations meet compliance and data sovereignty requirements while offering business continuity during major incidents.

- **Availability Zones:** Within some regions, Azure provides Availability Zones, which are physically separate locations within the region. Each Availability Zone is an independent failure domain, with its own power, cooling, and networking infrastructure. Deploying applications across different Availability Zones can enhance resilience against localized failures.

A visual representation of Azure's global infrastructure can be found in the Azure portal, where an interactive map showcases all active regions, paired regions, and datacenter locations. Azure also provides public roadmaps indicating upcoming datacenter launches, helping organizations plan their deployment strategies.

Another cornerstone of Azure's infrastructure is the **global network** that interconnects datacenters and regions. This network spans over 165,000 miles of fiber, providing a backbone for high-speed data transfer and low-latency communication across the globe. It is engineered to handle the robust demands of services like Azure Storage, Azure SQL Database, and high-volume networking services. The network's architecture supports redundancy and fault tolerance, ensuring constant availability even during maintenance or unexpected outages.

Azure's commitment to data residency and compliance is reflected in its infrastructure offerings. Data processed in an Azure region is not automatically moved outside that region without explicit direction from the customer. This assurance supports various compliance needs, such as GDPR in Europe, which mandates stringent data protection and privacy standards.

Resiliency is another fundamental attribute of Azure's global infrastructure. Azure employs various failure recovery strategies, such as data replication and service redundancy across Availability Zones and regions. In the event of a failure in one zone or region, applications can failover to another zone or region with minimal disruption. This resiliency is particularly critical for enterprise applications requiring high uptime and business continuity.

Azure also offers a range of geo-redundant storage options to enhance data durability and availability. For instance, the **Geo-Redundant Storage (GRS)** and **Read-Access Geo-Redundant Storage (RA-GRS)** options replicate data across primary and secondary regions, ensuring that data remains accessible even in the case of a regional outage. The following snippet provides an example of configuring geo-redundant storage using Azure CLI:

```
# Create a resource group
az group create --name myResourceGroup --location eastus

# Create a storage account with geo-redundant storage
az storage account create --name mystorageaccount \
    --resource-group myResourceGroup \
    --location eastus \
    --sku Standard_GRS
```

Additionally, **content delivery** is optimized through Azure's extensive Content Delivery Network (CDN), which uses a distributed set of nodes across multiple regions to cache content closer to end-users. This infrastructure reduces latency and accelerates the delivery of web applications, media, and large files.

Finally, Azure's global infrastructure supports a variety of network services, including Virtual Networks (VNet), ExpressRoute, and Azure Front Door. These services provide secure, high-performance networking solutions that enable hybrid cloud and edge computing capabilities. ExpressRoute, for example, allows private connections between Azure datacenters and on-premises infrastructure, bypassing the public internet to offer enhanced security and reliability.

Understanding Azure's robust and expansive global infrastructure empowers organizations to architect solutions that optimize performance, ensure compliance, and achieve high availability. The strategic deployment of resources across Azure's regions, leveraging Availability Zones and geo-redundant storage, can significantly improve application resilience and response times. Ensuring the correct configuration of these components is a fundamental step in maximizing the benefits of Microsoft's cloud platform.

1.4 Key Azure Concepts and Terminology

Understanding Microsoft Azure's key concepts and terminology is essential for navigating and leveraging its services effectively. This section outlines fundamental Azure terms, helping to build a strong foundational knowledge.

Azure provides a comprehensive suite of services, and it is essential to familiarize yourself with the nomenclature used within the platform. Below are some primary concepts:

Azure Subscription: An Azure subscription is a logical unit of Azure services linked to an Azure account. It is used to manage and track costs, as well as allocate resources and services. Each subscription has unique service and usage limits; multiple subscriptions can be used within an Azure account for different purposes, such as separating development and production environments.

Azure Region: An Azure region is a set of data centers deployed within a specific geographical area and connected via a low-latency network. Each region is designed to provide high availability and that customer's proximity to their services is optimized, reducing latency. Azure regions enable users to deploy resources close to their customers, ensuring efficiency and compliance with legal and regulatory requirements.

Resource Group: A resource group is a container that holds related resources for an Azure solution. It serves as a logical grouping mechanism to manage, deploy, monitor, and control access to resources. By using resource groups, users can simplify the organization of resources and manage them collectively according to their lifecycle.

Azure Resource Manager (ARM): The Azure Resource Manager is the deployment and management service for Azure. It provides a consistent management layer that enables you to create, update, and delete resources in your Azure account. ARM uses templates for deployment and maintains a unified structure for resources, facilitating the management of permissions, costs, and compliance.

Virtual Machine (VM): A Virtual Machine in Azure is an emulation of a computer system that provides the functionality of a physical computer. It includes an operating system and hardware configurations, deploying applications in various environments such as development, testing, and production. Users can choose from a wide selection of pre-configured VM images or create custom configurations.

Azure Virtual Network (VNet): An Azure Virtual Network is a representation of your own network in the cloud. It provides isolation, segmentation, and secure connections, allowing you to connect different resources securely and control traffic flow. VNets can be segmented into subnets to organize and secure resources effectively.

Storage Account: An Azure Storage Account provides a unique namespace to store and access data objects such as blobs, queues, files, and tables in Azure Storage. It supports scalable and durable storage solutions for various data types and sizes, ensuring high availability and redundancy.

Compute: Azure Compute provides the infrastructure required to run applications and services, including VMs, containers, and serverless computing. It supports scalable and resilient computing resources that can be adapted to meet fluctuating demands and high availability requirements.

Azure Active Directory (Azure AD): Azure Active Directory is a cloud-based identity and access management service. It provides authentication and authorization capabilities for users, applications, and services, enhancing security through single sign-on (SSO), multi-factor authentication (MFA), and conditional access policies.

Azure Policy: Azure Policy is a service in Azure that you can use to create, assign, and manage policies. These policies enforce different rules and effects over your resources so that those resources stay compliant with corporate standards and service level agreements. By using Azure Policy, you ensure consistency and enhance governance across your Azure environment.

Azure Monitor: Azure Monitor collects and analyzes telemetry data from both Azure and on-premises environments. It provides comprehensive monitoring capabilities to ensure applications' performance, availability, and reliability. Azure Monitor supports alerting, visualization through dashboards, and integration with other Azure services for a proactive approach to system maintenance.

Azure DevOps: Azure DevOps offers developer services to support teams in planning work, collaborating on code development, and building and deploying applications. It includes features such as Azure Pipelines, Azure Repos, Azure Boards, Azure Test Plans, and Azure Artifacts to provide an end-to-end DevOps toolchain.

Azure Marketplace: The Azure Marketplace is an online store offering thousands of certified, open-source, and community software applications and services. It allows users to discover, purchase, and deploy solutions that integrate seamlessly with Azure's infrastructure and services.

Below is an example of listing resources under a specific Azure Subscription using Azure CLI:

```
az resource list --subscription <Subscription_Id>
```

Executing this command produces a list of resources similar to the following format, displayed in JSON:

```
[
  {
    "id": "/subscriptions/<Subscription_Id>/resourceGroups/<Resource_Group>/providers/Microsoft.Compute/virtualMachines/<VM_Name>",
    "name": "<VM_Name>",
    "type": "Microsoft.Compute/virtualMachines",
    "location": "eastus",
    "resourceGroup": "<Resource_Group>"
  },
  ...
]
```

This provides a clear view of how resources are organized and managed within Azure, enhancing your ability to navigate the platform efficiently.

Understanding these key concepts and terminology allows for effective utilization of Azure's offerings and makes the process of managing cloud resources more intuitive and structured.

1.5 Azure Free Account and Pricing Tiers

Microsoft Azure offers various pricing tiers and free account options to help users start leveraging cloud services without an immediate financial commitment. Establishing a solid understanding of these pricing models and the benefits of a free account is instrumental in making informed decisions when planning and implementing Azure-based projects.

Azure provides a free tier account designed for new users to explore and experiment with its services at no cost for the first 12 months. This free tier includes certain limits, beyond which usage fees may apply. Additionally, Azure offers credits to students and professionals, enabling augmented learning and development experiences.

Azure Free Account

The Azure free account grants new users access to a range of services with no initial costs, encompassing a selection of Azure's most popular services. This account is beneficial for evaluating and testing different functionalities of Azure.

- **Twelve Months of Free Services:** Users receive access to popular products for 12 months. These include:
    - **Azure Virtual Machines (Linux/Windows)**: Users can utilize up to 750 hours of B1S Standard tier VM per month.
    - **SQL Database**: 250 GB of SQL Database storage is available per month.
    - **Azure Blob Storage**: 5 GB LRS (Locally Redundant Storage) Hot Blob is provided.
    - **Azure Cosmos DB**: 400 RU/s provisioned throughput with 5 GB storage.
    - **Azure Bandwidth**: 15 GB bandwidth egress per month.
- **Always Free Services:** Certain services remain free beyond the initial 12-month period, as long as consumption remains within the defined limits:
    - **Azure App Service (Linux/Windows)**: 10 web, mobile, or API apps.
    - **Azure Functions**: 1,000,000 requests per month.
    - **Azure Event Grid**: 100,000 operations per month.
- **$200 Credit**: Azure offers a $200 credit for the first 30 days to explore and use any service not covered or exceeding the limitations of the free tier.

To sign up, users need a Microsoft account and must provide credit card information for identity verification purposes. However, no charges are incurred unless users explicitly upgrade to a paid subscription or exceed the free tier limits.

Azure Pricing Tiers

Understanding Azure's pricing structure is critical for optimizing both cost management and resources. Azure's pricing model is predominantly pay-as-you-go, allowing users to pay only for what they use. This model is supplemented by various cost management and optimization tools, such as Azure Cost Management and Billing.

- **Pay-As-You-Go:**
  - Users pay for services on-demand, as they consume resources. This model provides flexibility and scalability, adjusting costs according to the specific usage patterns of the services.
  - Pricing is calculated on a per-second or per-minute basis, depending on the service.
  - Example: Virtual Machines are charged per second based on the VM's size, region, operating system, and other factors.
- **Reserved Instances (RI):**
  - Customers can significantly reduce costs by committing to one-year or three-year reservations for various services, including virtual machines and SQL databases.
  - This approach lets users lock in savings up to 72
- **Spot Instances:**
  - For workloads that can tolerate interruptions, spot instances offer unused compute capacity at substantial discounts.
  - Ideal for batch processing or stateless applications.
- **Dev/Test Pricing:**
  - Active Visual Studio subscribers can access discounted rates on various Azure services to support development and testing activities.
  - This pricing structure helps reduce the overall development cost by providing a conducive environment for testing new applications.

```
# Example: Checking the price of an Azure VM using the Azure CLI
# This command retrieves the price of a Standard_B1s VM in the East US region
az vm list-sizes --location eastus --output table
```

```
Output:
Name            NumberOfCores  OsDiskSizeInMB  ResourceDiskSizeInMB  MemoryInMB  MaxDataDiskCount
--------------- -------------- -------------- -------------------- ---------- ----------------
Standard_B1s    1              1047552        4096                 1024       2
...
```

The above example demonstrates how users can utilize the Azure CLI to retrieve pricing and resource information regarding virtual machine sizes and their associated configurations.

Maximizing cost efficiency often involves monitoring and analyzing resource usage through the Azure Cost Management tool. By setting budgets and alerts, users can remain within their planned expenditure, ensuring financial predictability.

1.6 Overview of Azure Services

Microsoft Azure provides a comprehensive set of cloud services that cater to a variety of business needs, spanning computing, storage, networking, databases, and analytics. This section will delve into these services, elucidating their fundamental components and applications.

Azure's service categories include:

- **Compute Services:** These services enable running applications in the cloud, accommodating virtual machines, containers, and serverless functions.
- **Networking Services:** Facilitating secure and high-performance connectivity, both within Azure and to on-premises environments.
- **Storage Services:** Offering scalable, durable, and cost-effective storage solutions for diverse data needs.
- **Database Services:** Providing a range of relational and NoSQL databases, as well as tools for database migration and management.
- **Analytics Services:** Enabling data analysis, business intelligence, and machine learning through sophisticated tools and frameworks.

Compute Services

Azure's compute services allow users to deploy, manage, and scale applications efficiently. These services include:

1. *Azure Virtual Machines:* Providing on-demand, scalable computing resources, Azure Virtual Machines (VMs) support various operating systems and configurations, ideal for workloads requiring high flexibility.

```
# Example command to create an Azure VM using Azure CLI
az vm create \
  --resource-group myResourceGroup \
  --name myVM \
  --image UbuntuLTS \
  --admin-username adminuser \
  --generate-ssh-keys
```


```
{
  "fqdns": "",
  "id": "/subscriptions/{subscription-id}/resourceGroups/myResourceGroup/providers/Microsoft.Compute/virtualMachines/myVM",
  "location": "eastus",
  "macAddress": "00-0D-3A-1D-FD-63",
  "powerState": "VM running",
  "privateIpAddress": "10.0.0.4",
  "publicIpAddress": "13.92.224.166",
  "resourceGroup": "myResourceGroup",
  "zones": ""
}
```


2. *Azure Kubernetes Service (AKS):* A managed container orchestration service that simplifies the deployment, management, and operations of Kubernetes clusters.

```
# Example command to create an AKS cluster using Azure CLI
az aks create \
  --resource-group myResourceGroup \
  --name myAKSCluster \
  --node-count 3 \
  --enable-addons monitoring \
  --generate-ssh-keys
```


```
{
  "agentPoolProfiles": [...],
  "dnsPrefix": "myAKSCluster-dc07fb",
  "fqdn": "myAKSCluster-dc07fb.hcp.eastus.azmk8s.io",
  ...
}
```


3. *Azure Functions:* An event-driven serverless compute service that enables the execution of code in response to triggers, reducing the need for managing infrastructure.

```
# Example command to create a function app using Azure CLI
az functionapp create \
  --resource-group myResourceGroup \
  --consumption-plan-location eastus \
  --runtime dotnet \
  --functions-version 3 \
  --name myFunctionApp \
```

```
  --storage-account myStorageAccount
```

```
{
  "id": "/subscriptions/{subscription-id}/resourceGroups/myResourceGroup/providers/Microsoft.Web/sites/myFunctionApp",
  "name": "myFunctionApp",
  "type": "Microsoft.Web/sites",
  ...
}
```

Networking Services

Azure provides robust networking solutions to ensure secure and efficient connectivity:

1. *Azure Virtual Network (VNet):* Allows for the creation of private networks within Azure, offering control over IP address blocks, DNS settings, security policies, and routing.

```
# Example command to create a virtual network using Azure CLI
az network vnet create \
  --resource-group myResourceGroup \
  --name myVNet \
  --address-prefix 10.0.0.0/16 \
  --subnet-name mySubnet \
  --subnet-prefix 10.0.0.0/24
```

```
{
  "addressSpace": {
    "addressPrefixes": [
      "10.0.0.0/16"
    ]
  },
  "id": "/subscriptions/{subscription-id}/resourceGroups/myResourceGroup/providers/Microsoft.Network/virtualNetworks/myVNet",
  "location": "eastus",
  ...
}
```

2. *Azure Load Balancer:* Distributes incoming traffic among multiple VMs, ensuring high availability and reliability.

```
# Example command to create a load balancer using Azure CLI
az network lb create \
  --resource-group myResourceGroup \
  --name myLoadBalancer \
  --frontend-ip-name myFrontEndPool \
  --backend-pool-name myBackEndPool \
  --public-ip-address myPublicIP
```

```
{
  "frontendIpConfigurations": [
    {
      "id": "/subscriptions/{subscription-id}/resourceGroups/myResourceGroup/providers/Microsoft.Network/loadBalancers/myLoadBalancer/frontendIPConfigurations/myFrontEndPool",
      "properties": {
        "provisioningState": "Succeeded",
        ...
      },
      ...
    }
  ],
  ...
}
```

Storage Services

Azure's storage offerings are designed for scalability, durability, and cost-effectiveness. Key services include:

1. *Azure Blob Storage:* Optimized for storing massive amounts of un-

structured data such as text or binary data.

```
# Example command to create a storage account using Azure CLI
az storage account create \
  --name mystorageaccount \
  --resource-group myResourceGroup \
  --location eastus \
  --sku Standard_LRS
```


```
{
  "accountType": "Standard_LRS",
  "creationTime": "2023-10-01T12:34:56.789Z",
  "primaryEndpoints": {
    "blob": "https://mystorageaccount.blob.core.windows.net/",
    ...
  },
  ...
}
```


2. Azure File Storage: Managed file shares in the cloud using the standard SMB protocol, accessible by Windows, macOS, and Linux clients.

```
# Example command to create a file share using Azure CLI
az storage share create \
  --account-name mystorageaccount \
  --name myshare
```


```
{
  "created": true
}
```


Database Services

Azure provides various database solutions to meet different data storage and management requirements:

1. Azure SQL Database: Fully managed relational database service optimized for performance and scalability.

```
# Example command to create an Azure SQL Database using Azure CLI
az sql db create \
  --resource-group myResourceGroup \
  --server myServer \
  --name myDatabase \
  --service-objective S1
```


```
{
  "kind": "v12.0,user",
  "location": "eastus",
  "resourceGroup": "myResourceGroup",
  ...
}
```


2. Azure Cosmos DB: Globally distributed, multi-model database service providing NoSQL and SQL APIs for high-performance applications.

```
# Example command to create an Azure Cosmos DB account using Azure CLI
```

```
az cosmosdb create \
  --name mycosmosdbaccount \
  --resource-group myResourceGroup \
  --kind MongoDB
```


```
{
  "id": "/subscriptions/{subscription-id}/resourceGroups/myResourceGroup/providers/Microsoft.DocumentDB/databaseAccounts/mycosmosdbaccount",
  ...
}
```


Analytics Services

Azure's analytics services empower organizations to extract valuable insights from their data:

1. Azure Synapse Analytics: An integrated analytics service that accelerates time to insight across data lakes and data warehouses.

```
# Example command to create an Azure Synapse workspace using Azure CLI
az synapse workspace create \
  --name mySynapseWorkspace \
  --resource-group myResourceGroup \
  --storage-account mystorageaccount \
  --file-system myfilesystem
```


```
{
  "id": "/subscriptions/{subscription-id}/resourceGroups/myResourceGroup/providers/Microsoft.Synapse/workspaces/mySynapseWorkspace",
  ...
}
```


2. Azure Machine Learning: A cloud-based service that provides capabilities for building, training, and deploying machine learning models at scale.

```
# Example command to create an Azure Machine Learning workspace using Azure CLI
az ml workspace create \
  --name myMLWorkspace \
  --resource-group myResourceGroup \
  --location eastus
```


```
{
  "location": "eastus",
  "name": "myMLWorkspace",
  "resourceGroup": "myResourceGroup",
  ...
}
```


This detailed overview encompasses the core categories and some of the primary services offered by Microsoft Azure. The utilization of these services can facilitate the development of scalable, reliable, and efficient applications and solutions in the cloud.

1.7 Getting Started with the Azure Portal

The Azure Portal is a web-based application that provides a unified console to access and manage all aspects of Microsoft Azure. It is a crucial tool for developers, IT administrators, and data scientists to monitor, manage, and model various services and resources hosted on Azure.

To access the Azure Portal, navigate to https://portal.azure.com. You will be prompted to sign in with your Microsoft account. If you do not already have an account, follow the on-screen instructions to create one. Once signed in, you will be greeted by the Azure Dashboard, which serves as the central hub for all your Azure activities.

The Azure Dashboard is customizable and presents a high-level view of your resources. You can add, remove, or rearrange tiles to suit your needs. The left-hand sidebar contains various menu items, which are essential for navigating through the different functionalities of the Azure Portal. Key sections in the sidebar include:

- **Home**: Takes you to the main dashboard view.
- **All Services**: Provides access to the full catalog of Azure services.
- **Resource Groups**: Allows for the organization of resources based on specific criteria.
- **Subscriptions**: Presents details about your Azure subscriptions, including usage and billing.
- **Dashboard**: Enables the creation and management of additional dashboards.
- **Help + Support**: Offers assistance and documentation from Microsoft support.

Navigating the Azure Portal

When you first log in, the experience can be overwhelming due to the sheer number of options and services available. Below are the foundational components you need to understand to navigate effectively:

- **Search Bar**: Located at the top of the portal, the search bar allows for quick access to resources, services, and documentation.

By typing keywords, you can efficiently find what you need without navigating through multiple menus.

- **Notifications**: Next to the search bar, the bell icon displays alerts and notifications related to your account and resources, such as deployment statuses, updates, and warnings.
- Cloud Shell: An integrated command-line interface accessible via the icon >_. It supports both Bash and PowerShell, enabling you to run scripts and commands directly in the portal.
- **Settings**: Accessible through the gear icon, settings allow you to personalize your portal experience, including theme adjustments, language preferences, and time zones.

Customizing the Dashboard

Customizing your dashboard can significantly enhance your workflow by displaying only the most relevant information. To customize the dashboard:

1. Click on the *Dashboard* in the sidebar.
2. Select the *Edit* button.
3. Use the *Add Tile* button to include new components such as monitoring charts, shortcuts to specific services, or custom queries.
4. Drag and drop tiles to rearrange and resize them based on your requirements.
5. Click *Done Customizing* to save the changes.

Creating and Managing Resources

Creating a resource follows a structured process that involves filling out forms with necessary details. For instance, to create a Virtual Machine (VM):

1. Navigate to *All Services* and search for *Virtual Machines*.
2. Click on *Add* to start the creation process.
3. Fill out the necessary details such as the *Subscription*, *Resource Group*, *VM Name*, *Region*, and *Image*. Choose an appropriate *Size* based on your workload.

4. Configure options such as networking, management, guest OS settings, and review the estimated cost.

5. Click *Review + Create* followed by *Create* after a final validation.

Below is an example of creating a Virtual Machine using the Azure CLI within the Cloud Shell:

```
az vm create \
  --resource-group MyResourceGroup \
  --name MyVm \
  --image UbuntuLTS \
  --admin-username azureuser \
  --generate-ssh-keys
```

Execution of the above command will yield a JSON output summarizing the VM details:


```
{
  "fqdns": "",
  "id": "/subscriptions/xxxxxxxx-xxxx-xxxx-xxxx-xxxxxxxxxxxx/resourceGroups/MyResourceGroup/providers/Microsoft.Compute/virtualMachines/MyVm",
  "location": "eastus",
  "macAddress": "xx-xx-xx-xx-xx-xx",
  ...
  "zones": ""
}
```


Monitoring and Alerts

Proactive monitoring of your resources and setting up alerts is essential for maintaining optimal performance and cost-efficiency. Azure Monitor provides a comprehensive solution for collecting, analyzing, and acting on telemetry data from your Azure and on-premises environments.

To set up an alert:

1. Select *Monitor* from the left-hand sidebar.

2. Navigate to *Alerts*, and then click on *New Alert Rule*.

3. Specify the *Target Resource*, which could be a VM, storage account, etc.

4. Define the alert condition, such as CPU utilization exceeding a threshold.

5. Set *Alert Details* and actions, like sending an email or triggering a logic app.

6. Review and create the alert rule.

Resource Groups

Organizing resources into resource groups simplifies resource management by grouping related resources that share the same lifecycle, permissions, and policies. To create a resource group:

1. Navigate to *Resource Groups*.
2. Click on *Add*.
3. Provide a *Subscription* and unique *Resource Group Name*.
4. Select a *Region* that best suits your geographic needs and regulatory requirements.
5. Click *Review + Create*, then *Create*.

Security & Compliance

Security is paramount in any cloud environment. Azure provides robust security configurations, including Role-Based Access Control (RBAC), predefined security roles, and compliance certifications. To manage roles and permissions:

1. Go to the *Resource Group* or specific *Resource* of interest.
2. Click on *Access Control (IAM)*.
3. Click on *Add* to assign a role to a user, group, or service principal.
4. Select a role such as *Owner*, *Contributor*, or *Reader*, and specify the user or group.
5. Click *Save* to apply the permissions.

Utilize these functionalities within the Azure Portal to manage resources effectively, ensuring that your applications and infrastructure operate smoothly and securely.

1.8 Basic Azure CLI Commands

The Azure Command-Line Interface (CLI) is a powerful tool for managing resources in Microsoft Azure. It provides a set of commands that can be run on any operating system with Python, making it a flexible and versatile choice for both beginners and experienced users. This section delves into fundamental Azure CLI commands, explaining their syntax and demonstrating practical uses.

Installing Azure CLI

Before using the Azure CLI, it is necessary to install it. The Azure CLI can be installed on Windows, macOS, and Linux. Here is an example of how to install Azure CLI on different operating systems.

On Windows: The CLI can be installed via the MSI installer available on the Azure download page. Running the downloaded installer and following the setup wizard will install the Azure CLI.

On macOS: Using the Homebrew package manager, you can install the Azure CLI with the following command:

```
brew update && brew install azure-cli
```

On Linux: For a Debian-based distribution, the Azure CLI can be installed with the apt package manager:

```
curl -sL https://aka.ms/InstallAzureCLIDeb | sudo bash
```

Logging In and Setting the Subscription

Once installed, log in to your Azure account using the CLI. Run the following command to prompt a web-based sign-in.

```
az login
```

If multiple subscriptions are associated with your account, set the desired subscription using the following command by replacing *<subscription-id>* with your actual subscription ID:

```
az account set --subscription <subscription-id>
```

Creating a Resource Group

A resource group is a logical container for Azure resources. Create a new resource group with the command:

```
az group create --name myResourceGroup --location eastus
```

Here, *myResourceGroup* is the name of the resource group, and *eastus* specifies the region where the resources will be located.

Creating a Virtual Machine

Deploy a virtual machine (VM) in the resource group using the following command:

```
az vm create
    --resource-group myResourceGroup
    --name myVM
    --image UbuntuLTS
    --admin-username azureuser
    --generate-ssh-keys
```

This command will create an Ubuntu virtual machine named *myVM* with the specified admin username and generate SSH keys for authentication.

Listing Resources

To list the resources within a resource group, use the command:

```
az resource list --resource-group myResourceGroup
```

Deleting a Resource Group

To remove a resource group and all associated resources, use the command:

```
az group delete --name myResourceGroup --yes --no-wait
```

Here, the *–yes* flag confirms the deletion, and *–no-wait* allows the command to return immediately rather than waiting for the operation to finish.

Scaling Your VM

Scaling operations can be performed to resize an existing virtual machine. Change the VM size using the command below:

```
az vm resize --resource-group myResourceGroup --name myVM --size
    Standard_DS2_v2
```

Replace *Standard_DS2_v2* with the desired size from the list of available VM sizes.

Updating CLI Commands

Azure is continuously evolving, and so is the Azure CLI. Ensure you have the latest version by running:

```
az upgrade
```

Querying and Filtering

Azure CLI commands often return output in JSON format, which can be queried and filtered using the *jq* tool or built-in CLI querying parameters. For instance, to list all virtual machines in a resource group and display only their names and locations, use:

```
az vm list --resource-group myResourceGroup --query "[].{name:name, location:location
    }" --output table
```

Automating Tasks

Automate repetitive tasks using scripts. Here is an example of a simple Bash script to create multiple VMs:

```
#!/bin/bash
for i in {1..5}
do
    az vm create \
      --resource-group myResourceGroup \
      --name myVM$i \
      --image UbuntuLTS \
      --admin-username azureuser \
      --generate-ssh-keys
done
```

Executing this script will create five virtual machines named *myVM1* through *myVM5.*

Integrating these fundamental commands into your workflow facilitates efficient and automated management of Azure resources through the Azure CLI. As you become more proficient, exploring additional features and advanced commands can further enhance your productivity and cloud resource management capabilities.

1.9 Creating Your First Azure Resource

Creating your first resource in Microsoft Azure is an essential step that demonstrates the power and flexibility of the cloud platform. This section will guide you through the process of provisioning a basic virtual machine (VM) using the Azure Portal.

Azure resources are manageable items available through Azure. They can be anything from virtual machines, databases, and storage accounts to more advanced services like cognitive APIs, IoT hubs, and Kubernetes clusters. For this introductory example, creating a virtual machine provides a clear and tangible way to experience the basics of resource management in Azure.

Start by logging into the Azure Portal using your credentials. If you have not yet created an account, refer to the "Azure Free Account and Pricing Tiers" section to get started.

Upon successful login, navigate to the Azure Portal home page. From here, follow these steps:

1. **Navigate to the VM Creation Page**: On the left-hand menu, click on "Create a resource". In the "New" page that appears, type "Virtual Machine" in the search bar and select "Virtual Machine" from the dropdown suggestions to open the VM creation wizard.

2. **Configure Basic VM Settings**: In the "Basics" tab, you will need to enter several key details:

    - **Subscription**: Select the appropriate subscription. If you're using a free account, there should be only one option.
    - **Resource Group**: Either select an existing resource group or create a new one by entering a name. Resource groups are logical containers for clustering related resources.
    - **Virtual Machine Name**: Enter a unique name for your VM, such as "myFirstVM".
    - **Region**: Choose a geographic region that is closest to you or best meets your needs. This affects latency and compliance with legal or company policies.
    - **Image**: Select an image from the dropdown. Common choices include Windows Server 2019, Ubuntu Server, or other OS images. For this example, select "Ubuntu Server 18.04 LTS".
    - **Size**: Click "Size" to select the VM size that fits your requirement. For initial exploration, a "B1s (1 vCPU, 1 GiB memory)" machine within the free tier is adequate.
    - **Authentication Type**: Choose the authentication type. We will use SSH public key. Enter your public key in the provided box.
    - **Username**: Define the administrative username to use when connecting to the VM, e.g., "azureuser".

3. **Networking Settings**: Click on the "Next: Disks >" button to proceed to the networking configuration. Default settings usually suffice, but you can review them:

    - **Virtual network**: The selected resource group will default to a virtual network; no change required.
    - **Subnet**: A subnet will be auto-selected.

- **Public IP**: Ensures your VM is accessible over the internet via a unique IP address.
- **NIC network security group**: Options for allowing selected inbound ports will be presented. For simplicity, select "Allow selected ports" and choose SSH (22) to allow secure SSH connections.

4. **Disks Configuration**: Click the "Next: Networking >" button and then proceed to the "Disks" tab. The default options can be used for basic setups:

   - **OS disk type**: Set to "Standard HDD" which is cost-effective for testing.

5. **Review + Create**: Continue through the tabs ("Management", "Advanced", and "Tags") using default settings or adding relevant configuration based on personal preference. Finally, review all settings in the "Review + create" tab. Ensure the validation rule is passed, then click "Create".

Azure will now start provisioning your virtual machine. This process might take a few minutes. Once the VM deployment is complete, navigate to the "Resource Group" section and select your newly created VM. Here, you will see details about the VM, such as its public IP address.

You can access your virtual machine using SSH from a terminal on your local computer. For this, use the public IP address and the username you provided during setup.

```
ssh azureuser@<public-ip-address>
```

It prompts for your private key passphrase if applicable. Once authenticated, you will be connected remotely to your virtual machine, and you can execute terminal commands as if you were operating on a local machine.

The process of creating a virtual machine on Azure demonstrates how cloud resources are provisioned and managed. Understanding this process sets the foundation for creating more complex resources as you advance further in your Azure journey.

1.10 Introduction to Azure Marketplace

Azure Marketplace is a critical component of the Microsoft Azure ecosystem, providing a comprehensive catalog of solutions from both Microsoft and its partners. This directory of cloud solutions enables users to find, acquire, and deploy software applications and services across various domains, seamlessly integrating with Azure services. The Azure Marketplace offers customers a curated, digital storefront comprising thousands of products, ranging from virtual machine images to application stacks, development tools, and industry-specific solutions.

Azure Marketplace is categorized to facilitate ease of navigation and tailored search capabilities. Categories include but are not limited to: *Compute*, *Networking*, *Databases*, *Internet of Things (IoT)*, *Artificial Intelligence (AI)*, and *Machine Learning (ML)*. Each category helps users quickly locate products relevant to their specific needs. Furthermore, the marketplace distinguishes between free, bring-your-own-license (BYOL), and paid solutions, offering flexibility to adapt to various budget constraints.

When using Azure Marketplace, users have the option to deploy software directly onto Azure Virtual Machines (VMs) or leverage preconfigured platform-as-a-service (PaaS) applications. This offers a broad spectrum of deployment models suited for different business cases and technical requirements, ensuring tailored solutions for both startups and large enterprises. For example, consider a company needing a managed database solution; the marketplace provides preconfigured options like MySQL and PostgreSQL, reducing the overhead of setup and configuration.

The Azure Marketplace simplifies the procurement process by ensuring that all listed products meet Microsoft's certification standards, guaranteeing compatibility, security, and efficiency within the Azure environment. This vetting process involves a series of compliance checks, performance assessments, and security validations. Thus, end-users can trust that the solutions they procure and deploy are reliable and maintain rigorous operational standards.

Administratively, managing transactions within Azure Marketplace is straightforward, as all purchases and subscriptions are integrated with your Azure billing account. The Azure portal offers comprehensive tools to track usage, monitor expenditures, and manage renewals, ensuring that users maintain complete financial oversight over their cloud investments. The billing model is flexible, accommodating ones that are pay-as-you-go, subscription-based, or BYOL.

The Azure Marketplace also provides extensive collaboration opportunities for ISVs (Independent Software Vendors), systems integrators, and service providers. Partners can reach a global customer base by listing their applications and services on the marketplace, thus enhancing visibility and accessibility. This symbiotic ecosystem fosters innovation and diversity within the cloud solutions domain.

To illustrate the deployment process from Azure Marketplace, consider the task of deploying a web application using a pre-configured virtual machine image. The following example demonstrates how to do this via the Azure portal:

```
# Step 1: Open Azure Portal and Navigate to Azure Marketplace
# Step 2: Search for the desired application, e.g., "WordPress"
# Step 3: Select the WordPress offer from Bitnami
# Step 4: Click on "Create" to initiate the deployment process
# Step 5: Configure basic settings
    - Subscription: Select your Azure subscription
    - Resource Group: Create new or select an existing resource group
    - Instance Details: Specify Virtual Machine name, region, and size
# Step 6: Configure admin username and authentication type (SSH key/password)
# Step 7: Review + create the VM instance
# Step 8: The deployment begins and will take a few minutes to complete
# Step 9: Access the deployed web application using the provided DNS name or public
    IP address
```

After deploying and accessing the web application, users can further customize and manage their application through the Azure portal. Users are encouraged to monitor VM performance, set up security protocols, and integrate other Azure services like Azure Monitor, Azure Security Center, and Azure Backup to ensure optimal functioning and robustness of their deployed solutions.

The Azure Marketplace also supports programmatic access via Azure CLI and REST APIs, enabling advanced users and automation engineers to deploy and manage marketplace resources programmatically. Here is an example of using the Azure CLI to find and deploy a solution from Azure Marketplace:

```
# Find available VM images from Azure Marketplace
az vm image list --all --output table

# Output a filtered list based on a specific publisher
az vm image list --publisher bitnami --output table

# Create a VM from Azure Marketplace Image
az vm create --resource-group MyResourceGroup \
--name MyVM \
--image bitnami:wordpress:5-6:latest \
```

```
--admin-username azureuser \
--generate-ssh-keys
```

In the above commands, the az vm image list helps filter and identify specific images provided by Bitnami. Furthermore, the az vm create command demonstrates how to instantiate a WordPress VM image, specifying essential attributes like resource group, VM name, and administrator details.

The integration of Azure Marketplace within the broader Azure ecosystem underscores its potential to streamline the deployment processes, ensuring efficient and secure operation of diverse workloads. For individuals and enterprises embarking on their cloud journey, Azure Marketplace provides a multitude of vetted, ready-to-use solutions to accelerate and bolster their digital transformation initiatives.

Chapter 2

Azure Architecture and Services

This chapter provides a detailed exploration of Azure's architectural components and services, including regions, availability zones, and the Azure Resource Manager. It covers essential compute options such as virtual machines, App Services, and Kubernetes. The chapter also delves into serverless computing with Azure Functions, container management, and various database services. Additionally, it includes an overview of advanced services like AI, machine learning, and IoT, as well as hybrid and multi-cloud solutions enabled by Azure Arc.

2.1 Understanding Azure Regions and Availability Zones

Cloud computing platforms like Microsoft Azure are distributed across physical locations called regions. An Azure region is a geographical area containing at least one, but potentially multiple, datacenters. Each datacenter within a region is designed to provide high availability and fault tolerance. Azure's global infrastructure is built up of several such regions worldwide, providing a resilient backbone that helps ensure services are highly available and performant.

Azure regions are the cornerstone for deploying services and applications. When creating resources in Azure, selecting the appropriate region is critical for optimizing performance, complying with data residency requirements, and achieving redundancy. Regions are fundamental for deploying services closest to the end users to minimize latency.

Azure introduces the concept of Availability Zones within each region to further enhance reliability. An Availability Zone is a physically separate zone within a region, having independent power, cooling, and networking. Zones are designed to be isolated from failures in other zones within the region.

To ensure resiliency within a region, Azure strategies include replicating resources across these Availability Zones. This zonal redundancy is crucial for building highly available applications. Each region typically consists of three Availability Zones, enabling true high availability capabilities. Resources can be distributed across multiple zones to protect against datacenter-level failures.

For instance, consider a deployment of virtual machines (VMs). By deploying VMs across different Availability Zones, an application can maintain high availability even if one zone experiences an outage. The architecture could be visualized as below:

Using Availability Zones, Azure ensures service availability and offers a Service-Level Agreement (SLA) of 99.99% uptime for services deployed across two or more zones. This setup is crucial for mission-critical applications and enterprise-level workloads where downtime could translate to significant operational or financial setbacks.

Additionally, some Azure services provide zone-redundant configurations natively. For example, Azure SQL Database and Azure Cosmos DB are designed to replicate data across multiple zones automatically. This automatic replication ensures data availability and durability even in the event of an Availability Zone failure.

Azure locations are carefully selected to comply with various regulatory requirements, such as data residency laws. This is especially important for companies needing to ensure their data does not leave specific geographical boundaries. Azure's locations are also influenced by considerations such as latency and proximity to major internet exchanges.

When planning deployments, understanding the network latency implications of different regions is essential. Azure provides tools like Network Performance Monitor (NPM) to analyze latency between regions and optimize for the best performance. Below is an example of how to use az network CLI commands to measure inter-region latency.

```
# Measure latency between two Azure regions
az network watcher show-next-hop --resource-group MyResourceGroup --network-
    watcher-name MyNetworkWatcher --source-ip 10.0.0.4 --source-port 80 --
    destination-ip 10.2.0.4 --destination-port 80 --protocol Tcp
```

Selecting regions also plays a vital role in achieving compliance with industry-specific standards such as HIPAA, GDPR, or FedRAMP, which may dictate specific geographical constraints for data storage and processing. Azure provides documentation and tools to ensure that customers can align their deployments with these regulatory requirements.

Azure's global footprint consists of various types of regions:

- Country/Region-specific Regions: These regions serve specific countries or regions to meet local data residency requirements.

- Government Regions: Special regions designed to meet stringent government regulations for data residency and security, e.g., Azure Government.

- Specialized Regions: These are optimized for specific purposes, such as regions with availability zones designed to support the highest service availability.

The distribution and categorization of Azure regions provide customers with the flexibility to tailor their deployments according to business needs, compliance requirements, and performance considerations.

Understanding the configuration and utilization of Azure regions and Availability Zones is critical for optimizing both the reliability and performance of deployments. By leveraging these fundamental building blocks of Azure's global infrastructure, enterprises can build resilient, high-performing, and compliant solutions tailored to their specific needs.

2.2 Introduction to Azure Resource Manager

Azure Resource Manager (ARM) is the deployment and management service for Azure. It provides a consistent management layer that enables you to create, update, and delete resources in your Azure account. All resources are managed through this uniform interface, ensuring seamless integration and operation of various Azure services.

Resource Groups: In Azure, each resource, such as a virtual machine (VM) or database, is created inside a resource group. A resource group is a logical container into which Azure resources are deployed and managed. Resource groups provide a means to manage and provision infrastructure within a contained scope.

Syntax Example: Creating a resource group using the Azure CLI can be demonstrated with the following command:

```
az group create --name MyResourceGroup --location eastus
```

It is essential to note that all resources in a resource group should share the same lifecycle. You can deploy, update, or delete all the resources in a resource group together. If one resource in the group requires updates, this updates the management and security parameters for that specific resource across the entire group.

Declarative Templates: ARM templates are JSON files that define the infrastructure and configuration of your Azure deployment. ARM templates are declarative, meaning you define what you want to deploy, and Azure takes care of the rest. This can be instrumental in scenarios such as Infrastructure as Code (IaC).

Template Example: Here is a simplified example of an ARM template which deploys a single storage account:

```
{
  "$schema": "https://schema.management.azure.com/schemas/2019-04-01/
       deploymentTemplate.json#",
  "contentVersion": "1.0.0.0",
  "resources": [
    {
      "type": "Microsoft.Storage/storageAccounts",
      "apiVersion": "2019-04-01",
      "name": "mystorageaccount",
      "location": "eastus",
      "sku": {
        "name": "Standard_LRS"
      },
      "kind": "StorageV2",
      "properties": {}
    }
  ]
}
```

An ARM template like the example above enables repeatable deployments and can be parameterized to allow flexibility across deployments.

Benefits of Using ARM:

- **Consistency:** ARM provides a standardized way to manage resources, ensuring consistency across deployments.
- **Security:** Role-Based Access Control (RBAC) can be applied to all services managed through ARM, improving security and governance.
- **Tagging:** ARM provides the capability to tag resources, making it simpler to locate and manage resources based on certain criteria such as environment, department, or cost center.
- **Auditing:** Comprehensive auditing capabilities via Azure Activity Log.

Resource Manageability: Through ARM, resources can be managed individually or as a group. This is beneficial for not only deployment automation but also for ongoing management tasks such as scaling and monitoring. ARM also enables the implementation of advanced governance features such as resource locks and policies.

Automation and Scripts: ARM significantly enhances the automation capabilities in Azure. Resources can be managed using predefined scripts and templates, which can either be created manually or exported after resource creation. This automation can be implemented through Azure CLI, Azure PowerShell, or REST API.

Azure CLI Example: Deploying an ARM template using Azure CLI:

```
az deployment group create \
  --resource-group MyResourceGroup \
  --template-file storage-template.json
```

Resource Dependencies: ARM supports defining dependencies between resources, ensuring that resources are deployed in the correct order. This feature is crucial when a resource must be set up before another resource relies on it for stable deployment.

Execution Example: The output of creating a resource group using the Azure CLI might look like this:


```
{
  "id": "/subscriptions/{subscription-id}/resourceGroups/MyResourceGroup",
  "location": "eastus",
  "managedBy": null,
  "name": "MyResourceGroup",
  "properties": {
    "provisioningState": "Succeeded"
  },
  "tags": null,
  "type": "Microsoft.Resources/resourceGroups"
}
```


This JSON output indicates the successful creation of a resource group, providing details such as the location, provisioning state, and unique identifier of the resource group.

Azure Policies: Azure Policies can be used in conjunction with ARM to enforce organizational standards and assess compliance at-scale. Policies enable you to create, assign, and manage policy definitions to ensure resources comply with your required standards. This allows for governance and compliance capabilities to be applied across all resources deployed via ARM.

In Azure, ARM acts as the backbone for resource management, ensuring that all deployments are consistent, secure, and easily manageable.

2.3 Core Azure Architectural Components

Azure's architectural foundation is built upon several key components that enable a high degree of scalability, availability, and resilience. These components are globally distributed to support a wide range of enterprise IT needs. In this section, we will explore the core architectural components of Azure, their functions, and how they interact with each other to provide a robust cloud platform.

Azure Regions and Availability Zones

Azure's infrastructure is divided into regions, which are geographic areas containing one or more datacenters. Each region is designed to be completely isolated from others to ensure data residency and compliance requirements. Availability Zones, on the other hand, are physically separate locations within each region, equipped with independent power, cooling, and networking, providing high availability.

Azure Resource Manager (ARM)

The Azure Resource Manager (ARM) is the deployment and management service for Azure. It provides a consistent management layer that enables you to create, update, and delete resources within your Azure subscription. ARM allows you to manage these resources using a declarative syntax through ARM templates or imperative commands through Azure CLI or PowerShell.

```
# Example of deploying resources using Azure CLI and ARM template
az group create --name MyResourceGroup --location eastus
az deployment group create --resource-group MyResourceGroup --template-file template.
    json
```

ARM organizes resources into **resource groups**, which act as containers for logically grouping and managing resources. This helps in tracking billing costs and simplifying access control. Additionally, ARM supports resource tagging, enabling further categorization and management.

Virtual Networks (VNet)

Azure Virtual Networks (VNets) are fundamental components for building private networks in Azure, allowing the isolation and secure communication of Azure resources. VNets provide several crucial functionalities:

- **Subnets**: VNets can be divided into subnets, each with its own IP address range within the VNet.

- **Network Security Groups (NSG)**: NSGs can be used to filter traffic to and from Azure resources within a VNet.
- **Peering**: VNet peering allows VNets to connect with each other, enabling cross-VNet traffic.

Azure Load Balancer

The Azure Load Balancer distributes incoming network traffic across multiple virtual machines (VMs) to ensure no single VM is overwhelmed. It provides both public and internal load balancing capabilities and supports various distribution algorithms, including round-robin and hash-based distribution.

Azure Application Gateway

Azure Application Gateway is a web traffic load balancer that manages application traffic. It operates at the application layer (Layer 7) and provides features such as URL-based routing, SSL termination, and Web Application Firewall (WAF). It is particularly useful for managing HTTP and HTTPS traffic and providing advanced routing capabilities based on URL paths or host headers.

```
# Example of creating an Application Gateway
az network application-gateway create --name MyAppGateway --resource-group
    MyResourceGroup --vnet-name MyVNet --subnet MySubnet --http-settings-cookie
    -based-affinity Enabled
```

Azure Storage Services

Azure Storage Services provide scalable and durable storage options for various types of data:

- **Blob Storage**: Optimized for storing massive amounts of unstructured data such as text or binary data.
- **Queue Storage**: Provides reliable messaging for large workloads.
- **Table Storage**: Offers structured NoSQL data storage.
- **File Storage**: Managed file shares for cloud or on-premises deployments.

For example, Blob Storage allows the storage of large amounts of unstructured data with high availability, while Table Storage is suitable for structured data with a schemaless design to handle millions of records efficiently.

```
# Azure Blob Storage example
az storage blob upload --container-name mycontainer --file myfile.txt --name myfile.txt
```

Azure SQL Database

Azure SQL Database is a fully managed relational database service based on the SQL Server engine. It provides high availability, automated backups, scaling, and compliance features, making it suitable for mission-critical applications. Key features include:

- **Hyperscale Mode**: Supports enormous database sizes with fast backups and restores.
- **Serverless Option**: Automatically pauses and resumes based on workload, saving costs.

```
# Example of creating an Azure SQL Database
az sql server create --name mydemoserver --resource-group MyResourceGroup --location
        eastus --admin-user myadmin --admin-password mypassword
az sql db create --resource-group MyResourceGroup --server mydemoserver --name
        mySampleDatabase --service-objective S0
```

Azure Active Directory (AD)

Azure Active Directory (AD) is Microsoft's multi-tenant cloud-based directory and identity management service, enabling authentication and management for users and integrated applications. It supports various authentication methods including Single Sign-On (SSO), multifactor authentication, and conditional access policies to secure access to resources.

Azure Key Vault

Azure Key Vault stores and manages cryptographic keys, secrets, and certificates. It helps safeguard secrets and keys used by cloud applications and services. It provides audit logs to track activities and can be integrated with other Azure services for automated secret management.

```
# Example of creating a Key Vault and storing a secret
az keyvault create --name MyKeyVault --resource-group MyResourceGroup --location
        eastus
az keyvault secret set --vault-name MyKeyVault --name MySecret --value
        MySecretValue
```

Azure Monitor

Azure Monitor provides comprehensive monitoring solutions for collecting, analyzing, and acting on telemetry data from Azure and on-premises environments. It helps you understand how your applications are performing and proactively identifies issues affecting them. Azure Monitor includes features such as Metrics, Logs, Alerts, and Application Insights.

```
# Example of creating a metric alert rule
az monitor metrics alert create --name MyAlertRule --resource-group
    MyResourceGroup --scopes MyVirtualMachine --condition "avg Percentage CPU
    > 80" --description "Alert when CPU percentage exceeds 80%"
```

These core components of Azure's architecture provide a robust foundation for building, deploying, and managing enterprise-grade applications. Understanding and effectively utilizing these components ensures that applications are scalable, resilient, and secure. Different components work together seamlessly, allowing developers and IT professionals to create sophisticated solutions tailored to diverse business needs.

2.4 Virtual Machines and Compute Services

Azure Virtual Machines (VMs) provide the ability to provision scalable compute resources on-demand within the cloud infrastructure. VMs in Azure are versatile, supporting various operating systems and configuration settings, making them suitable for diverse workloads. This section delves into the intricacies of Azure Virtual Machines and other compute services that Azure offers, explaining their core functionalities, configurations, and practical applications.

Azure VMs run on hypervisor-based virtualization, specifically leveraging Hyper-V to ensure isolated execution environments. Users can choose from a variety of VM sizes and configurations, each optimized for different workloads, including general-purpose, compute-optimized, memory-optimized, storage-optimized, GPU-optimized, and high-performance compute scenarios.

Creating an Azure Virtual Machine

Creating and configuring a VM in Azure involves several steps, from selecting the VM image and size to configuring network settings and storage options. The process can be expeditiously achieved using the Azure Portal, Azure CLI, or Azure PowerShell. Below is an example of creating a VM using Azure CLI:

```
az vm create \
  --resource-group myResourceGroup \
```

```
--name myVM \
--image UbuntuLTS \
--admin-username azureuser \
--generate-ssh-keys
```

This command provisions an Ubuntu LTS VM named myVM in the specified resource group, setting up SSH key authentication for secure access.

VM Sizes and Configurations

Azure VMs come in several sizes, denoted by a series of letters and numbers indicating their optimized use cases:

- **B-series (Burstable VMs):** Ideal for workloads with variable CPU usage, offering cost-efficiency by utilizing credits accumulated during idle periods.
- **D-series (General Purpose):** Balanced for both compute and memory, suitable for many applications.
- **E-series (Memory Optimized):** Enhanced memory capabilities, optimal for in-memory workloads like SAP HANA.
- **F-series (Compute Optimized):** High CPU-to-memory ratio, designed for compute-intensive tasks.
- **L-series (Storage Optimized):** Optimized for low latency storage needs.
- **G-series and H-series (High Performance):** Tailored for heavy computational tasks and applications requiring substantial resources such as scientific simulations.

Disks and Storage Options

Azure offers a variety of storage options tailored for VMs to ensure high performance and reliability. The two primary types are:

- **Standard HDD:** Cost-effective storage for less critical, lower IOPS applications.
- **Premium SSD:** High-performance, low-latency storage for mission-critical applications.

Networking Features

Azure VMs integrate seamlessly with Azure Virtual Networks (VNets) to connect resources and secure communications. For enhanced security and management, networking features such as Network Security Groups (NSGs), Azure Load Balancer, and Azure Application Gateway are utilized.

Below is an example of associating a VM with a virtual network and a network security group using Azure CLI:

```
az vm create \
  --resource-group myResourceGroup \
  --name mySecureVM \
  --image UbuntuLTS \
  --admin-username azureuser \
  --ssh-key-value ~/.ssh/id_rsa.pub \
  --nsg myNetworkSecurityGroup \
  --vnet-name myVNet \
  --subnet mySubnet
```

Scale Sets

Virtual Machine Scale Sets provide an efficient way to create and manage a set of auto-scaling VMs. They enable you to centrally manage, configure, and update a large number of VMs, ensuring that workloads can scale out and in based on demand.

```
az vmss create \
  --resource-group myResourceGroup \
  --name myScaleSet \
  --image UbuntuLTS \
  --admin-username azureuser \
  --generate-ssh-keys \
  --instance-count 3
```

Azure Compute Services

Beyond virtual machines, Azure offers a variety of other compute services designed for unique workloads. These include:

- **Azure App Services:** A fully managed platform for building, deploying, and scaling web apps, APIs, and mobile backends.
- **Azure Batch:** Enables large-scale parallel and high-performance computing (HPC) applications, distributing workloads across thousands of cores.
- **Azure Functions:** Supports serverless compute, allowing event-driven code execution without managing infrastructure.

Azure App Services provide an environment to deploy and scale web applications quickly. Azure Batch allows for efficient execution of large-scale parallel jobs. Azure Functions offer a serverless compute experience, ideal for event-driven tasks.

Azure's comprehensive suite of compute services, including virtual machines and additional compute offerings, facilitates solutions for every conceivable workload. The subsequent sections will expand on specific services like Azure App Services, Azure Kubernetes Service (AKS), and serverless computing options.

2.5 Azure App Services

Azure App Services is a platform-as-a-service (PaaS) offering designed to enable users to build, deploy, and scale web applications and APIs quickly and efficiently. This service provides a fully managed platform for the creation of applications using various programming languages and frameworks, including .NET, Java, Node.js, Python, PHP, and Ruby.

At its core, Azure App Services includes several specific services: Web Apps, API Apps, Logic Apps, and Mobile Apps. Each of these services caters to different development needs, offering a unified platform for building a wide array of application types with flexibility and ease.

Web Apps enable developers to deploy website content and applications with a high degree of scalability, and they support multiple programming languages and frameworks. Key features include:

- **Continuous Deployment and Integration:** Easily integrate with development tools and services like GitHub, Bitbucket, Azure DevOps, and Git to enable continuous deployment of applications.
- **High Availability:** With built-in load balancing and autoscaling, Web Apps ensure that applications remain available and performant under varying loads.
- **Security and Compliance:** SSL/TLS, custom domain support, and compliance with standards such as ISO, SOC, and GDPR ensure that applications meet modern security and compliance requirements.

API Apps offer a set of tools and features specifically designed to facilitate the development and hosting of APIs. These include:

- **API Gateways:** These gateways provide functionalities to handle API routing, rate limiting, and security.
- **Swagger Integration:** Swagger or OpenAPI support enables the automatic generation of API definitions, simplifying documentation and client generation processes.
- **Authentication and Authorization:** Easily implement OAuth 2.0, Azure Active Directory, and other authentication mechanisms to secure APIs.

Logic Apps allow the automation of workflows and business processes using a visual designer. Logic Apps are particularly useful for:

- **Integration:** Connect disparate systems and services, both on-premises and in the cloud, to automate business processes.
- **Flexibility:** Use connectors to integrate with services like Office 365, Azure SQL Database, Dynamics 365, and many others.
- **Event-Driven Workflows:** Respond to triggers such as HTTP requests, timers, or specific events from integrated services.

Mobile Apps offer features tailored to mobile development, including:

- **Offline Sync:** Provide a seamless user experience by allowing apps to function offline and then synchronize data once connection is restored.
- **Push Notifications:** Send targeted notifications to user devices based on different criteria, enhancing user engagement.
- **Authentication Integration:** Utilize various authentication providers, such as Microsoft, Google, Twitter, and Facebook, to authenticate users.

Azure App Services' underlying infrastructure abstracts the complexities of server management, allowing developers to focus on writing code and improving application functionality. It further includes features such as:

- **Autoscaling:** Automatically scales applications up or down based on traffic demands, ensuring optimal performance while controlling costs.

- **Custom Domains and SSL:** Configure custom domain names and secure applications using SSL certificates to enhance security and brand consistency.
- **Deployment Slots:** Deploy different versions of applications to various slots (e.g., development, staging, production) and swap them without downtime.
- **Monitoring and Diagnostics:** Use Azure's built-in monitoring and diagnostics tools, including Application Insights, to gain insights into application performance and issues.

Deployment of an application to Azure Web Apps can be demonstrated using the following example of a Node.js application. This example assumes that the user is working within a local environment set up with Node.js and Git.

```
$ git clone https://github.com/example/repository.git
$ cd repository
$ npm install
$ az webapp up --name my_unique_app_name --resource-group myResourceGroup --
    runtime "node|14-lts"
```

This series of commands clones a repository, installs the necessary Node.js packages, and creates and deploys the app to an Azure Web App service. The `az webapp up` command handles much of the configuration and deployment steps automatically.

Upon successful deployment, the application's accessibility can be verified via a web browser. For example, if the app was deployed using the custom domain my_unique_app_name.azurewebsites.net, navigating to this URL should display the deployed application.

```
Welcome to your Node.js application running on Azure!
```

The comprehensive management capabilities provided by Azure App Services ensure that developers can efficiently deploy, monitor, and manage applications at scale with minimal overhead.

2.6 Azure Kubernetes Service (AKS)

Azure Kubernetes Service (AKS) is a managed container orchestration service provided by Microsoft Azure, offering a rich set of features to deploy, manage, and scale containerized applications using Kubernetes.

By facilitating the management of Kubernetes clusters without the complexity, AKS allows developers to focus on building applications rather than infrastructure concerns. This section delves deeply into the intricacies of AKS, covering cluster creation, management, scaling, and integration with other Azure services.

AKS simplifies the process of Kubernetes cluster creation through the Azure portal, Azure CLI, or ARM templates. When creating a cluster, the following elements are defined:

- **Cluster Name**: A unique identifier within the selected resource group.
- **Node Count**: The initial number of nodes in the cluster, which can later be scaled up or down.
- **Node Pools**: Provide isolation and custom configurations for groups of nodes within the same cluster.
- **Virtual Network**: The network configuration for the nodes, typically defined by subnets within an Azure Virtual Network (VNet).
- **Authentication Methods**: Options such as Azure Active Directory (AAD) integration for secure access to the cluster.

To create a basic AKS cluster using the Azure CLI, the following command is used:

```
az aks create --resource-group MyResourceGroup --name MyAKSCluster --node-count 3
    --enable-addons monitoring --generate-ssh-keys
```

The command above specifies the resource group, cluster name, initial node count, and adds the monitoring addon using Azure Monitor. The –generate-ssh-keys flag generates SSH keys for node access.

Cluster management in AKS includes upgrading Kubernetes versions, node scaling, and monitoring. To upgrade the cluster to a new Kubernetes version:

```
az aks upgrade --resource-group MyResourceGroup --name MyAKSCluster --kubernetes-
    version 1.21.2
```

For scaling the node pool, the following command can be issued:

```
az aks scale --resource-group MyResourceGroup --name MyAKSCluster --node-count 5
```

Cluster operation and maintenance are facilitated through the Kubernetes Dashboard, role-based access control (RBAC), and integration with Azure DevOps for continuous integration and continuous delivery (CI/CD). AKS also supports Helm for package management, enabling easy deployment of pre-configured Kubernetes applications.

The following configuration allows Helm to connect to an AKS cluster:

```
az aks get-credentials --resource-group MyResourceGroup --name MyAKSCluster
helm init
```

This sets up the Kubernetes configuration in the local context and initializes Helm to work with the AKS cluster.

AKS provides robust networking capabilities, supporting both basic and advanced configurations. Basic networking uses Azure CNI networking, integrating tightly with Azure Virtual Network (VNet), enabling secure and private networking. Advanced configurations support network policies for controlling traffic flow and network security within the cluster.

Below is an example of a network policy implemented using a Kubernetes NetworkPolicy resource:

```
apiVersion: networking.k8s.io/v1
kind: NetworkPolicy
metadata:
  name: allow-frontend
  namespace: default
spec:
  podSelector:
    matchLabels:
      app: frontend
  policyTypes:
  - Ingress
  ingress:
  - from:
    - podSelector:
        matchLabels:
          app: backend
    ports:
    - protocol: TCP
      port: 80
```

This policy allows ingress traffic to pods labeled 'frontend' only from pods labeled 'backend' on port 80.

Scaling AKS clusters involves automatic scaling of nodes and pods. AKS supports the Cluster Autoscaler, which adjusts the number of nodes based on resource requirements. To enable the Cluster Autoscaler:

```
az aks update --resource-group MyResourceGroup --name MyAKSCluster --enable-
      cluster-autoscaler --min-count 1 --max-count 5
```

Moreover, AKS supports the Kubernetes Horizontal Pod Autoscaler (HPA) for scaling individual application pods based on CPU or other select metrics. An example HPA configuration:

```
apiVersion: autoscaling/v1
kind: HorizontalPodAutoscaler
metadata:
  name: frontend-autoscaler
spec:
  scaleTargetRef:
    apiVersion: apps/v1
    kind: Deployment
    name: frontend
  minReplicas: 1
  maxReplicas: 10
  targetCPUUtilizationPercentage: 50
```

This HPA adjusts the number of replicas for the 'frontend' deployment based on average CPU utilization, maintaining it around 50

Integrating AKS with other Azure services enhances the platform's capabilities. For instance, integrating with Azure Container Registry (ACR) facilitates private Docker image storage. Configuring an AKS cluster to authenticate with ACR involves the following commands:

```
az aks update -n MyAKSCluster -g MyResourceGroup --attach-acr MyACRRegistry
```

Monitoring and logging are integral to AKS operations, achieved through Azure Monitor and Azure Log Analytics. Enabling monitoring, as shown earlier, with the 'monitoring' addon provides insights into the cluster's health and performance.

Finally, security is a critical aspect of AKS. AKS integrates with Azure Security Center to provide security recommendations, compliance checks, and threat protection. Moreover, AKS supports secrets management using Azure Key Vault, ensuring sensitive information is securely stored and accessed by applications as needed.

By combining extensive capabilities with streamlined management, Azure Kubernetes Service (AKS) provides a comprehensive solution for deploying, managing, and scaling containerized applications on Kubernetes, leveraging the power and flexibility of Microsoft's Azure platform.

2.7 Serverless Computing with Azure Functions

Serverless computing allows developers to build and deploy applications without managing the underlying infrastructure. Azure Functions, a key component of Microsoft's serverless computing offer, provides a highly scalable and efficient solution for executing code. The primary advantage of using Azure Functions lies in its ability to dynamically allocate resources and scale execution without manual intervention.

Azure Functions supports multiple programming languages, including C#, JavaScript, F#, Java, and Python, among others, allowing developers to write code in the language of their choice. The platform follows an event-driven model, where functions are triggered by specific events such as HTTP requests, changes in data, messages from queues, or schedules.

Key Features:

- **Automatic Scaling:** Azure Functions automatically scales out to handle increased load, scaling back down when demand decreases.
- **Event-Driven:** Functions are triggered by various events, making it suitable for tasks such as handling HTTP requests, processing queues, or running scheduled tasks.
- **Pay-per-Execution:** Billing is based on the actual number of executions and resource consumption, leading to cost efficiency.
- **Multiple Language Support:** Developers can write functions in various languages, providing flexibility and encouraging cross-language functionality.
- **Integration:** Deep integration with other Azure services like Cosmos DB, Event Hubs, and Azure Blob Storage.

Creating an Azure Function:

Creating an Azure Function involves a series of steps, starting from setting up an Azure Functions app in the Azure portal to deploying the function code. The following example illustrates how to create a simple HTTP-triggered function using C#.

Step 1: Create an Azure Functions App

1.1 Navigate to the *Azure portal*.

1.2 Select *Create a resource*, and then search for *Function App*.

1.3 Configure the *Function App* with essential settings such as *Subscription*, *Resource Group*, *Function App name*, *Runtime stack*, *Region*, and *Operating system*.

1.4 Click *Create* to deploy the Function App.

Step 2: Create a Function in the App

2.1 Navigate to the newly created *Function App* in the Azure portal.

2.2 Select the *Functions* option from the left-hand menu.

2.3 Click *Create* and select the *HTTP trigger* template. Configure the function name and authorization level.

2.4 Once created, you will see a default function code editor.

Here is a sample code snippet for the HTTP-triggered function in C#:

```
using System.IO;
using Microsoft.AspNetCore.Mvc;
using Microsoft.Azure.WebJobs;
using Microsoft.Azure.WebJobs.Extensions.Http;
using Microsoft.AspNetCore.Http;
using Microsoft.Extensions.Logging;
using Newtonsoft.Json;

public static class HttpTriggerFunction
{
    [FunctionName("HttpTriggerFunction")]
    public static async Task<IActionResult> Run(
        [HttpTrigger(AuthorizationLevel.Function, "get", "post", Route = null)]
            HttpRequest req,
        ILogger log)
    {
        log.LogInformation("C# HTTP trigger function processed a request.");

        string name = req.Query["name"];
        string requestBody = await new StreamReader(req.Body).ReadToEndAsync();
        dynamic data = JsonConvert.DeserializeObject(requestBody);
        name = name ?? data?.name;

        return name != null
            ? (ActionResult)new OkObjectResult($"Hello, {name}")
            : new BadRequestObjectResult("Please pass a name on the query string or
                in the request body");
    }
}
```

Step 3: Test the Function

3.1 After deploying the function, open the *Functions* menu again in the Azure portal.

3.2 Select the function and click on *Code + Test*.

3.3 Use the *Test/Run* capability in the portal to test the function by providing parameters and executing it. Observe the logs and results directly in the portal.

Bindings in Azure Functions:

Bindings provide a declarative way to connect the function to other Azure services. Azure Functions supports both input and output bindings. Input bindings help the function to read data from various services, while output bindings write data to these services. Below is an example of adding a Blob storage output binding to the existing function.

```
public static class HttpTriggerFunction
{
    [FunctionName("HttpTriggerFunction")]
    public static async Task<IActionResult> Run(
        [HttpTrigger(AuthorizationLevel.Function, "get", "post", Route = null)]
            HttpRequest req,
        [Blob("output-container/{rand-guid}.txt", FileAccess.Write, Connection = "
            AzureWebJobsStorage")] TextWriter outputBlob,
        ILogger log)
    {
        log.LogInformation("C# HTTP trigger function processed a request.");

        string name = req.Query["name"];
        string requestBody = await new StreamReader(req.Body).ReadToEndAsync();
        dynamic data = JsonConvert.DeserializeObject(requestBody);
        name = name ?? data?.name;

        await outputBlob.WriteLineAsync($"Hello, {name}");

        return name != null
            ? (ActionResult)new OkObjectResult($"Hello, {name}")
            : new BadRequestObjectResult("Please pass a name on the query string or
                in the request body");
    }
}
```

Durable Functions:

Durable Functions extend Azure Functions by enabling long-running, stateful workflows. These workflows are written in code using familiar programming constructs and are based on the Durable Task Framework. Durable Functions provide abstractions for function chaining, fan-out/fan-in workflows, and human interaction into the orchestration, ensuring reliable execution flow.

Example: Orchestrator Function for Chaining

An example of a simple Durable Function orchestrator in C#:

```
using System.Collections.Generic;
using System.Threading.Tasks;
```

```
using Microsoft.Azure.WebJobs;
using Microsoft.Azure.WebJobs.Extensions.Http;
using Microsoft.Extensions.Logging;
using Microsoft.AspNetCore.Mvc;
using Microsoft.AspNetCore.Http;

public static class DurableOrchestrator
{
    [FunctionName("OrchestratorFunction")]
    public static async Task<List<string>> RunOrchestrator(
        [OrchestrationTrigger] IDurableOrchestrationContext context)
    {
        var outputs = new List<string>();

        outputs.Add(await context.CallActivityAsync<string>("SayHello", "Tokyo"));
        outputs.Add(await context.CallActivityAsync<string>("SayHello", "Seattle"));
        outputs.Add(await context.CallActivityAsync<string>("SayHello", "London"));

        return outputs;
    }

    [FunctionName("SayHello")]
    public static string SayHello([ActivityTrigger] string name, ILogger log)
    {
        log.LogInformation($"Saying hello to {name}.");
        return $"Hello, {name}!";
    }
}
```

Integrating Azure Functions into applications facilitates seamless scalability and efficient resource usage. These properties make them a versatile component in modern cloud-native application development.

2.8 Introduction to Azure Containers

Azure provides a comprehensive suite of services for running and managing containers at scale. Containers encapsulate an application along with its dependencies, providing a consistent computing environment for deployment. This enables applications to run reliably when moved from one computing environment to another. Azure's container ecosystem includes multiple services catering to various use cases, with Azure Kubernetes Service (AKS) being the central offering.

Containers excel in microservices architectures, where complex applications are decomposed into smaller, independent services. Each microservice can be deployed, updated, and scaled independently, which facilitates continuous development and deployment practices.

Azure Container Instances (ACI)

Azure Container Instances (ACI) is a fast and straightforward way to run containers in Azure. ACI supports Docker containers and provides isolated, ephemeral environments to run containerized applications without managing the underlying infrastructure. ACI is ideal for applications that require a quick response and do not need complex orchestration features.

```
az container create --resource-group myResourceGroup --name mycontainer \
  --image myapp:latest --cpu 1 --memory 1.5 --dns-name-label myapp
```

This command deploys a container instance with specified CPU and memory resources. It uses an existing Docker image and assigns a DNS name label for access.

Azure Kubernetes Service (AKS)

AKS provides a managed Kubernetes environment, enabling simplified cluster management. Kubernetes is an open-source system for automating deployment, scaling, and operations of application containers. AKS handles critical tasks such as cluster monitoring, automatic updates, and scaling, alleviating the operational burden on developers.

```
az aks create --resource-group myResourceGroup --name myAKSCluster \
  --node-count 3 --enable-addons monitoring --generate-ssh-keys
```

This command initializes an AKS cluster with three nodes and monitoring capabilities.

Azure Container Registry (ACR)

Azure Container Registry (ACR) is a managed Docker container registry service used for storing and managing container images. ACR supports Docker CLI commands, making it easy to push and pull container images within Azure environments. It integrates seamlessly with AKS and ACI, enabling a streamlined container deployment pipeline.

```
az acr create --resource-group myResourceGroup --name myContainerRegistry \
  --sku Basic
```

This command creates a basic ACR instance for storing container images.

Deployment and Management

Azure provides robust tools for deploying and managing containerized applications at scale. ACI is more suited for lightweight, temporary deployments, while AKS handles complex orchestrations. Deployment manifests, typically written in YAML, define the configuration for deploying containers in AKS.

```
apiVersion: apps/v1
kind: Deployment
metadata:
  name: myapp-deployment
spec:
  replicas: 3
  selector:
    matchLabels:
      app: myapp
  template:
    metadata:
      labels:
        app: myapp
    spec:
      containers:
      - name: myapp
        image: myContainerRegistry.azurecr.io/myapp:latest
        ports:
        - containerPort: 80
```

This manifest specifies the deployment configuration for a containerized application, detailing the number and replica set of pods along with container images and ports.

Security and Compliance

Azure ensures container security by offering integration with Azure Active Directory (AAD) for role-based access control (RBAC). Azure Policy can be applied to enforce security practices across all container resources. Azure's built-in security features, network policies, and isolation mechanisms safeguard containers and their communications.

Monitoring and Logging

Monitoring and logging are crucial for maintaining containerized applications. Azure Monitor and Azure Log Analytics help track performance metrics, resource utilization, and logs. These tools provide insights for troubleshooting and optimizing container deployments. Integration with tools like Prometheus and Grafana is also supported, enriching the monitoring ecosystem.

The Azure container services ecosystem constitutes a versatile, scalable, and secure platform for deploying and managing containerized applications. The managed nature of these services minimizes operational overhead, allowing developers to focus on innovation and rapid delivery.

```
Successfully deployed container instance 'mycontainer'
DNS Name: myapp.westus.azurecontainer.io
```

2.9 Azure Database Services

Azure Database Services provide a comprehensive solution for modern data storage and management needs, offering scalability, flexibility, and powerful features. This section presents an in-depth examination of various Azure Database Services, including Azure SQL Database, Azure Cosmos DB, Azure Database for MySQL, PostgreSQL, and MariaDB. Furthermore, it addresses considerations for selecting appropriate database solutions and best practices for implementation and optimization within an Azure environment.

Azure SQL Database is a fully managed relational database service based on the latest stable version of Microsoft SQL Server. It offers high availability, automated backups, and advanced security features. To create an Azure SQL Database, the following Azure CLI command can be utilized:

```
az sql db create --resource-group myResourceGroup --server myServer --name
    myDatabase --service-objective S0
```

Moreover, Azure SQL Database supports dynamic scaling to meet varying workload demands, ensuring performance and cost-efficiency. The built-in intelligence capabilities, such as automatic tuning and performance recommendations, assist developers in maintaining and optimizing database performance.

Azure Cosmos DB is a globally distributed, multi-model database service designed for high availability and low latency. It provides support for multiple data models, including document (e.g., MongoDB), key-value, graph (e.g., Gremlin), and column-family (e.g., Cassandra). A key feature of Azure Cosmos DB is its ability to elastically and independently scale throughput and storage across any number of Azure regions worldwide.

To create an Azure Cosmos DB account:

```
az cosmosdb create --name myCosmosDBAccount --resource-group myResourceGroup --
    kind MongoDB
```

Azure Cosmos DB offers SLAs for uptime, consistency, throughput, and latency. It also includes multiple consistency models: Strong, Bounded Staleness, Session, Consistent Prefix, and Eventual, providing flexibility to optimize for performance and availability based on specific application requirements.

Azure Database for MySQL, PostgreSQL, and MariaDB are fully managed database services designed to handle mission-critical workloads with automated maintenance, automated backups, and built-in security features. These services are compatible with commonly used open-source database technologies, making it easier to migrate existing MySQL, PostgreSQL, or MariaDB databases to Azure with minimal changes to application code.

To create an Azure Database for PostgreSQL instance:

```
az postgres server create --resource-group myResourceGroup --name myPostgresServer
    --location westus --admin-user myadmin --admin-password mypassword --sku-
    name B_Gen5_1
```

Azure supports scaling for compute, storage, and IOPS resources independently, providing flexibility to adapt to changing workload requirements. Additionally, these database services benefit from advanced security measures like Azure AD authentication, data encryption at rest, and virtual network service endpoints.

Choosing the right Azure Database Service depends on several factors, including data model requirements, consistency needs, geographic distribution, expected workload, and integration considerations with existing systems. Here is a quick comparison of key Azure Database Services:

- **Azure SQL Database**: Ideal for relational data requiring high transaction throughput, advanced security, automatic tuning, and integrations with SQL Server ecosystem tools.
- **Azure Cosmos DB**: Suitable for globally distributed applications needing low latency, high availability, and flexibility in choosing consistency models.
- **Azure Database for MySQL/PostgreSQL/MariaDB**: Best for applications depending on open-source relational databases, offering customizable performance and cost-effective scaling.

Effective use of these database services requires understanding and applying best practices for design, performance optimization, and maintenance. Key considerations include indexing strategies, query optimization, data partitioning/sharding, automated monitoring, and applying security best practices.

The following Python script demonstrates connecting to an Azure SQL Database and executing a basic query:

```
import pyodbc

# Configuration
server = 'tcp:myServer.database.windows.net'
database = 'myDatabase'
username = 'myUser'
password = 'myPassword'
driver = '{ODBC Driver 17 for SQL Server}'

# Connection string
connection_string = f'DRIVER={driver};SERVER={server};PORT=1433;DATABASE
    ={database};UID={username};PWD={password}'

# Connect and execute query
with pyodbc.connect(connection_string) as conn:
    with conn.cursor() as cursor:
        cursor.execute('SELECT * FROM myTable')
        row = cursor.fetchone()
        while row:
            print(f'Row: {row}')
            row = cursor.fetchone()
```

Example output from running the script:

```
Row: ('Value1', 'Value2', ...)
Row: ('Value3', 'Value4', ...)
...
```

This comprehensive exploration of Azure Database Services equips users with the necessary information to select, deploy, and manage databases effectively within the Azure ecosystem.

2.10 Azure AI and Machine Learning Services

Azure AI and Machine Learning services provide a robust platform for building, training, and deploying machine learning models and AI applications. These services cater to a wide range of machine learning needs, from basic algorithm training to sophisticated deep learning and reinforcement learning applications. Azure's ecosystem offers a suite of tools and services designed to make machine learning accessible and scalable for developers and data scientists.

The primary service offerings include Azure Machine Learning, Azure Cognitive Services, and Azure Bot Service. Each of these services addresses different aspects of AI and machine learning, enabling versatile and powerful solutions.

Azure Machine Learning (Azure ML) is a comprehensive, end-to-end service for managing the entire machine learning lifecycle. This includes data preparation, model training, deployment, monitoring, and management. One of the core features of Azure ML is the Azure Machine Learning Studio, an integrated development environment that provides a user-friendly interface, facilitating drag-and-drop capabilities for experiment creation and management.

```
from azureml.core import Workspace, Dataset

# Connect to the Azure ML workspace
ws = Workspace.from_config()

# Load a dataset from the workspace
dataset = Dataset.get_by_name(ws, 'my_dataset')
data = dataset.to_pandas_dataframe()
```

Azure ML supports a variety of frameworks and libraries, including TensorFlow, PyTorch, Scikit-learn, and many others. It also integrates with Azure Databricks, providing a powerful environment for collaborative and interactive analytics. Additionally, Azure ML offers automated machine learning (AutoML) capabilities that streamline the process of developing predictive models.

```
from azureml.train.automl import AutoMLConfig
from azureml.core.experiment import Experiment

# Define the AutoML configuration
automl_config = AutoMLConfig(task='classification',
                             primary_metric='accuracy',
                             training_data=data,
                             label_column_name='target',
                             n_cross_validations=5)

# Create an experiment and submit the run
experiment = Experiment(ws, 'automl_experiment')
run = experiment.submit(automl_config)
```

Azure Cognitive Services provide pre-built APIs that enable applications to see, hear, speak, understand, and interpret the needs through natural methods of communication. Cognitive Services are categorized into several groups, including Vision, Speech, Language, Decision, and Search.

The Vision category encompasses Computer Vision, Custom Vision, Face, and Form Recognizer APIs. These tools enable capabilities such as image analysis, facial recognition, and optical character recognition (OCR).

```
from azure.cognitiveservices.vision.computervision import ComputerVisionClient
from msrest.authentication import CognitiveServicesCredentials

# Authenticate to the Computer Vision service
```

```
cv_key = 'your_computer_vision_key'
cv_endpoint = 'your_computer_vision_endpoint'
credentials = CognitiveServicesCredentials(cv_key)
cv_client = ComputerVisionClient(cv_endpoint, credentials)

# Analyze an image
image_url = 'https://example.com/image.jpg'
analysis = cv_client.analyze_image(image_url, visual_features=['Description', 'Tags'])

# Print the result
for tag in analysis.tags:
    print(tag.name, tag.confidence)
```

The Speech category offers services like Speech-to-Text, Text-to-Speech, and Speech Translation. These services can be integrated into applications to enhance user interaction through voice commands and real-time translation.

```
from azure.cognitiveservices.speech import SpeechConfig, SpeechRecognizer

# Configure the Speech service
speech_key = 'your_speech_service_key'
service_region = 'your_service_region'
speech_config = SpeechConfig(subscription=speech_key, region=service_region)

# Recognize speech from the microphone
recognizer = SpeechRecognizer(speech_config=speech_config)
result = recognizer.recognize_once()

# Print the result
print(f"Recognized: {result.text}")
```

Azure Bot Service enables the development of intelligent, enterprise-grade bots that can interact with users naturally. This service integrates with the Bot Framework SDK, supporting multiple channels such as Microsoft Teams, Skype, Slack, and more. Bots developed using Azure Bot Service can leverage Cognitive Services to enhance their capabilities.

```
from botbuilder.core import BotFrameworkAdapter, TurnContext
from botbuilder.schema import Activity
import asyncio

# Define the bot's logic
async def handle_message(turn_context: TurnContext):
    await turn_context.send_activity(Activity(type="message", text="Hello, World!"))

# Set up the bot framework
adapter = BotFrameworkAdapter()
loop = asyncio.get_event_loop()

# Run the bot
try:
    loop.run_until_complete(adapter.process_activity(handle_message))
except Exception as ex:
    raise ex
```

These services collectively provide a powerful platform for developing AI and machine learning applications that can scale and perform at an enterprise level. Leveraging the capabilities of Azure AI and Machine Learning services can significantly reduce the time and complexity involved in building intelligent applications, allowing developers and data scientists to focus on the innovative aspects of their projects.

2.11 Hybrid and Multi-cloud Solutions with Azure Arc

Azure Arc is a breakthrough service that extends Azure management and services to any infrastructure, both on-premises and in other cloud environments, providing a unified management interface across hybrid and multi-cloud landscapes. Azure Arc plays a crucial role in digital transformation, enabling organizations to harness the power of Azure in scenarios where data residency, latency requirements, or existing on-premises investments necessitate a hybrid approach.

Azure Arc enables central management of a wide range of resources, including Windows and Linux servers, Kubernetes clusters, and a variety of databases, regardless of their location. It allows you to adopt Azure's governance, compliance, and security tools across a dispersed ecosystem of resources.

Azure Arc for Servers provides seamless management and monitoring capabilities for Windows and Linux machines running outside of Azure. This is accomplished by installing an agent on the non-Azure machines, which then registers them with Azure Arc. Once onboarded, these servers are treated as native Azure resources, enabling the use of various Azure management services such as Azure Policy, Azure Monitor, and Azure Security Center.

To illustrate this, consider the registration and management of a Linux server through Azure Arc. The following steps demonstrate the process:

```
# Install the Azure Arc agent
curl -sSL https://aka.ms/InstallAzureArcAgent | sudo bash

# Register the server with Azure Arc
sudo azcmagent connect --resource-group 'resource_group_name' --tenant-id '
    tenant_id' --location 'location'
```

In a multi-cloud environment, where organizations leverage services from multiple cloud providers to take advantage of specific service strengths, cost benefits, or compliance requirements, Azure Arc's capabilities become even more significant. Azure Arc-enabled Kubernetes simplifies the management of Kubernetes clusters across various environments. By connecting any certified Kubernetes cluster to Azure Arc, you can deploy and manage containerized applications with the same Azure tools you use for Azure Kubernetes Service (AKS).

Once a Kubernetes cluster is connected, Azure Monitor and Azure Policy can be applied consistently, ensuring uniform governance and visibility. The process of connecting a Kubernetes cluster to Azure Arc involves the following steps:

```
# Log in to Azure
az login

# Register the connectedk8s Azure CLI extension
az extension add --name connectedk8s

# Connect the cluster to Azure Arc
az connectedk8s connect --name 'cluster_name' --resource-group '
    resource_group_name'
```

A key advantage of Azure Arc is the flexibility it affords in database management. Azure Arc-enabled data services operate consistently across environments. You can deploy and manage Azure SQL Managed Instance or PostgreSQL Hyperscale on any infrastructure. This consistency is pivotal for scenarios requiring on-premises data residency or specific performance constraints.

Azure Arc-enabled SQL Managed Instance offers hybrid flexibility. It allows deploying enterprise-grade SQL Server databases in local datacenters while maintaining the robust capabilities of Azure SQL. The arcdata extension manages this by deploying instances through Kubernetes. The following demonstrates deployment steps:

```
# Add arcdata extension
az extension add --name arcdata

# Create custom location for the data service
az customlocation create --name 'custom_location_name' --resource-group '
    resource_group_name' --cluster-name 'cluster_name'

# Deploy SQL managed instance
az sql mi-arc create --name 'sql_instance_name' --resource-group '
    resource_group_name' --custom-location 'custom_location_id'
```

Beyond on-premises integration, Azure Arc extends to other cloud environments, enabling seamless management across AWS, Google Cloud Platform, and others. This cross-cloud integration ensures consistent security policies and comprehensive compliance adherence, centralizing management to simplify administrative overhead.

Azure Arc also facilitates DevOps practices in hybrid and multi-cloud setups. Developers can utilize GitOps configurations, enhancing deployment consistency across environments. By deploying policies and configurations via Git repositories, organizations leverage version control, fostering a clear, auditable paradigm for infrastructure as code.

Azure Arc's integration capabilities are enhanced by its interoperability with a wide array of Azure services. Services such as Azure App Services, Azure Functions, and Azure Logic Apps support hybrid deployments, allowing for elasticity and modern application practices across traditional and modern infrastructures.

Unified operations brought by Azure Arc address complexities traditional hybrid solutions face, ensuring security, compliance, and management across the entire IT ecosystem. This comprehensive approach simplifies the orchestration of complex environments, bolstering resilience and agility critical to modern business landscapes.

2.12 Overview of Azure IoT Services

Azure IoT Services provide a comprehensive suite of tools and services enabling the creation, deployment, and management of Internet of Things (IoT) solutions. These services facilitate seamless connectivity between devices, provision robust cloud-based analytics, enable device management, and integrate advanced security features. Central to these offerings are several key Azure services, including Azure IoT Hub, Azure IoT Edge, Azure Digital Twins, and the Azure IoT Central.

Azure IoT Hub is a fully managed service that acts as the central messaging hub for bi-directional communication between IoT applications and the devices it manages. The IoT Hub ensures secure and reliable communication and can process vast amounts of data from numerous IoT devices. Through device-to-cloud telemetry data and cloud-to-device messaging, IoT Hub underpins the entire IoT ecosystem with elaborate routing rules and connection methodologies using protocols such as MQTT, HTTPS, and AMQP.

The following example demonstrates a Python script for sending device-to-cloud messages using the IoT Hub SDK:

```
from azure.iot.device import IoTHubDeviceClient, Message
```

```
CONNECTION_STRING = "HostName=<IoTHubName>.azure-devices.net;DeviceId
    =<DeviceId>;SharedAccessKey=<SharedAccessKey>"
MESSAGE_TEXT = "This is a message from the device!"

client = IoTHubDeviceClient.create_from_connection_string(
    CONNECTION_STRING)

def send_message():
    message = Message(MESSAGE_TEXT)
    client.send_message(message)
    print("Message successfully sent")

if __name__ == "__main__":
    send_message()
```

The output of the script:

```
Message successfully sent
```

Azure IoT Edge extends cloud intelligence and analytics to the edge of the network. By deploying modules that contain cloud workloads to IoT Edge devices, developers can run data processing directly on the devices, significantly reducing latency and dependence on cloud connectivity. It allows for improved response times and local action while continuing to leverage cloud services. IoT Edge provides a runtime environment that enables execution of functionality such as stream analytics, machine learning, and custom code.

Azure Digital Twins is an IoT service that models and creates comprehensive digital representations of environments, allowing for the simulation of real-world environments. It enables spatial intelligence graphs to model the relationships and interactions between people, spaces, and devices. Digital Twins can be utilized to optimize operations, improve planning, enhance the understanding of asset usage, and provide actionable insights by unifying disparate data streams and sources.

Azure IoT Central offers a fully managed IoT application platform, simplifying the deployment and management of IoT solutions without requiring deep knowledge of cloud development. It provides dashboards, customizable user interfaces, and pre-configured templates for rapid deployment and iteration. IoT Central ensures built-in scalability and security, integrates with other Azure services seamlessly, and reduces the complexity associated with developing IoT applications.

Security in IoT is paramount, and Azure IoT Suite addresses this need comprehensively. Azure Sphere is a comprehensive solution encompassing integrated hardware, operating systems, and a cloud-based security service to secure IoT devices. The layered security approach ensures robust defense against evolving threats, enabling devices to retain the integrity, confidentiality, and availability of data.

Considering the coexistence of numerous components within Azure IoT Services, integration and interaction facilitate more impactful solutions. Leveraging Azure's advanced analytics services like Azure Stream Analytics and Azure Time Series Insights enables real-time analytics, visualization of time-series data, and historical trend analysis, enhancing predictive maintenance and operational efficiencies.

Utilizing these capabilities, businesses can transform raw telemetry data into actionable insights, optimizing resource utilization, reducing downtime, and driving informed decision-making. The holistic approach of Azure IoT services ensures unified management, seamless connectivity, robust security, and unrivaled scalability for IoT solutions across various industries.

Chapter 3

Deploying and Managing Azure Resources

This chapter focuses on the tools and practices for deploying and managing resources in Azure. It covers the use of ARM Templates, Azure Portal, Azure CLI, and PowerShell for resource management. Key topics include the basics of Azure Bicep, resource tracking and tagging, and implementing Role-Based Access Control (RBAC). Additionally, the chapter discusses deploying and managing virtual machines, scaling applications, utilizing Azure DevTest Labs, enforcing resource governance with Azure Policy, and managing costs and budgets effectively.

3.1 Azure Resource Manager (ARM) Templates

Azure Resource Manager (ARM) templates provide a declarative way to define and deploy Azure resources. With ARM templates, one can specify the resources needed for a project in a JSON format. This allows for consistent and reproducible deployments, making infrastructure as code (IaC) a reality on the Azure platform.

The JSON format used by ARM templates is divided into several key sections: schema, contentVersion, parameters, variables, resources, and outputs.

- Schema: Defines the location of the JSON schema file that describes the structure and syntax of the template. It ensures that the template complies with the expected format. The latest schema can be referenced via the URL: https://schema.management.azure.com/schemas/2019-04-01/deploymentTemplate.json#
- contentVersion: Specifies the version of the template content. This value is defined by the user and not linked to the schema version. It is typically used to manage template changes and versioning.
- parameters: Allows developers to define parameters to make the template more flexible and reusable. Parameters can be customized for different environments or configurations.
- variables: Provides a mechanism to define values that can be reused throughout the template. Variables help to simplify templates by avoiding repetition.
- resources: The core section where actual Azure resources are defined and configured. Each resource is defined as an object with various properties such as type, name, apiVersion, location, and properties.
- outputs: Defines the values that will be returned after the deployment. Outputs can be used to retrieve important information about deployed resources, such as connection strings or resource IDs.

Below is an example of an ARM template that deploys a simple Azure Storage Account:

```
{
 "$schema": "https://schema.management.azure.com/schemas/2019-04-01/
     deploymentTemplate.json#",
 "contentVersion": "1.0.0.0",
 "parameters": {
   "storageAccountType": {
     "type": "string",
     "defaultValue": "Standard_LRS",
     "allowedValues": [
       "Standard_LRS",
       "Standard_GRS",
       "Standard_ZRS",
       "Premium_LRS"
     ],
     "metadata": {
       "description": "The type of storage account to create."
     }
```

```
    },
    "storageAccountName": {
      "type": "string",
      "metadata": {
        "description": "Name of the storage account"
      }
    }
  },
  "variables": {
    "location": "[resourceGroup().location]"
  },
  "resources": [
    {
      "type": "Microsoft.Storage/storageAccounts",
      "apiVersion": "2021-01-01",
      "name": "[parameters('storageAccountName')]",
      "location": "[variables('location')]",
      "sku": {
        "name": "[parameters('storageAccountType')]"
      },
      "kind": "StorageV2",
      "properties": {}
    }
  ],
  "outputs": {
    "storageAccountId": {
      "type": "string",
      "value": "[resourceId('Microsoft.Storage/storageAccounts', parameters('
          storageAccountName'))]"
    }
  }
}
```

In this template, the parameters section defines two parameters: storageAccountType and storageAccountName. storageAccountType has a default value of Standard_LRS and allows for multiple storage replication options.

The variables section defines a variable called location that retrieves the location of the resource group in which the resources are being deployed.

In the resources section, a storage account resource is defined with the type Microsoft.Storage/storageAccounts. The name and location of the storage account are dynamically assigned based on the parameter and variable values. The storage account SKU (Stock Keeping Unit) is configured based on the storageAccountType parameter. The kind property specifies the type of storage account.

The outputs section returns the resource ID of the newly created storage account, which can be useful for subsequent operations or scripts.

To deploy this ARM template, various tools can be used, including Azure Portal, Azure CLI, and PowerShell.

Using Azure CLI, the following command deploys the template:

```
az deployment group create --resource-group myResourceGroup --template-file
    storageaccount.json --parameters storageAccountName=myUniqueStorageAccount
```

The output will be similar to:


```
{
 "id": "/subscriptions/{subscription-id}/resourceGroups/myResourceGroup/providers/Microsoft.Resources/deployments/myDeployment",
 "name": "myDeployment",
 "properties": {
  "outputs": {
   "storageAccountId": {
    "type": "String",
    "value": "/subscriptions/{subscription-id}/resourceGroups/myResourceGroup/providers/Microsoft.Storage/storageAccounts/myUniqueStorageAccount"
   }
  }
 }
}
```


This JSON output confirms successful deployment and provides the resource ID of the storage account.

Understanding ARM templates is fundamental for managing Azure resources programmatically. With ARM templates, one can automate processes, enforce consistency, and enable version control on infrastructure setups.

3.2 Deploying Resources with Azure Portal

The Azure Portal provides a user-friendly, web-based interface for managing and deploying resources within Microsoft's cloud environment. It facilitates the creation, configuration, and monitoring of various Azure services without requiring scripting or command-line tools, making it accessible for both beginners and experienced professionals.

To deploy resources using the Azure Portal, follow these steps:

1. **Accessing the Azure Portal:** Open a web browser and navigate to https://portal.azure.com. Log in with your Azure credentials.

2. **Navigation to the Resource Creation Interface:** On the Azure Portal homepage, select the **Create a resource** button located on the top left corner. This action brings up the **Create a resource** blade, where you can choose from a plethora of Azure services and resources such as Virtual Machines, Web Apps, Databases, and Storage Accounts.

3. **Selecting a Resource:** For example, to create a Virtual Machine (VM), in the **Create a resource** blade, type *Virtual Machine* into the search bar. Select *Virtual Machine* from the search results, which navigates you to the **Virtual Machine** creation blade.

4. **Configuring the Resource:** The resource creation blade for a Vir-

tual Machine includes several tabs for different configuration options:

- - **Basics:** Here, you enter information such as the subscription, resource group, virtual machine name, region, and availability options. You also select an image, such as *Windows Server 2019* or *Ubuntu 18.04*, and choose the size of the VM.
- - **Disks:** Configure the OS disk and any data disks. Options include managed disks and selecting disk types like Standard HDD, Standard SSD, or Premium SSD.
- - **Networking:** Set up the public IP address, network interfaces, subnet, and network security group. Additionally, you can specify virtual network peering and configure load balancer settings if needed.
- - **Management:** Configure monitoring, backup, and guest OS diagnostics. You can enable features such as boot diagnostics, system-assigned managed identity, and automatic shutdown.
- - **Advanced:** Customize extensions, cloud-init for Linux VMs, and custom data for Windows VMs.
- - **Tags:** Apply tags to your resources to manage and categorize them effectively. Tags consist of {key, value} pairs, such as {Environment, Production}.

Complete the required fields and navigate through the configuration tabs. Azure validates the configuration to ensure that all necessary fields are correctly filled.

5. **Review and Create:** After configuring the resource, select the **Review + create** button. This tab provides a summary of your configurations and validates the inputs. If there are any configuration issues, Azure displays error messages pointing to the fields that need attention.

6. **Deployment:** Once validation is successful, click on the **Create** button. Azure initiates the deployment process, and a progress notification appears on the Azure Portal interface. The deployment typically involves the allocation of resources, network setup, and initialization of the virtual machine.

7. **Monitoring and Managing Deployed Resources:** Upon successful deployment, navigate to the **Resource Groups** blade from the left-hand menu. Select the resource group containing your newly created

VM to view all associated resources such as network interfaces, public IP addresses, storage accounts, and virtual networks.

You can manage the deployed VM by accessing its specific blade. Here, perform tasks such as starting, stopping, resizing, and configuring networking settings. Additionally, you can view performance metrics, set up alerts, and access the VM via Remote Desktop Protocol (RDP) for Windows VMs or Secure Shell (SSH) for Linux VMs.

```
# Example Output: Success message and details in Azure Portal
Deployment succeeded. Click here to navigate to your resource.
```

Deploying resources through the Azure Portal is an intuitive and efficient way to leverage Azure's capabilities. The portal's comprehensive interface allows for meticulous configuration and management of resources, ensuring that they meet the specific requirements of various applications and services.

3.3 Using Azure CLI for Resource Management

Azure Command-Line Interface (CLI) is a set of commands used to create and manage Azure resources. Designed for flexibility and automation, Azure CLI is ideal for users who are familiar with shell scripting and seeking efficient management of their Azure infrastructure.

Azure CLI can be installed on multiple platforms including Windows, macOS, and Linux. Additionally, you can use it via the Azure Cloud Shell within the Azure Portal. To install Azure CLI on your local machine, refer to the official Azure documentation for specific instructions for your operating system.

After installation, verify the CLI by checking the version. Open your terminal or command prompt and execute:

```
az --version
```

This command returns the current version of Azure CLI along with detailed information on dependencies and extensions.

To start using Azure CLI, you must log in to your Azure account. Execute the following command:

```
az login
```

Your browser will open prompting you to enter your Azure credentials. Upon successful authentication, the CLI session in your terminal will display details of your subscription.

Azure CLI uses a structure of commands followed by arguments and specific options. The general syntax is:

```
az <command-group> <command> <sub-commands> [arguments]
```

For example, to create a new resource group, use:

```
az group create --name MyResourceGroup --location eastus
```

Below is a detailed examination of some critical commands for managing Azure resources using Azure CLI.

Creating Resources

To create a resource, specify the 'create' command within the resource's command group. For instance, to create a virtual machine (VM):

```
az vm create --resource-group MyResourceGroup --name MyVM --image UbuntuLTS --
    admin-username azureuser --generate-ssh-keys
```

This command creates a VM in the specified resource group using the Ubuntu LTS image and generates SSH keys for secure access.

Listing Resources

To list resources within a resource group, use the following command:

```
az resource list --resource-group MyResourceGroup
```

This lists all resources in 'MyResourceGroup', showing details such as their names, types, and locations.

Updating Resources

To update a resource, use the 'update' sub-command within the resource group. For example, to change the tags of a resource group:

```
az group update --name MyResourceGroup --set tags.Environment=Production
```

This command adds the 'Environment=Production' tag to 'MyResourceGroup'.

Deleting Resources

Deleting resources can be done with the 'delete' command. Always exercise caution with this command as it permanently removes the specified resource. To delete a resource group and all its content:

```
az group delete --name MyResourceGroup --yes --no-wait
```

The '–yes' flag bypasses the confirmation prompt, and '–no-wait' allows the command to return immediately without waiting for the operation to finish.

Managing Virtual Machines

Azure CLI provides comprehensive commands for managing VMs. To start a VM, use:

```
az vm start --resource-group MyResourceGroup --name MyVM
```

To stop a VM, execute:

```
az vm stop --resource-group MyResourceGroup --name MyVM
```

To list all VMs in a resource group:

```
az vm list --resource-group MyResourceGroup --output table
```

The '–output table' argument formats the output in a readable table.

Deploying ARM Templates

Azure CLI allows direct deployment of Azure Resource Manager (ARM) templates. To deploy a template file:

```
az deployment group create --resource-group MyResourceGroup --template-file template.
    json --parameters @parameters.json
```

The command above deploys an ARM template specified in 'template.json' with parameters provided in 'parameters.json' to the specified resource group.

By leveraging Azure CLI, users can script and automate many of their resource management tasks, driving efficiency and consistency. Azure CLI's wide range of options and support for automated workflows make it a powerful tool for both simple and complex operations within Azure.

3.4 Managing Resources with PowerShell

PowerShell is a powerful scripting language and command-line shell designed for task automation and configuration management. Within the context of Azure, PowerShell provides a versatile platform for managing and automating Azure resources through the Azure PowerShell module. This section will explore the installation and configuration of Azure PowerShell, authenticating with Azure, managing resources like virtual machines, storage accounts, resource groups, and more.

Installation and Configuration of Azure PowerShell

Installing the Azure PowerShell module can be achieved using the PowerShellGet module. First, open the PowerShell terminal with administrative privileges and execute the following command to install the Az module:

```
Install-Module -Name Az -AllowClobber -Scope CurrentUser
```

The -AllowClobber switch ensures that existing cmdlets with the same name will be overridden if necessary. Following the successful installation, it's vital to verify the installation and import the module:

```
Import-Module Az
Get-InstalledModule -Name Az
```

Authenticating with Azure

To interact with Azure resources, authentication is a prerequisite. Azure PowerShell supports both interactive login and service principal authentication. For interactive login, use the Connect-AzAccount cmdlet:

```
Connect-AzAccount
```

Upon execution, this command will prompt a login window where your Azure credentials should be entered. To verify the currently logged-in account and available subscriptions, execute:

```
Get-AzContext
```

For scenarios requiring non-interactive authentication, such as automated scripts, service principal authentication is often employed. Create a service principal using:

```
$sp = New-AzADServicePrincipal -DisplayName "MyServicePrincipal"
```

Store the service principal credentials securely. Use these credentials in scripts for authentication:

```
$TenantId = "xxxxxxxx-xxxx-xxxx-xxxx-xxxxxxxxxxxx"
$ClientId = "xxxxxxxx-xxxx-xxxx-xxxx-xxxxxxxxxxxx"
$ClientSecret = "xxxxxxxxxxxxxxxxxxxxxxxxxxxxxxxx"
$SecureClientSecret = ConvertTo-SecureString $ClientSecret -AsPlainText -Force
$Credential = New-Object -TypeName System.Management.Automation.PSCredential -
    ArgumentList $ClientId, $SecureClientSecret
```

```
Connect-AzAccount -ServicePrincipal -TenantId $TenantId -Credential $Credential
```

Managing Azure Resources

Once authenticated, managing resources such as resource groups, virtual machines, and storage accounts becomes feasible.

Resource Groups

Resource groups act as logical containers for resources. Create a new resource group with the New-AzResourceGroup cmdlet:

```
New-AzResourceGroup -Name "MyResourceGroup" -Location "EastUS"
```

Retrieve information about an existing resource group using the Get-AzResourceGroup cmdlet:

```
Get-AzResourceGroup -Name "MyResourceGroup"
```

To remove a resource group and all its contained resources, the Remove-AzResourceGroup cmdlet is used:

```
Remove-AzResourceGroup -Name "MyResourceGroup" -Force
```

Virtual Machines

Virtual machines (VMs) are integral to many Azure deployments. To create a new VM, use the following sequence of commands to specify the VM configuration:

```
$vmName = "MyVM"
$resourceGroup = "MyResourceGroup"
$location = "EastUS"
$credential = Get-Credential -Message "Enter VM credentials"

# Create a virtual network
$vnet = New-AzVirtualNetwork -ResourceGroupName $resourceGroup -Location
      $location -Name "$vmName-VNet" -AddressPrefix "10.0.0.0/16"
$subnet = Add-AzVirtualNetworkSubnetConfig -Name "default" -AddressPrefix "
      10.0.0.0/24" -VirtualNetwork $vnet
Set-AzVirtualNetwork -VirtualNetwork $vnet

# Create a public IP address
$pip = New-AzPublicIpAddress -ResourceGroupName $resourceGroup -Location
      $location -Name "$vmName-PublicIP" -AllocationMethod Dynamic

# Create a network interface
$nic = New-AzNetworkInterface -Name "$vmName-NIC" -ResourceGroupName
      $resourceGroup -Location $location -SubnetId $vnet.Subnets[0].Id -
      PublicIpAddressId $pip.Id

# Specify VM configuration
$vmConfig = New-AzVMConfig -VMName $vmName -VMSize "Standard_DS1_v2" |
  Set-AzVMOperatingSystem -Windows -ComputerName $vmName -Credential
```

```
    $credential |
  Set-AzVMSourceImage -PublisherName "MicrosoftWindowsServer" -Offer "
    WindowsServer" -Skus "2019-Datacenter" -Version "latest" |
  Add-AzVMNetworkInterface -Id $nic.Id

# Create the VM
New-AzVM -ResourceGroupName $resourceGroup -Location $location -VM $vmConfig
```

To start, stop, and deallocate a VM, the following cmdlets are employed respectively:

```
Start-AzVM -ResourceGroupName $resourceGroup -Name $vmName
Stop-AzVM -ResourceGroupName $resourceGroup -Name $vmName
Stop-AzVM -ResourceGroupName $resourceGroup -Name $vmName -StayProvisioned
```

The Stop-AzVM cmdlet with the -StayProvisioned switch deallocates the VM, thus stopping billing for the compute resources while retaining the VM configuration.

Storage Accounts

Storage accounts are necessary for storing data and ensuring high availability. Create a new storage account with the New-AzStorageAccount cmdlet:

```
New-AzStorageAccount -ResourceGroupName $resourceGroup -AccountName "
    mystorageaccount" -Location $location -SkuName "Standard_LRS" -Kind "
    StorageV2"
```

Retrieve storage account details with the Get-AzStorageAccount cmdlet:

```
Get-AzStorageAccount -ResourceGroupName $resourceGroup -Name "
    mystorageaccount"
```

Remove a storage account using the Remove-AzStorageAccount cmdlet:

```
Remove-AzStorageAccount -ResourceGroupName $resourceGroup -Name "
    mystorageaccount"
```

The flexibility of PowerShell facilitates the automation of complex tasks and is an invaluable tool for managing Azure resources effectively. Combining PowerShell scripts with other Azure services like Azure Automation and Logic Apps can result in a robust and scalable management framework for your Azure environment.

Throughout this section, we have utilized various essential cmdlets to interact with and manage Azure resources via PowerShell. Mastery of these cmdlets and their parameters is crucial for efficient resource management and automation in Azure, ultimately leading to more streamlined and cost-effective operations.

3.5 Introduction to Azure Bicep

Azure Bicep is a domain-specific language (DSL) that provides an efficient and concise way to deploy Azure resources declaratively. Bicep is designed to simplify the authoring experience compared to JSON-based Azure Resource Manager (ARM) templates by providing clearer syntax and improved tooling. As a transpiler to ARM JSON, Bicep encapsulates the same capabilities while enhancing readability and manageability.

Bicep files are denoted with the .bicep extension. They define resources and configurations in a high-level language similar to other template-based languages. The Bicep language offers various features such as variables, resource loops, conditional resource deployment, and modularity. This section begins by examining the syntax and structure of a Bicep file.

```
param location string = resourceGroup().location

resource storageAccount 'Microsoft.Storage/storageAccounts@2021-02-01' = {
  name: 'mystorageaccount${uniqueString(resourceGroup().id)}'
  location: location
  sku: {
    name: 'Standard_LRS'
  }
  kind: 'StorageV2'
}
```

In the Bicep file above, the param keyword declares a parameter for the location, which defaults to the resource group's location. The resource keyword declares an Azure Storage account with a dynamically generated name. The properties name, location, sku, and kind are specified within the resource block. The uniqueString function generates a unique name using the resource group ID.

Parameters in Bicep allow for customizable deployment configurations. Parameters can be of several types, including string, int, bool, and array. The following example demonstrates how to use different parameter types and their default values.

```
param environment string = 'production'
param instanceCount int = 3
param enableDiagnostics bool = true
param allowedLocations array = [
```

```
  'WestUS'
  'EastUS'
  'CentralUS'
]
```

Bicep supports outputs, which can be retrieved after deployment. The output keyword specifies the values to return. Outputs are useful for automation workflows that consume deployment results.

```
output storageAccountName string = storageAccount.name
output storageAccountKey string = listKeys(storageAccount.id, '2021-02-01')[0].value
```

Modules in Bicep promote reusability by allowing common sets of resources to be defined in separate files. Modules can be parametrized and included in main Bicep files. The module's .bicep file is referenced using the module keyword.

Consider a module to define a Logging account in logging.bicep:

```
param logAnalyticsWorkspaceName string
param location string

resource logAnalyticsWorkspace 'Microsoft.OperationalInsights/workspaces@2020-08-01'
    = {
  name: logAnalyticsWorkspaceName
  location: location
  sku: {
    name: 'PerGB2018'
  }
}

output workspaceId string = logAnalyticsWorkspace.id
```

To utilize the module in a main Bicep file:

```
param location string = resourceGroup().location

module logging 'logging.bicep' = {
  name: 'loggingModule'
  params: {
    logAnalyticsWorkspaceName: 'myLogAnalyticsWorkspace'
    location: location
  }
}
output logAnalyticsWorkspaceId string = logging.outputs.workspaceId
```

The example above specifies a logging module's inclusion, passing parameters and retrieving the output workspaceId.

Bicep supports resource definitions in loops, which allow for dynamic resource creation based on specified count or array parameters. This feature is highly beneficial for deploying identical resources, such as multiple virtual machines or storage accounts.

```
param instanceCount int = 3

resource myStorageAccounts 'Microsoft.Storage/storageAccounts@2021-02-01' = [for i
    in range(0, instanceCount): {
  name: 'storagaccount${i}${uniqueString(resourceGroup().id)}'
  location: resourceGroup().location
  sku: {
    name: 'Standard_LRS'
  }
  kind: 'StorageV2'
}]
```

The code snippet demonstrates iterating over a range with specified instanceCount to create multiple Storage accounts.

Lastly, it is crucial to test Bicep templates for correctness. Azure provides the az bicep CLI command and the Visual Studio Code Bicep extension for local development and validation. Converting Bicep to ARM JSON is straightforward using the bicep build command, ensuring compatibility and ease of deployment.

By presenting a simpler yet powerful templating language, Bicep aims to improve the Azure resource management experience, fostering better practices through modular, maintainable, and expressive infrastructure code.

3.6 Resource Tracking and Tagging

Resource tracking and tagging are fundamental practices for maintaining an organized and efficient cloud environment in Microsoft Azure. These practices enable administrators to identify, categorize, and manage resources systematically, which is crucial for operational efficiency, cost management, and governance.

Resource tagging is the process of applying descriptive metadata, known as tags, to Azure resources. Tags consist of key-value pairs that help you categorize resources based on various attributes such as department, environment, project, or owner. This categorization is essential for filtering, sorting, and managing resources across subscriptions.

Tag Structure: Tags in Azure are structured as key-value pairs. Each tag consists of a key, which serves as the tag name, and a value that represents the tag's content. The following illustrates the syntax for applying tags using an Azure Resource Manager (ARM) template:

```
{
  "$schema": "https://schema.management.azure.com/schemas/2019-04-01/
      deploymentTemplate.json#",
  "contentVersion": "1.0.0.0",
  "resources": [
    {
      "type": "Microsoft.Compute/virtualMachines",
      "apiVersion": "2019-12-01",
      "name": "myVM",
      "location": "West US",
      "tags": {
        "department": "finance",
        "environment": "production",
        "owner": "JohnDoe"
      },
      "properties": {
        ...
      }
    }
  ]
}
```

Tagging Best Practices:

- **Consistent Tagging Scheme:** Establish a consistent tagging strategy across your organization. Ensure that everyone uses the same key names and follows the guidelines for values.

- **Automate Tagging:** Use policies and templates to enforce tagging automatically during resource creation.

- **Limit the Number of Tags:** While tags are useful, too many tags can lead to complexity. Azure allows a maximum of 50 tags per resource.

- **Update Tags Regularly:** Periodically review and update your tags to ensure they remain relevant and accurate.

Applying Tags via Azure Portal: To apply tags using the Azure Portal, navigate to the resource you want to tag. In the resource's settings, find the Tags option, and add your desired key-value pairs. The interface allows for easy addition, modification, and deletion of tags.

Applying Tags via Azure CLI: Azure CLI provides a simple command-line interface for managing tags. The following command shows how to add a tag to a virtual machine:

```
az resource tag --tags department=finance environment=production owner=JohnDoe --
    name myVM --resource-group MyResourceGroup --resource-type Microsoft.
    Compute/virtualMachines
```

Applying Tags via Azure PowerShell: PowerShell can also be used to apply tags to resources. The following example demonstrates tagging a virtual machine:

```
$tags = @{
    department = "finance"
    environment = "production"
    owner = "JohnDoe"
}
Set-AzResource -ResourceName "myVM" -ResourceGroupName "MyResourceGroup" -
    ResourceType "Microsoft.Compute/virtualMachines" -Tag $tags
```

Resource Tracking: Resource tracking encompasses monitoring and analyzing resource usage and performance. Azure provides various tools for comprehensive resource tracking:

- **Azure Monitor:** Collects and analyzes logs, metrics, and diagnostic data from Azure resources. You can create alerts and dashboards to monitor resource performance and health.
- **Azure Resource Graph Explorer:** Enables querying and exploring your Azure resources at scale. It helps in finding resources based on specific criteria, such as tags or locations.
- **Cost Management + Billing:** Offers insights into your cloud spend across multiple subscriptions, and helps identify cost-saving opportunities by analyzing resource usage patterns.

Example Usage of Azure Resource Graph Explorer: To use the Azure Resource Graph Explorer for finding all resources tagged with the key environment and value production:

```
Resources
| where tags.environment == 'production'
| project name, type, location, tags
```

Azure Resource Graph Explorer provides a powerful query language that allows detailed and complex investigation of the resources across your Azure environment.

Integrating resource tracking and tagging in your Azure deployments enhances resource management, operational efficiency, and cost control. Employing a consistent and automated tagging strategy, along with utilizing comprehensive tracking tools, ensures your resources are easily identifiable, manageable, and aligned with organizational standards.

3.7 Role-Based Access Control (RBAC) for Resource Management

Role-Based Access Control (RBAC) is a critical mechanism in Azure that simplifies the management of permissions and access to resources. RBAC allows administrators to assign specific roles to users, groups, and applications, which then grant the appropriate level of access to resources. This approach enhances security by adhering to the principle of least privilege, ensuring users only have access to the resources necessary for their role.

To facilitate a comprehensive understanding of RBAC in Azure, we will delve into various aspects, including the architecture of RBAC, built-in roles, custom roles, assignment procedures, and best practices for managing access.

RBAC utilizes a declarative model where permissions are granted through role assignments. A role assignment consists of three main elements:

- **Security principal**: A security principal can be a user, group, service principal, or managed identity that needs access to Azure resources.
- **Role definition**: Roles contain a set of permissions. A role definition lists operations that can be performed, such as read, write, or delete.
- **Scope**: Scope defines the boundaries within which the role assignment is valid. It can be specified at multiple levels including subscription, resource group, or individual resources.

Built-In Roles:

Azure provides several built-in roles tailored to common usage scenarios, making it simpler to apply standardized permissions. Some of the key built-in roles include:

- **Owner**: Full access to all resources including the ability to delegate access to others.
- **Contributor**: Access to create and manage all types of Azure resources but cannot grant access to others.

- **Reader**: Read-only access to the Azure resources.
- **User Access Administrator**: Manages user access to Azure resources.

To view the built-in roles available in Azure, you can use the following Azure CLI command:

```
az role definition list --output table
```

Custom Roles:

While built-in roles cover many scenarios, custom roles allow for more granular control tailored to unique requirements. Custom roles are defined using JSON templates that specify the allowed actions. Below is an example of a custom role definition that grants read access to storage accounts:

```
{
  "Name": "Storage Account Reader",
  "IsCustom": true,
  "Description": "Can read storage account information.",
  "Actions": [
    "Microsoft.Storage/storageAccounts/read"
  ],
  "NotActions": [],
  "DataActions": [],
  "NotDataActions": [],
  "AssignableScopes": [
    "/subscriptions/{subscriptionId}"
  ]
}
```

This role can be created using the following Azure CLI command:

```
az role definition create --role-definition roleDefinition.json
```

Role Assignment:

Assigning a role to a user, group, or application involves specifying the security_principal and the appropriate scope. The following Azure CLI command demonstrates how to assign the Contributor role to a user at the resource group level:

```
az role assignment create --assignee user@example.com --role Contributor --resource-
    group MyResourceGroup
```

Similarly, the same operation can be performed using PowerShell:

```
New-AzRoleAssignment -SignInName user@example.com -RoleDefinitionName
    Contributor -ResourceGroupName MyResourceGroup
```

Best Practices for RBAC Management:

To effectively manage RBAC, consider the following best practices:

- **Least Privilege**: Assign only the minimum permissions necessary for users to perform their tasks.
- **Role Optimization**: Prefer built-in roles when possible as they are optimized and maintained by Azure. Use custom roles only when necessary.
- **Audit and Review**: Regularly review role assignments and audit access to ensure compliance and detect any unauthorized access.
- **Group Assignments**: Assign roles to groups instead of individual users to streamline role management and reduce complexity.
- **Principle of Segregation**: Separate duties among multiple users to reduce the risk of malicious activities.
- **Conditional Access**: Use Azure Active Directory (AAD) conditional access policies to enforce additional access controls such as Multi-Factor Authentication (MFA).

Executing the following command in Azure CLI lists all role assignments in a subscription:

```
az role assignment list --all --output table
```

By adhering to these best practices and utilizing the tools and commands demonstrated, administrators can efficiently manage access to Azure resources, enhancing both security and operational efficiency without compromising on flexibility.

3.8 Deploying and Managing Virtual Machines

Virtual machines (VMs) are a fundamental component of modern cloud computing environments. Azure provides a robust platform to deploy, manage, and scale VMs with ease. In this section, we will explore the processes and tools available in Azure for effectively managing virtual machines.

Azure VMs provide compute resources as needed, making them suitable for various workloads, including web applications, databases, and batch processing. The deployment and management of these VMs can be achieved using several methods: Azure Portal, Azure CLI, PowerShell, and ARM Templates.

1. Deploying a Virtual Machine Using Azure Portal

The Azure Portal provides a graphical interface that simplifies VM creation:

- Navigate to the Azure Portal.
- Click on + Create a resource and select Virtual machine.
- Fill out the necessary fields in the Basics tab, such as Subscription, Resource Group, and VM details (e.g., name, region, image, size).
- Choose an administrative username and an authentication method (SSH public key or password).
- Configure additional settings in the Disks, Networking, Management, and Advanced tabs as needed.
- Review the settings and click Create to deploy the VM.

2. Deploying a Virtual Machine Using Azure CLI

Azure CLI offers a command-line interface for managing Azure resources. Here is a sample command to create a VM:

```
az vm create \
    --resource-group MyResourceGroup \
    --name MyVM \
    --image UbuntuLTS \
    --admin-username azureuser \
    --authentication-type ssh \
    --ssh-key-value ~/.ssh/id_rsa.pub
```

The above command performs the following actions:

- Specifies the resource group with –resource-group MyResourceGroup.
- Names the VM MyVM.
- Selects the Ubuntu LTS image with –image UbuntuLTS.

- Sets the administrator username to azureuser.
- Uses SSH for authentication with the public key path specified.

3. Managing Virtual Machines Using PowerShell

Azure PowerShell provides cmdlets to create and manage VMs. Here is an example of creating a VM:

```
New-AzVM `
    -ResourceGroupName "MyResourceGroup" `
    -Name "MyVM" `
    -Location "EastUS" `
    -VirtualNetworkName "MyVnet" `
    -SubnetName "MySubnet" `
    -SecurityGroupName "MyNetworkSecurityGroup" `
    -PublicIpAddressName "MyPublicIpAddress" `
    -OpenPorts 80,3389
```

This script accomplishes:

- Specifies the resource group and name for the VM.
- Sets the location to EastUS.
- Creates or specifies the virtual network, subnet, and network security group.
- Opens ports 80 (HTTP) and 3389 (RDP) on the VM.

4. ARM Templates for Virtual Machine Deployment

ARM Templates are JSON files that define infrastructure and configuration for Azure resources. An ARM Template for deploying a VM includes the schema, parameters, variables, and resources sections:

Example template snippet:

```
{
  "$schema": "https://schema.management.azure.com/schemas/2019-04-01/
      deploymentTemplate.json#",
  "contentVersion": "1.0.0.0",
  "parameters": {
    "vmName": {
      "type": "string",
      "defaultValue": "myVM",
      "metadata": {
        "description": "Name of the virtual machine"
      }
    }
  },
  "resources": [
    {
      "type": "Microsoft.Compute/virtualMachines",
```

```
      "apiVersion": "2020-06-01",
      "name": "[parameters('vmName')]",
      "location": "[resourceGroup().location]",
      "properties": {
        "hardwareProfile": {
          "vmSize": "Standard_DS1_v2"
        },
        "osProfile": {
          "computerName": "[parameters('vmName')]",
          "adminUsername": "azureuser",
          "linuxConfiguration": {
            "disablePasswordAuthentication": true,
            "ssh": {
              "publicKeys": [
                {
                  "path": "/home/azureuser/.ssh/authorized_keys",
                  "keyData": "[parameters('sshKeyData')]"
                }
              ]
            }
          }
        },
        "networkProfile": {
          "networkInterfaces": [
            {
              "id": "[resourceId('Microsoft.Network/networkInterfaces', variables('
                   nicName'))]"
            }
          ]
        }
      }
    }
  ]
}
```

5. Scaling and Monitoring Virtual Machines

Scaling VMs involves adjusting their size or instance count to meet demand. Azure offers several scaling options:

- Vertical scaling (scale-up): Change the VM size to a larger instance.
- Horizontal scaling (scale-out): Increase the number of VM instances in an availability set or scale set.

For scaling-out, Azure Virtual Machine Scale Sets (VMSS) can be used. VMSS allow you to deploy and manage a set of identical VMs. Commands or templates can automate scaling actions based on metrics or schedules.

Monitoring VMs involves tracking performance and availability. Azure Monitor and Log Analytics provide comprehensive monitoring and diagnostics capabilities, including:

- Metrics: CPU usage, memory usage, disk I/O, network traffic.
- Logs: Application logs, OS logs, Azure Diagnostic logs.
- Alerts: Notifications based on metric thresholds or log conditions.

For example, to check the status of a VM using Azure CLI:

```
az vm get-instance-view --resource-group MyResourceGroup --name MyVM --query
    instanceView.statuses[1]
```

The output displays the current state of the VM:

```
{
  "code": "PowerState/running",
  "level": "Info",
  "displayStatus": "VM running",
  "message": ""
}
```

Effective VM management in Azure leverages a combination of deployment options, scaling strategies, and robust monitoring to ensure optimal performance and cost-efficiency. The integration of these tools and practices empowers users to manage their cloud infrastructure dynamically and proactively.

3.9 Scaling Azure Applications

Scaling Azure applications involves adjusting the number of resources allocated to your application to meet the demands of incoming workloads. This process can be primarily divided into two categories: vertical scaling (scaling up) and horizontal scaling (scaling out).

Vertical scaling involves adding more power (CPU, RAM) to an existing machine, while horizontal scaling refers to adding more instances of a machine to distribute the load. Azure provides several mechanisms to implement both types of scaling to ensure your applications remain responsive and cost-effective under varying load conditions.

Azure Scale Sets

Azure Virtual Machine Scale Sets (VMSS) allow you to create and manage a group of identical, load-balanced VMs. Scale Sets ensure that the VMs can automatically increase or decrease to match the current demand or a defined schedule. They provide high availability to your application and make it easier to build large-scale services targeting big compute, big data, and container workloads.

An example of creating a Virtual Machine Scale Set using Azure CLI:

```
az vmss create \
  --resource-group myResourceGroup \
  --name myScaleSet \
  --image UbuntuLTS \
  --upgrade-policy-mode automatic \
  --admin-username azureuser \
  --generate-ssh-keys
```

This command creates a scale set named myScaleSet in the myResourceGroup resource group, using the Ubuntu LTS image and setting the upgrade policy to automatic.

Scaling Rules

Azure provides two primary methods to define scaling rules: manual and autoscale. Manual scaling allows you to set instance counts explicitly, while autoscale dynamically adjusts the number of instances based on real-time metrics.

For autoscaling, you can define rules that trigger based on metrics such as CPU utilization, memory usage, or queue length. An example of setting an autoscale rule for a VM scale set might look like:

```
az monitor autoscale create \
  --resource-group myResourceGroup \
  --resource myScaleSet \
  --resource-type Microsoft.Compute/virtualMachineScaleSets \
  --name autoscaleVMSS \
  --min-count 2 \
  --max-count 10 \
  --count 3
```

In this example, the autoscale settings will keep a minimum of 2 instances and a maximum of 10, usually maintaining 3 instances unless the defined conditions change.

App Service Plan Scaling

Azure App Service Plans provide another layer of scaling at the platform as a service (PaaS) level. For web apps, mobile app backends, and RESTful APIs, apps run and scale on App Service Plans.

To scale up an App Service Plan using Azure Portal, navigate to the scale up option in the App Service Plan blade, where you can change the pricing tier to add more CPU, memory, or storage.

Additionally, for scaling out, you can set autoscale settings based on usage patterns or schedules. Here is an example using Azure CLI to scale an App Service Plan to five instances:

```
az appservice plan update \
  --name myAppServicePlan \
  --resource-group myResourceGroup \
  --number-of-workers 5
```

Scaling Azure Databases

Scaling Azure databases such as Azure SQL Database or Cosmos DB involves changing the service tier or the number of throughput units respectively.

For example, you can scale an Azure SQL Database by changing its performance level:

```
az sql db update \
  --resource-group myResourceGroup \
  --server myServer \
  --name myDatabase \
  --service-objective S3
```

Here, S3 denotes the new service tier aimed at improving performance.

For Cosmos DB, you can adjust the throughput by changing the number of Request Units (RUs):

```
az cosmosdb collection update \
  --resource-group myResourceGroup \
  --name myCosmosDBAccount \
  --database-name myDatabase \
  --collection-name myCollection \
  --throughput 10000
```

In this command, the throughput is set to 10,000 RUs, allowing the database to handle more requests per second.

Azure Kubernetes Service (AKS)

For containers and microservices, Azure Kubernetes Service (AKS) provides a robust platform for automating the management, deployment, and scaling of containerized applications. Scaling in AKS can be managed both manually and through autoscaling features provided by Kubernetes.

The Horizontal Pod Autoscaler in Kubernetes automatically adjusts workloads by scaling the number of pods based on observed CPU utilization or other select application-provided metrics. To configure:

```
kubectl autoscale deployment my-deployment --cpu-percent=50 --min=1 --max=10
```

In this scenario, the deployment my-deployment will scale automatically, ensuring the average CPU utilization remains at 50

Integration of these scaling methods ensures your Azure applications remain efficient, responsive, and economical, regardless of the load they encounter. Proper configuration and management of scaling policies are essential, aligning resource allocation with demand and optimizing overall application performance.

3.10 Introduction to Azure DevTest Labs

Azure DevTest Labs is a service provided by Microsoft Azure that facilitates the creation and management of environments for testing, development, and experimentation. It enables developers and testers to efficiently provision Windows and Linux environments, utilizing reusable templates and artifacts to customize virtual machines (VMs) according to specific project requirements. The primary goal of Azure DevTest Labs is to enable rapid iteration while maintaining cost control and resource governance.

Azure DevTest Labs offers several features designed to streamline the process of setting up and managing lab environments. These include the ability to create custom images, define formulas, schedule automatic shutdowns, and set cost controls. These attributes collectively contribute to improved productivity, enhanced collaboration, and optimized resource utilization.

To begin using Azure DevTest Labs, it is essential to understand its core components and functionalities. This section provides an overview of how to create a DevTest Lab, manage and utilize templates and artifacts, and implement cost management strategies.

The first step in utilizing Azure DevTest Labs is to create a new lab. This can be done through the Azure Portal. To create a new DevTest Lab, navigate to the Azure Portal and search for *DevTest Labs*. Select *+ Add* and provide the required details such as the lab name, subscription, resource group, and region. Once the lab is created, you can begin adding virtual machines and configuring the lab settings.

```
az lab create \
  --resource-group MyResourceGroup \
  --lab-name MyDevTestLab \
  --location eastus
```

With the lab created, the next step involves configuring the lab settings to align with your team's requirements. Azure DevTest Labs allows you to set policies that govern the usage of the lab. For example, you can enable or disable sharing of the lab VMs, set expiration dates for VMs, and configure auto-shutdown schedules to save costs.

```
az lab policy set \
  --resource-group MyResourceGroup \
  --lab-name MyDevTestLab \
  --name vmExpirationPolicy \
  --threshold 14d \
  --action delete
```

One of the essential features of Azure DevTest Labs is the use of templates and artifacts. Templates are reusable images that can be used to create new VMs with predefined configurations. Artifacts are scripts or applications that can be applied to VMs during creation or after, allowing you to customize VMs further.

```
az lab vm apply-artifacts \
  --resource-group MyResourceGroup \
  --lab-name MyDevTestLab \
  --name MyVM \
  --artifacts @artifacts.json
```

The artifacts.json file would specify the list of artifacts to be applied, as shown below:

```
[
  {
    "artifactId": "myArtifactId1",
    "parameters": {
      "param1": "value1",
      "param2": "value2"
    }
  },
  {
    "artifactId": "myArtifactId2",
    "parameters": {
      "paramA": "valueA"
    }
  }
]
```

Implementing cost control measures is paramount to ensuring that the use of Azure DevTest Labs remains within budget. Azure DevTest Labs provides several mechanisms to manage costs, including setting usage quotas, defining auto-shutdown policies, and tracking spending through built-in cost metrics. You can specify a daily usage quota for the lab, which restricts the total number of VM hours consumed.

```
az lab policy set \
  --resource-group MyResourceGroup \
  --lab-name MyDevTestLab \
  --name dailyUsageQuotaPolicy \
  --threshold 720 \
  --action shut-down
```

When considering compliance and collaboration, Azure DevTest Labs integrates with Azure Active Directory (Azure AD) to manage user access and permissions, enabling RBAC (Role-Based Access Control). This integration allows organizations to control who can create or access VMs within the lab, thus maintaining security and compliance.

Moreover, the ability to schedule automatic shutdowns and startups is highly beneficial for managing operational costs. Users can configure auto-startup and auto-shutdown policies directly from the Azure Portal or programmatically using the Azure CLI or PowerShell scripts.

Azure DevTest Labs is designed to support a wide range of use cases, from individual developers requiring isolated environments for testing new features to large teams needing sandbox environments for conducting robust testing and development iterations. By leveraging the flexibility and control offered by Azure DevTest Labs, teams can achieve a more streamlined and cost-effective development process.

3.11 Using Azure Policy for Resource Governance

Azure Policy is a critical service designed to enforce organizational standards and assess compliance at scale. It enables users to create, assign, and manage policies to control and mitigate risks by ensuring that resources remain compliant with organizational standards. This section delves into the various aspects and functionalities of Azure Policy, providing a comprehensive understanding of its application and benefits.

Understanding Azure Policy Structure

Azure Policy operates through a combination of policy definitions, initiatives, and assignments.

- **Policy Definition**: The fundamental unit in Azure Policy, a policy definition outlines the desired criteria and the effect if the criteria are not met. A policy definition includes properties like display name, description, mode, and the policy rule. The policy rule is at the heart of the policy definition, specifying the conditions and the effect.
- **Policy Initiative**: Also known as policy set definitions, initiatives allow you to group multiple policy definitions to achieve a compre-

hensive, larger scope of control. This is useful for implementing complex compliance requirements that involve numerous individual policies.

- **Policy Assignment**: This is the application of a policy definition or initiative to specific resources or resource groups within an Azure subscription. An assignment applies the policy to the chosen scope, determining where the policy's rules and effects are enforced.

Creating a Policy Definition

To create a new policy definition in Azure, follow these steps:

```
# Using Azure CLI to create a policy definition
az policy definition create --name 'requireTag' --rules '{ "if": { "field": "tags", "
    notContainsKey": "environment" }, "then": { "effect": "modify", "details": { "
    roleDefinitionIds": [ "/providers/Microsoft.Authorization/roleDefinitions/
    XXXXXXXX-XXXX-XXXX-XXXX-XXXXXXXXXXXX" ], "operations": [ { "
    operation": "add", "field": "tags.environment", "value": "production" } ] } } }' --
    display-name 'Require environment tag' --description 'Automatically add an
    environment tag to resources without one' --mode All
```

This command creates a policy definition that mandates the existence of the tag 'environment' and, if absent, automatically adds it to the resource.

The policy rule in JSON format specifies:

- **If condition**: Checks for resources lacking the 'environment' tag.
- **Then condition**: Ensures resources missing the tag get one with the value 'production'.

Assigning a Policy

Once the policy definition is in place, you must assign it to the necessary scope.

```
# Assigning the policy to a resource group using Azure CLI
az policy assignment create --name 'require-environment-tag' --scope '/subscriptions/{
    subscription-id}/resourceGroups/{resource-group-name}' --policy "{policy-id}"
```

Replace 'subscription-id', 'resource-group-name', and 'policy-id' with appropriate values. This command ensures that all resources within the specified resource group comply with the 'requireTag' policy.

Evaluating Compliance

Azure Policy continuously evaluates resources for compliance. You can review compliance status within the Azure Policy service in the

Azure portal. By navigating to *Policy -> Compliance*, users can see an overview of the compliance state across assigned policies. This dashboard helps identify non-compliant resources and areas needing attention.

Built-in Policies and Initiatives

Azure provides numerous built-in policies and initiatives to expedite governance efforts. These cover a wide array of standards, such as:

- Enforcing geographic compliance for data residency.
- Applying security configurations in line with benchmarks like CIS or ISO 27001.
- Standardizing tag usage for resource management and chargeback.

For example, the *Audit VMs without disaster recovery* initiative integrates multiple policies to ensure virtual machines have appropriate disaster recovery measures. It audits whether virtual machines are enabled and configured correctly in Azure Site Recovery.

Policy Effects

Policy definitions can trigger various effects, such as:

- **Deny**: Prevents the creation or updates of resources that do not comply with policy rules.
- **Audit**: Evaluates resources but does not enforce compliance; instead, it logs non-compliant resources for review.
- **Append**: Adds specified configurations to resources if they do not exist during their creation or update.
- **Modify**: Alters resource properties to ensure compliance with policy requirements.

These effects empower organizations to enforce governance through both soft and hard compliance measures.

Remediation Tasks

In cases where resources already exist in non-compliant states, Azure Policy can use remediation tasks to bring them into compliance. This process involves defining a policy with effects like 'Modify' or 'DeployIfNotExists', which proactively enforce the necessary changes.

For instance, a remediation task might automatically enable encryption on storage accounts that lack it, based on a predefined policy.

Policy as Code

Azure Policy supports infrastructure-as-code paradigms, allowing policy definitions and assignments to be managed through source control and CI/CD pipelines. By using tools like Azure DevOps or GitHub Actions, teams can codify their governance policies, ensuring consistency and version control across environments.

Here's an example of deploying a policy definition through an Azure Resource Manager (ARM) template:

```
{
  "type": "Microsoft.Authorization/policyDefinitions",
  "apiVersion": "2019-09-01",
  "name": "requireTag",
  "properties": {
    "displayName": "Require environment tag",
    "description": "Automatically adds an 'environment' tag if missing.",
    "mode": "All",
    "policyRule": {
      "if": {
        "not": {
          "field": "tags.environment",
          "exists": true
        }
      },
      "then": {
        "effect": "modify",
        "details": {
          "roleDefinitionIds": [
            "/providers/Microsoft.Authorization/roleDefinitions/XXXXXXXX-XXXX-
                XXXX-XXXX-XXXXXXXXXXXX"
          ],
          "operations": [
            {
              "operation": "add",
              "field": "tags.environment",
              "value": "production"
            }
          ]
        }
      }
    }
  }
}
```

This JSON template can be deployed via Azure CLI or Azure DevOps pipelines, ensuring that policy definitions are part of the infrastructure lifecycle.

By leveraging Azure Policy, organizations can systematically enforce compliance and governance across their Azure environments, ensuring resources adhere to internal and regulatory standards efficiently.

3.12 Managing Costs and Budgets in Azure

Effective cost management is vital for leveraging the full potential of Microsoft Azure while ensuring financial efficiency. Managing costs and budgets within Azure involves a strategic approach based on monitoring, analyzing, and controlling expenditures. This section delves into several core features and techniques available to manage costs and budgets effectively, including Azure Cost Management and Billing, setting up budgets, forecasting, and analyzing cost drivers.

Azure Cost Management and Billing

Azure Cost Management and Billing is a comprehensive suite of tools provided by Azure to track and manage the costs associated with running Azure resources. This service enables resource administrators to understand how and where their money is being spent, and to identify inefficient or underutilized resources. The granular insights provided by Azure Cost Management and Billing facilitate more informed decision-making.

Monitoring your costs can be started by navigating to the Azure Cost Management section in the Azure Portal. Here, there's a detailed breakdown of costs:

```
# Navigate to Azure Cost Management and Billing in Azure Portal
1. Azure Portal > Cost Management + Billing > Cost Management
```

Within this section, you can explore accumulated costs, forecast future expenses based on current usage trends, and drill down into specific services to analyze their individual contributions to your overall expense.

Setting Up Budgets

Setting up budgets in Azure allows you to define a spending threshold, receive alerts, and take actions when these thresholds are reached. Budgets are part of the Azure Cost Management suite and can be configured through the Azure Portal or by using Azure CLI.

To create a budget via the Azure Portal:

```
1. Azure Portal > Cost Management + Billing > Budgets > Add
```

```
2. Enter budget details (name, amount, time period, scope)
3. Define alert conditions
4. Click 'Create'
```

To create a budget using Azure CLI, the following commands can be utilized:

```
# Create a budget using Azure CLI
az consumption budget create --resource-group <ResourceGroupName> --amount 1000
    \
--time-grain monthly --name MyMonthlyBudget --category cost \
--start-date 2023-01-01 --end-date 2023-12-31
```

Forecasting Costs

Azure Cost Management provides forecasting capabilities that predict future spending based on historical data. The forecasting tool helps in anticipating future costs and making proactive adjustments to align with financial constraints.

To access cost forecasting:

```
1. Azure Portal > Cost Management + Billing > Forecast
2. Review historical costs
3. View forecasted costs based on selected time frames
```

The forecast data assists in understanding potential cost trends and enables better financial planning for upcoming projects or scaling activities.

Analyzing Cost Drivers

Understanding the primary contributors to your Azure costs is crucial. The Cost Analysis feature allows you to view and breakdown costs based on various dimensions such as resources, resource groups, services, and tags.

To analyze cost drivers:

```
1. Azure Portal > Cost Management + Billing > Cost Analysis
2. Select the desired scope (subscription, resource group)
3. Apply filters (e.g., service name, resource type)
4. Analyze costs using charts and tables
```

The ability to dissect costs enables identification of inefficiencies, such as underutilized resources or cost-intensive services that might need review or optimization.

Utilizing Azure Advisor for Cost Recommendations

Azure Advisor provides actionable recommendations to improve resource utilization and reduce costs. These recommendations include suggestions for resizing or shutting down underutilized virtual machines, or using more cost-effective storage options.

Accessing Azure Advisor:

```
1. Azure Portal > Advisor
2. Review cost recommendations
3. Implement recommended actions
```

Implementing these recommendations can lead to significant cost savings and better resource efficiency.

Setting Up Cost Alerts

Cost alerts help in staying informed about spending and taking timely action to prevent budget overruns. Cost alerts can be configured to notify you when spending exceeds a predefined threshold.

To set up a cost alert:

```
1. Azure Portal > Cost Management + Billing > Alerts > Add
2. Define alert conditions (target, threshold)
3. Configure alert notifications (email, SMS)
4. Click 'Create'
```

Cost alerts ensure that stakeholders are promptly informed about financial deviations, allowing for rapid response to unexpected expenses.

Maintaining cost efficiency in Azure is an ongoing process that requires continuous monitoring, analysis, and adjustment. By leveraging the tools and strategies outlined above, organizations can manage their Azure expenditures effectively, ensuring optimal use of resources and adherence to budgetary constraints.

Chapter 4

Azure Networking

This chapter covers the essential components and configurations of Azure networking. It includes an introduction to Azure Virtual Networks (VNet) and subnetting, as well as network security with Network Security Groups (NSG) and Application Security Groups (ASG). The chapter discusses connectivity options like Azure VPN Gateway, Site-to-Site connectivity, and Azure ExpressRoute. Key networking services such as Azure Load Balancer, Application Gateway, DNS, Traffic Manager, and Front Door are explored. Additionally, it addresses configuring Azure Firewall and monitoring network performance.

4.1 Introduction to Azure Virtual Networks (VNet)

Azure Virtual Networks (VNet) constitute the core foundation of Microsoft's Azure networking stack, providing isolation, security, and the capability to have a manageable, scalable network in the cloud. Each VNet is logically isolated from other VNets, ensuring that the resources within a VNet can operate securely and independently. VNets allow resources like virtual machines (VMs) and other services to communicate with each other, the internet, and on-premises networks. This section covers VNet architecture, addressing, routing, and essential configuration elements to provide a comprehensive understanding.

A Virtual Network allows for the creation of a virtual private cloud (VPC) within the Azure environment. It is similar to the traditional network utilized within an on-premises data center, but with enhanced flexibility, scale, and integration capabilities.

Addressing and Subnetting

VNets are configured with IPv4 or IPv6 address spaces based on private IP addresses (RFC 1918). Upon creating a VNet, a CIDR (Classless Inter-Domain Routing) block must be specified which determines the address space for the VNet. Example of CIDR blocks include 10.0.0.0/16, 192.168.0.0/16, or 172.16.0.0/12.

Resources within a VNet can be segmented into subnets. Subnets segment a larger network into smaller, manageable sections, and assign IP addresses within that range to resources. Each subnet must have a unique CIDR block within the VNet address space.

Below is an example of a VNet and subnets configuration in Azure.

```
# Create Resource Group
az group create --name myResourceGroup --location eastus

# Create Virtual Network with CIDR block 10.1.0.0/16 and a Subnet
az network vnet create --resource-group myResourceGroup --name myVNet --address-
    prefix 10.1.0.0/16 --subnet-name mySubnet --subnet-prefix 10.1.1.0/24
```

The above script constructs a Virtual Network named $myVNet$ with an address space defined by the CIDR block $10.1.0.0/16$. The network is further divided into a subnet named $mySubnet$ with a subnet prefix $10.1.1.0/24$.

Routing and Security

The routing within a VNet can be either system routes or user-defined routes. System routes are automatically created by Azure, enabling resources within a VNet to communicate with each other, across peered VNets, and with on-premises networks (in case of a hybrid setup). User-defined routes allow for the customization of traffic paths between subnets. This is particularly useful for scenarios requiring traffic to flow through a network virtual appliance (NVA) or other specific routing needs.

Network security for VNets can be significantly enhanced using Network Security Groups (NSGs). NSGs contain a list of security rules that allow or deny network traffic to resources within a virtual network. These rules are composed of security rules that can be defined based on various parameters such as source and destination IP address, port, and protocol.

```
# Create Network Security Group and a rule to allow HTTP traffic
az network nsg create --resource-group myResourceGroup --name myNSG

az network nsg rule create --resource-group myResourceGroup --nsg-name myNSG --
    name myNSGRuleAllowHTTP --protocol tcp --direction inbound --priority 1000 --
    source-address-prefix '*' --source-port-range '*' --destination-address-prefix '*' --
    destination-port-range 80 --access allow
```

Peering VNets

VNet peering enables direct traffic routes between VNets, allowing resources in different VNets to communicate with each other. This feature is particularly useful when isolating workloads across VNets but requiring operational communication. Peering can be configured within the same region or across different regions, referred to as global VNet peering.

```
# Create peering between two VNets
az network vnet peering create --name myVNet1ToMyVNet2 --resource-group
    myResourceGroup --vnet-name myVNet1 --remote-vnet myVNet2Id --allow-vnet-
    access
```

The command above establishes a peering relationship between myVNet1 and myVNet2, allowing traffic to flow between them.

A structured and well-planned design and configuration of VNets are essential for the proper functioning of resources within the Azure ecosystem. It enhances security, ensures seamless communication between resources, and provides scalability. All subsequent networking components or services can leverage the VNet architecture for optimized operations.

4.2 Subnetting in Azure

Azure Virtual Networks (VNets) provide an isolated and highly secure environment for your applications. Within a VNet, subnetting is the mechanism that allows you to segment your network into smaller, more manageable chunks, which can then be allocated more precisely to different purposes and security requirements. In Azure, subnets play a critical role in organizing and securing your network topology.

Azure Subnet Basics

A subnet is a range of IP addresses within a VNet. When you define a subnet, you specify a subset of the VNet's address space, identifying a contiguous range of IP addresses. For instance, if your VNet has an address space of 10.0.0.0/16, you can divide this into smaller subnets like 10.0.0.0/24, 10.0.1.0/24, and so on.

Each subnet facilitates network segmentation, which can enhance security and improve network management. By segregating different types of resources into dedicated subnets, you can apply specific policies and route traffic more efficiently.

CIDR Notation and IP Address Ranges

In Azure, IP address ranges for VNets and their subnets are defined using Classless Inter-Domain Routing (CIDR) notation. CIDR notation is a compact representation of an IP address and its associated network mask. For example, 10.0.0.0/24 indicates that the first 24 bits of the IP address are the network part, and the remaining bits are for host addresses.

Configuring Subnets in Azure

To configure subnets in Azure, you use the Azure Portal, PowerShell, or the Azure CLI. Below is an example using the Azure CLI to create a VNet and then add subnets to it.

```
# Create a resource group
az group create --name MyResourceGroup --location eastus

# Create a virtual network with a 16-bit address space
az network vnet create \
  --resource-group MyResourceGroup \
  --name MyVNet \
  --address-prefix 10.0.0.0/16

# Add a subnet with a /24 address space
az network vnet subnet create \
  --resource-group MyResourceGroup \
  --vnet-name MyVNet \
  --name MySubnet1 \
  --address-prefix 10.0.0.0/24

# Add another subnet with a /24 address space
az network vnet subnet create \
  --resource-group MyResourceGroup \
  --vnet-name MyVNet \
  --name MySubnet2 \
  --address-prefix 10.0.1.0/24
```

In the above script, a resource group named MyResourceGroup is created in the East US region. Subsequently, a VNet named MyVNet is created with a 16-bit address space. Finally, two subnets (MySubnet1 and MySubnet2) are added to the VNet, each with a 24-bit subnet mask, effectively creating two subnets with 256 IP addresses each.

Subnet Constraints

It's important to understand the constraints Azure imposes on subnets:

- **IP Address Reservation:** Azure reserves the first four and the last IP address of each subnet for internal use. This reduces the number of usable IP addresses within a subnet. For a /24 subnet, you have 251 usable IP addresses (256-5 reserved).
- **Subnet Size:** Azure supports subnet sizes starting from /29 (8 IP addresses) to /8 (16,777,216 IP addresses), though larger subnets are less commonly used for practical reasons.
- **Address Space Overlap:** Subnets within a VNet must not have overlapping address ranges, ensuring each subnet has a unique address space.

Routing and Security within Subnets

Each subnet within a VNet can be associated with its own Network Security Groups (NSGs) that control inbound and outbound traffic rules. By defining NSGs, you can create fine-grained security policies that tailor access and egress rules specific to the subnet's role.

Example of Creating NSGs and Associating with a Subnet

Below is an example illustrating how to create an NSG and associate it with a subnet using Azure CLI.

```
# Create a Network Security Group
az network nsg create \
  --resource-group MyResourceGroup \
  --name MyNSG

# Create a rule to allow HTTP traffic
az network nsg rule create \
  --resource-group MyResourceGroup \
  --nsg-name MyNSG \
  --name AllowHTTP \
  --priority 100 \
  --protocol Tcp \
  --destination-port-range 80 \
  --access Allow

# Associate the NSG with a subnet
az network vnet subnet update \
  --resource-group MyResourceGroup \
  --vnet-name MyVNet \
  --name MySubnet1 \
  --network-security-group MyNSG
```

The above script first creates an NSG named MyNSG. A rule is added to MyNSG to allow HTTP traffic (port 80). Finally, MyNSG is associated with the subnet $\mathrm{MySubnet1}$, thereby applying the defined security rules to all resources within this subnet.

Design Considerations for Subnetting

When designing your subnet architecture in Azure, several best practices should be considered to optimize performance, manageability, and security:

- **Network Segmentation:** Group similar resources into the same subnet. For instance, place web servers in one subnet and database servers in another.
- **Security:** Use NSGs to enforce security boundaries between subnets. Apply least privilege principle by only allowing necessary traffic.
- **Addressing:** Plan your IP address space allocation to avoid overlaps and ensure efficient utilization of IP addresses.
- **Scenario-specific Subnets:** Create subnets based on function—such as public-facing and private subnets. Azure services like VPN Gateway and Azure Bastion can reside in purpose-specific subnets.

Understanding and employing these practices while creating and managing subnets ensures an organized, secure, and scalable Azure network architecture.

4.3 Network Security Groups (NSG) and Application Security Groups (ASG)

Network Security Groups (NSGs) and Application Security Groups (ASGs) are fundamental components for implementing network security in Microsoft Azure. They allow for controlling inbound and outbound traffic to Azure resources, thereby providing a robust mechanism for safeguarding applications and data.

NSGs are used to filter network traffic to and from Azure resources within an Azure Virtual Network (VNet). They contain security rules that allow or deny traffic based on source and destination IP address, port, and protocol. By associating NSGs with subnets and network interfaces, administrators can control the flow of traffic at various levels of granularity.

The following is an example of creating an NSG using Azure CLI:

```
az network nsg create \
    --resource-group myResourceGroup \
    --name myNetworkSecurityGroup
```

In addition to creating an NSG, security rules must be defined. Security rules can be added to an NSG to control the traffic flow. For example, the following command creates an inbound rule to allow HTTP traffic:

```
az network nsg rule create \
    --resource-group myResourceGroup \
    --nsg-name myNetworkSecurityGroup \
    --name Allow-HTTP \
    --protocol Tcp \
    --direction Inbound \
    --priority 100 \
    --source-address-prefix '*' \
    --source-port-range '*' \
    --destination-address-prefix '*' \
    --destination-port-range 80 \
    --access Allow
```

The rule created above allows inbound TCP traffic on port 80 from any source to any destination within the associated NSG. The priority parameter is vital as it dictates the order of rule evaluation; lower numbers have higher priority. If multiple rules match the same traffic, the rule with the highest priority (lowest numerical value) is applied.

Similarly, ASGs enable fine-grained network security by grouping virtual machine (VM) network interfaces based on application-specific requirements. This grouping abstracts the rules from specific IP addresses, allowing administrators to craft more readable and maintainable security policies. ASGs work in tandem with NSGs by acting as the source and destination in security rules.

An ASG can be created using the Azure CLI as follows:

```
az network asg create \
    --resource-group myResourceGroup \
    --name myApplicationSecurityGroup
```

Once the ASG is created, it can be included in an NSG rule. For instance, to govern traffic between ASGs:

```
az network nsg rule create \
    --resource-group myResourceGroup \
    --nsg-name myNetworkSecurityGroup \
    --name ASG-Rule \
    --protocol Tcp \
```

```
--direction Inbound \
--priority 200 \
--source-asgs mySourceASG \
--destination-asgs myDestinationASG \
--destination-port-ranges 8080 \
--access Allow
```

In the aforementioned rule, traffic is allowed from VMs in the mySourceASG Application Security Group to VMs in the myDestinationASG Application Security Group on TCP port 8080. This demonstrates the flexibility and abstraction benefits provided by ASGs.

NSGs and ASGs are also essential for compliance and auditing. Security rules can be fine-tuned to meet specific regulatory requirements, and activity logs can be reviewed to ensure adherence to security policies. Azure provides detailed logs that include information on rule processing and traffic flows, available through Azure Monitor, which facilitates effective tracking and analysis.

To visualize the security rules in place and their effectiveness, administrators can use Azure Network Watcher. It offers network diagnostic and visualization tools, such as Topology, which illustrates the relationships and rule associations across the network infrastructure.

Combining NSGs and ASGs affords a layered and coherent security strategy tailored to complex application environments. Understanding their capabilities and deployment options is critical for ensuring a secure and efficient Azure network configuration.

Carefully managing and applying these security tools optimizes network performance while maintaining stringent security standards, balancing access and protection.

4.4 Azure VPN Gateway and Site-to-Site Connectivity

Azure VPN Gateway is a critical component for enabling hybrid cloud solutions by securely linking on-premises networks to Azure Virtual Networks over the public Internet. It provides a mechanism for both point-to-site and site-to-site VPN connections, facilitating robust and scalable network communication. We'll delve into the concepts, configuration steps, and practical considerations for implementing site-to-site connectivity using an Azure VPN Gateway.

An Azure VPN Gateway is a type of virtual network gateway that sends encrypted traffic between an Azure virtual network and an on-premises location over the public internet. This form of network connectivity is designed to help network engineers build hybrid infrastructure securely and efficiently.

To create a VPN Gateway, practitioners typically follow these steps:

1. **Create a Virtual Network (VNet):** Ensure that you have a VNet with at least one subnet. This subnet is usually referred to as the GatewaySubnet.
2. **Create the VPN Gateway:** Define the specifics, such as the gateway type (VPN gateway), SKU (gateway performance level), and the region.
3. **Configure the On-Premises VPN Device:** This involves setting up a compatible on-premises VPN appliance. IPsec/IKE configurations will be necessary to establish a secure VPN tunnel.
4. **Create a Local Network Gateway:** Represent the on-premises location, specifying the public IP address of your VPN appliance and the address space that will traverse the VPN tunnel.
5. **Create the VPN Connection:** Link the Azure VPN Gateway to the Local Network Gateway, specifying the connection type (site-to-site).

The scripts to perform these steps in Azure PowerShell are illustrated below:

```
# Define variables
$resourceGroupName = "MyResourceGroup"
$location = "East US"
$virtualNetworkName = "VNet1"
$subnetName = "GatewaySubnet"
$vnetAddressPrefix = "10.1.0.0/16"
$subnetPrefix = "10.1.0.0/24"
$gatewayName = "VNet1GW"
$publicIPName = "VNet1GWIP"
$gatewaySku = "VpnGw1"
$localNetworkGatewayName = "MyOnPremisesSite"
$localNetworkAddressPrefix = "10.2.0.0/16"
$onPremisesPublicIP = "198.51.100.1"
$connectionName = "VNet1toOnPrem"
$sharedKey = "A1b2C3d4"

# Create a resource group
New-AzResourceGroup -Location $location -Name $resourceGroupName

# Create a virtual network
```

```
$vnet = New-AzVirtualNetwork -ResourceGroupName $resourceGroupName -Location
    $location -Name $virtualNetworkName -AddressPrefix $vnetAddressPrefix
Add-AzVirtualNetworkSubnetConfig -Name $subnetName -AddressPrefix $subnetPrefix
    -VirtualNetwork $vnet
$vnet | Set-AzVirtualNetwork

# Request a public IP
$publicIp = New-AzPublicIpAddress -ResourceGroupName $resourceGroupName -
    Location $location -Name $publicIPName -AllocationMethod Dynamic

# Create the gateway subnet
$gatewaySubnet = Add-AzVirtualNetworkSubnetConfig -Name $subnetName -
    AddressPrefix $subnetPrefix -VirtualNetwork $vnet
$vnet | Set-AzVirtualNetwork

# Create the virtual network gateway
$gatewayIPConfig = New-AzVirtualNetworkGatewayIpConfig -Name "
    GatewayIPConfig" -SubnetId $gatewaySubnet.Id -PublicIpAddressId $publicIp.Id
$vnetGateway = New-AzVirtualNetworkGateway -ResourceGroupName
    $resourceGroupName -Location $location -Name $gatewayName -IpConfigurations
     $gatewayIPConfig -GatewayType Vpn -VpnType RouteBased -GatewaySku
    $gatewaySku

# Configure the local network gateway
$localNetworkGateway = New-AzLocalNetworkGateway -ResourceGroupName
    $resourceGroupName -Location $location -Name $localNetworkGatewayName -
    GatewayIpAddress $onPremisesPublicIP -AddressPrefix
    $localNetworkAddressPrefix

# Create the VPN connection
New-AzVirtualNetworkGatewayConnection -ResourceGroupName $resourceGroupName
    -Name $connectionName -Location $location -VirtualNetworkGateway1
    $vnetGateway -LocalNetworkGateway2 $localNetworkGateway -ConnectionType
    IPsec -SharedKey $sharedKey
```

The output of these commands would confirm the successful creation of the Azure VPN Gateway and the site-to-site VPN connection establishment. A typical output snippet is shown below:

```
ResourceGroupName   : MyResourceGroup
Location            : eastus
GatewayType          : Vpn
VpnType             : RouteBased
EnableBgp           : False
GatewayDefaultSite  :
Sku                 : VpnGw1
ConnectedDevices    :
0/1 subnet/nics connected
ProvisioningState   : Succeeded
```

Several advances in Azure VPN technology ensure that such connections remain secure and reliable:

- **IPsec/IKE Protocols:** Azure VPN Gateway uses industry-standard IPsec/IKE protocols to secure the VPN tunnel.
- **Redundancy and High Availability:** Azure supports active-active and active-passive redundancy configurations to guaran-

tee high availability.

- **Performance Tiers:** Multiple gateway SKUs are available to match performance needs.

When configuring the on-premises VPN device, be sure to refer to vendor-specific documentation, as supported configurations may vary. It's also important to note that certain advanced configurations, such as BGP (Border Gateway Protocol) for route exchange, are supported should your environment require dynamic routing.

By configuring Azure VPN Gateway and establishing site-to-site connectivity, organizations can seamlessly extend their on-premises networks into Azure, allowing for a hybrid IT architecture. This capability not only facilitates migration and disaster recovery scenarios but also provides a robust environment for ongoing workloads that span both on-premises and cloud infrastructure.

4.5 Azure ExpressRoute

Azure ExpressRoute enables the creation of private connections between Azure datacenters and on-premises infrastructure, without going through the public internet. This type of connection offers higher speed, lower latency, more reliability, and greater security compared to typical internet-based connections. Enterprises looking for robust and predictable network performance can leverage ExpressRoute to extend their own on-premises networks into the Azure cloud.

ExpressRoute circuits are established through a connectivity provider. These circuits can connect to Azure at ExpressRoute locations such as exchange points or directly from any WAN network through an Ethernet connectivity provider.

Key Features of Azure ExpressRoute:

- **High Availability**: ExpressRoute offers redundant circuits with dual connections for high availability.
- **Increased Security**: With no exposure to public internet, ExpressRoute ensures data is transferred more securely.
- **Consistent Network Experience**: Dedicated circuits provide consistent network performance with reduced jitter and lower latency.

- **Scalability**: Capacity to scale bandwidth from 50 Mbps to 100 Gbps, accommodating different organizational needs.
- **Global Reach**: Integrate on-premises networks with cloud regions across the world.

ExpressRoute Circuit Types:

- **Local**: Directly connects your on-premises to a specific Azure region.
- **Standard**: Connects to multiple Azure regions within a geopolitical region.
- **Premium**: Extends connectivity to Azure regions globally, providing a broader reach.

Setting Up an Azure ExpressRoute Circuit: To configure an ExpressRoute circuit, execute the following steps through the Azure Portal. As an example, the commands below illustrate typical configuration steps:

```
# Create a resource group
az group create --name MyResourceGroup --location "West US"

# Create an ExpressRoute circuit
az network express-route circuit create --name MyCircuit --resource-group
    MyResourceGroup --bandwidth 200 --peering-location "Silicon Valley" --sku-
    family MeteredData --sku-tier Standard
```

Configuring ExpressRoute Peerings: ExpressRoute supports three types of peering:

- **Private Peering**: For extended on-premises networks into Azure virtual networks.
- **Microsoft Peering**: For accessing Microsoft services such as Microsoft 365 and Azure PaaS services.
- **Public Peering (Deprecated)**: Was previously used for accessing the public IP addresses for Azure services but is now deprecated.

For configuring Private and Microsoft peerings, you need to set up BGP sessions. Below is an example of configuring private peering:

```
# Configure private peering
az network express-route peering create --circuit-name MyCircuit --resource-group
    MyResourceGroup --peering-type AzurePrivatePeering --peer-asn 12345 --primary-
    peer-subnet 192.168.1.0/30 --secondary-peer-subnet 192.168.2.0/30 --vlan-id 200
```

Monitoring ExpressRoute Circuits: Keeping track of the performance and status of your ExpressRoute circuits is critical to maintain network health. Azure provides tools to monitor these metrics effectively.

- **Azure Monitor**: Use this service to track metrics and logs related to your ExpressRoute circuits.
- **Network Performance Monitor**: Utilize this tool to detect and diagnose issues across your networks.

To view the metrics of an ExpressRoute circuit via Azure CLI:

```
# List metrics for ExpressRoute circuits
az monitor metrics list --resource /subscriptions/{subscriptionId}/resourceGroups/
    MyResourceGroup/providers/Microsoft.Network/expressRouteCircuits/MyCircuit
     --metric-names PeeringsTotalReceivedBytes,PeeringsTotalSentBytes --aggregation
     Total
```

```
Result:
Name                         Value
----                         -----
PeeringsTotalReceivedBytes   325689
PeeringsTotalSentBytes       128734
```

The concept of ExpressRoute simplifies the challenges of extending enterprise networks into the cloud environment by ensuring high reliability, increasing security standards, and providing scalable, consistent performance. Understanding how to effectively set up and monitor these circuits ensures the continuity and seamless integration of cloud resources with on-premises infrastructure.

4.6 Azure Load Balancer

Azure Load Balancer is a Layer 4 (TCP/UDP) load balancer that provides high availability and network performance to your applications. It distributes incoming network traffic across multiple instances of a service, ensuring no single instance becomes a bottleneck. There are two types of Azure Load Balancer: Basic and Standard.

Azure Load Balancer operates at the OSI model's transport layer and is capable of handling millions of requests per second. It offers ultra-low latency, scalable load balancing, and efficient packet flow.

To get a working Azure Load Balancer, it must be linked to a backend pool, health probes, and load balancing rules. The backend pool consists of virtual machines or instances, health probes monitor the status of backend instances, and load balancing rules define how traffic is distributed.

Creating an Azure Load Balancer

Creating an Azure Load Balancer involves setting up the resource and configuring its components. Below is an example illustrating the creation and configuration of an Azure Load Balancer using Azure CLI.

```
# Create a virtual network and a subnet
az network vnet create \
  --resource-group MyResourceGroup \
  --name MyVnet \
  --subnet-name MySubnet

# Create a public IP address if needed
az network public-ip create \
  --resource-group MyResourceGroup \
  --name MyPublicIP

# Create the Load Balancer
az network lb create \
  --resource-group MyResourceGroup \
  --name MyLoadBalancer \
  --frontend-ip-name MyFrontEndPool \
  --backend-pool-name MyBackEndPool \
  --public-ip-address MyPublicIP
```

This sequence of commands sets up a virtual network, a public IP address, and finally, creates a Load Balancer.

Backend Pools

The backend pool contains the virtual machine instances that will receive traffic from the Load Balancer. Each VM instance must have a NIC (Network Interface Card) with an associated network configuration assigned to it. Configuring the backend pool effectively distributes traffic among several instances, providing higher availability.

To add a virtual machine to the backend pool, use the following Azure CLI command:

```
# Add a VM to the backend pool
az network nic ip-config address-pool add \
  --resource-group MyResourceGroup \
  --nic-name MyNic \
  --lb-name MyLoadBalancer \
  --address-pool MyBackEndPool
```

Health Probes

Health probes are used to determine the health status of the instances in the backend pool. If an instance fails to respond appropriately to the health probe, it is temporarily removed from the pool until it regains a healthy status.

A health probe can be created using HTTP, TCP, or HTTPS protocols. The following example creates an HTTP health probe:

```
# Create a health probe
az network lb probe create \
  --resource-group MyResourceGroup \
  --lb-name MyLoadBalancer \
  --name MyHealthProbe \
  --protocol Http \
  --port 80 \
  --path "/"
```

This command sets up an HTTP probe checking the root path (/) on port 80 of each backend instance.

Load Balancing Rules

Load balancing rules define how traffic is distributed to the VMs in the backend pool. Rules include frontend IP configuration, protocol, load distribution, and other settings.

Here is an example of creating a load balancing rule:

```
# Create a load balancer rule
az network lb rule create \
  --resource-group MyResourceGroup \
  --lb-name MyLoadBalancer \
  --name MyLoadBalancingRule \
  --protocol Tcp \
  --frontend-port 80 \
  --backend-port 80 \
  --frontend-ip-name MyFrontEndPool \
  --backend-pool-name MyBackEndPool \
  --probe-name MyHealthProbe
```

This example sets up a load balancing rule that listens on port 80 and forwards traffic to instances on the same port as long as they are healthy according to the specified health probe.

Outbound Rules

Outbound rules control the outbound traffic from instances in the backend pool. For instance, you can define how outbound connectivity is handled from the VMs using a Load Balancer public IP.

To configure an outbound rule, the following command may be used:

```
# Create an outbound rule
az network lb outbound-rule create \
  --resource-group MyResourceGroup \
  --lb-name MyLoadBalancer \
  --name MyOutboundRule \
  --frontend-ip-configs MyFrontEndPool \
  --address-pool MyBackEndPool \
  --protocol All \
  --enable-tcp-reset false \
  --idle-timeout 4
```

Types of Azure Load Balancer

Basic Load Balancer: Suitable for small-scale applications. Features include a single availability set, limited scalability, and a single front-end IP configuration.

Standard Load Balancer: Suitable for production workloads, providing higher scalability, more sophisticated metrics, and diagnostics. Features include multi-dimensional metrics through Azure Monitor, multiple front-end IP configurations, and support across availability zones.

Both Basic and Standard Load Balancers have near real-time latency monitoring and provide logs for diagnostic purposes.

This section has elaborated on the core functionality of Azure Load Balancer, from creating the resource to configuring backend pools, health probes, load balancing rules, and outbound rules. Azure Load Balancer is an essential tool for designing scalable, high-availability applications on the Azure platform.

4.7 Azure Application Gateway and Web Application Firewall

Azure Application Gateway is a web traffic load balancer that enables you to manage traffic to your web applications. It operates at Layer 7 (Application layer) of the OSI model, providing advanced routing capabilities based on HTTP/HTTPS requests. One of its key features is the integration of Web Application Firewall (WAF), which helps protect web applications from common threats and vulnerabilities as defined by the OWASP Top 10.

Application Gateway Components

An Azure Application Gateway consists of several components:

- **Frontend IP Configuration:** It can be public or private, depending on whether you wish to expose your application to the internet or keep it internal.
- **Listeners:** These are used to check the incoming traffic. You can configure HTTP and HTTPS listeners. For HTTPS listeners, you must provide a certificate for TLS termination.
- **Backend Pools:** This is a collection of IP addresses, FQDNs, or NICs of virtual machines that the Application Gateway will forward traffic to.
- **Backend HTTP Settings:** Defines settings like port, protocol, cookie-based affinity, and connection draining for backend communication.
- **HTTP Load Balancing rules:** These rules define how to route the traffic received at configured listeners to the backend pools.
- **Health Probes:** Ensures that the endpoints within a backend pool are healthy and capable of receiving traffic.
- **URL-based Routing:** Traffic can be routed to different backend servers based on URL path (e.g., domain.com/images goes to Image Server pool).
- **Path-based Routing:** Also known as URL path-based routing, forwards requests based on the URL path of the request.
- **Multi-site Hosting:** Enables hosting multiple websites behind a single Application Gateway.
- **Redirection:** Directs HTTP traffic to HTTPS, or to another URL.

Web Application Firewall (WAF)

The Web Application Firewall (WAF) is integrated with Azure Application Gateway to provide protection against many common attack patterns, including SQL injection, cross-site scripting, and other web application vulnerabilities. This protection is primarily accomplished through the use of rulesets provided and maintained by OWASP.

WAF Features

- **Managed Rulesets:** These are pre-configured rules provided by Microsoft and updated automatically.
- **Custom Rules:** You can define your own custom rules to handle specific protection requirements.
- **Policy Modes:** WAF operates in Detection mode, which logs attacks without blocking traffic, and Prevention mode, which blocks detected attacks.
- **Exclusions:** Allows you to exclude certain attributes from inspection.
- **Geo-Filtering:** Restrict access based on geographic location.
- **Bot Protection:** Rules to mitigate unwanted and potentially harmful bots.

Here is an example of creating an Application Gateway with WAF using Azure CLI:

```
# Variables for configuring the Application Gateway
RESOURCE_GROUP="myResourceGroup"
AG_NAME="myAppGateway"
VNET_NAME="myVNet"
SUBNET_NAME="mySubnet"
PUBLIC_IP_NAME="myPublicIP"

# Create a resource group
az group create --name $RESOURCE_GROUP --location eastus

# Create a virtual network
az network vnet create \
  --resource-group $RESOURCE_GROUP \
  --name $VNET_NAME \
  --subnet-name $SUBNET_NAME

# Create a public IP address
az network public-ip create \
  --resource-group $RESOURCE_GROUP \
  --name $PUBLIC_IP_NAME \
  --allocation-method Static \
  --sku Standard
```

```
# Create the application gateway
az network application-gateway create \
  --resource-group $RESOURCE_GROUP \
  --name $AG_NAME \
  --sku WAF_v2 \
  --capacity 2 \
  --vnet-name $VNET_NAME \
  --subnet $SUBNET_NAME \
  --frontend-port 80 \
  --http-settings-port 80 \
  --public-ip-address $PUBLIC_IP_NAME \
  --routing-rule-type Basic
```

The preceding command creates an Azure Application Gateway with WAF v2 SKU. It specifies the virtual network, subnet, public IP, and port settings.

Configuring WAF Policies

To configure a WAF policy and associate it with an Application Gateway, you can use the Azure Portal, Azure CLI, or PowerShell. Below is an example using Azure CLI to create and associate a WAF policy:

```
# Create a WAF Policy
az network application-gateway waf-policy create \
  --resource-group $RESOURCE_GROUP \
  --name myWafPolicy

# Add managed ruleset
az network application-gateway waf-policy rule-set add \
  --resource-group $RESOURCE_GROUP \
  --policy-name myWafPolicy \
  --type OWASP \
  --version 3.1

# Associate WAF Policy with the Application Gateway
az network application-gateway update \
  --name $AG_NAME \
  --resource-group $RESOURCE_GROUP \
  --waf-policy myWafPolicy
```

The managed ruleset included in this example is OWASP 3.1. Custom rules and exclusions can be defined and added as needed.

Output from the creation and association steps in CLIs typically includes JSON responses detailing the configurations:

```
{
  "managedRules": {
    "ruleSets": [
      {
        "ruleGroupOverrides": null,
        "ruleSetType": "OWASP",
        "ruleSetVersion": "3.1"
      }
    ]
  },
  "name": "myWafPolicy",
  "resourceGroup": "myResourceGroup"
}
```

By configuring an Application Gateway with WAF, you ensure that your web applications are protected from common threats while also benefiting from the scalable and highly available infrastructure provided by Azure's load balancing solutions.

4.8 Azure DNS

Azure DNS is a hosting service for DNS domains, providing name resolution by using Microsoft Azure infrastructure. By hosting your domains in Azure, you can manage your DNS records using the same credentials, APIs, tools, and billing as your other Azure services. It is an efficient and reliable DNS service offering features such as fast DNS responses and high availability.

Azure DNS supports all common DNS record types such as A, AAAA, CNAME, MX, NS, PTR, SOA, SRV, and TXT. It also supports alias records, which can refer to Azure resources like public IP addresses, traffic manager profiles, and CDN endpoints, enabling easier management of DNS records linked to Azure services.

DNS Zone and Records:

A DNS zone is used to host the DNS records for a particular domain. For example, if you own the domain "contoso.com", you could create a DNS zone for "contoso.com" in Azure DNS and then manage its DNS records. Below is the process of creating a DNS zone and adding DNS records using Azure CLI.

```
# Create a resource group
az group create --name MyResourceGroup --location eastus

# Create a DNS zone
az network dns zone create -g MyResourceGroup -n contoso.com

# Add a record set in the DNS zone
az network dns record-set a add-record -g MyResourceGroup -z contoso.com -n www -a
```

```
    10.0.0.1
```

Aliases and Azure Resources:

Azure DNS allows you to map DNS records directly to the IP addresses of Azure resources. Alias records can automatically track the IP addresses associated with these resources, simplifying management, particularly in dynamic environments.

For example, to create an alias record for an Azure public IP address, you can follow these steps:

1. Create a public IP address.

```
az network public-ip create --resource-group MyResourceGroup --name MyPublicIP
```

2. Add an alias record that references the public IP address.

```
az network dns record-set a add-alias -g MyResourceGroup -z contoso.com -n www --
    target-resource /subscriptions/{subscriptionId}/resourceGroups/
    MyResourceGroup/providers/Microsoft.Network/publicIPAddresses/MyPublicIP
```

Role-based Access Control (RBAC) for Azure DNS:

Granular access control is essential to manage DNS zones effectively. Azure provides Role-Based Access Control (RBAC) which enables you to assign roles to users, groups, and applications to control who has access to Azure resources.

Example of assigning the "DNS Zone Contributor" role to a user:

```
az role assignment create --assignee user@contoso.com --role "DNS Zone Contributor" --
    scope /subscriptions/{subscriptionId}/resourceGroups/MyResourceGroup/
    providers/Microsoft.Network/dnszones/contoso.com
```

DNS Security:

The security of DNS records and zones is critical. Azure DNS comes with built-in security features including: - **Role-based access control (RBAC)**: Detailed control over who can manage DNS zones and records. - **DNS Security Extensions (DNSSEC)**: Currently not supported by Azure DNS, understanding the implications of its absence is crucial for your security planning. - **Audit logs**: Trace and monitor changes to DNS zone and record resources.

Azure DNS Private Zones:

Azure DNS Private Zones provide a reliable and secure DNS service for your virtual networks. It allows you to manage and resolve domain names in a virtual network and includes built-in zone redundancy.

To create a Private DNS Zone:

```
az network private-dns zone create --resource-group MyResourceGroup --name contoso.
    private
```

Link the Private DNS Zone to a virtual network:

```
az network private-dns link vnet create --resource-group MyResourceGroup --zone-name
    contoso.private --name MyLinkName --virtual-network MyVNet --registration-
    enabled false
```

Add an A record to the Private DNS Zone:

```
az network private-dns record-set a add-record --resource-group MyResourceGroup --
    zone-name contoso.private --record-set-name www --ipv4-address 10.0.0.4
```

Azure DNS offers a robust, scalable, and secure solution for managing DNS records, both for public and private domains. By leveraging the seamless integration with other Azure services and comprehensive management capabilities, Azure DNS enables efficient and effective DNS management aligned with modern cloud application requirements.

4.9 Azure Traffic Manager

Azure Traffic Manager is a DNS-based traffic load balancer that enables the distribution of traffic optimally to services across global Azure regions. Utilizing Traffic Manager enhances the performance and availability of applications by directing client requests to the most optimal endpoint based on a set of customizable traffic-routing methods.

Traffic Routing Methods

Azure Traffic Manager supports several traffic routing methods to cater to different scenarios and requirements:

- **Priority** - This routing method provides a primary endpoint for your service. Secondary and tertiary endpoints are used only when the primary endpoint is unavailable. Traffic Manager routes all traffic to the primary endpoint until it becomes unavailable. If the primary endpoint fails, traffic is routed to the secondary endpoint, ensuring maximum availability.

- **Weighted** - The weighted routing method allows defining weights to different endpoints, and traffic is distributed proportionally based on the weights assigned. This method is useful for load testing and gradually shifting traffic from one endpoint to another.

- **Performance** - This routing method directs traffic to the endpoint with the lowest latency for the user, thus optimizing performance by considering the user's geographical location and the available endpoints.
- **Geographic** - Geographic routing enables directing traffic based on the geographic location of the user, aligning with data sovereignty, localization of content, and ensuring regulatory compliance.
- **Multivalue** - This method returns multiple healthy endpoints in the DNS response for the client to choose from, increasing redundancy and providing options for connection.
- **Subnet** - Traffic is routed based on the IP address range of users. It is useful for directing specific user groups to certain endpoints, optimizing resource use.

Endpoint Types

Azure Traffic Manager supports a variety of endpoint types, providing flexibility in different deployment architectures:

- **Azure Endpoints** - These endpoints can be any Azure service such as Azure App Service, Cloud Services, or Public IP of Virtual Machine Scale Sets.
- **External Endpoints** - These endpoints can be non-Azure endpoints, allowing integration with hybrid cloud solutions and other cloud platforms.
- **Nested Endpoints** - Nested endpoints enable the creation of a more complex hierarchy in traffic management by allowing another Traffic Manager profile to be used as an endpoint.

Configuration of Traffic Manager Profile

To configure Azure Traffic Manager, follow these steps:

```
1. Sign in to the Azure portal.
2. In the Azure portal menu, select "Create a resource".
3. In the "New" pane, select "Networking" and then "Traffic Manager Profile".
4. In the "Create Traffic Manager Profile" pane, configure the necessary settings:
   a. Name: Enter a unique profile name.
```

b. Routing Method: Select the desired traffic-routing method.
c. Subscription: Choose the Azure subscription.
d. Resource Group: Select an existing resource group or create a new one.
e. Resource Group Location: Choose the location for the resource group.
5. Click "Create" to create the Traffic Manager profile.

Once the Traffic Manager profile has been created, you need to configure the endpoints as follows:

1. In the Azure portal menu, select "All services" and search for "Traffic Manager profiles".
2. Select the Traffic Manager profile you created.
3. In the "Settings" pane, select "Endpoints".
4. Click "+ Add" to add new endpoints.
5. In the "Add endpoint" pane:
   a. Type: Choose the type of endpoint (Azure, External, or Nested).
   b. Name: Provide a name for the endpoint.
   c. Target resource type: Select the target resource type.
   d. Target resource: Specify the target resource based on the chosen type.
6. Click "OK" to add the endpoint.
7. Repeat the process to add additional endpoints.

Monitoring and Alerting

Traffic Manager includes built-in monitoring and alerts to ensure that endpoints are available and responsive. Health checks are performed at configurable intervals to verify the status of endpoints. If an endpoint is deemed unhealthy, Traffic Manager automatically reroutes traffic to healthy endpoints based on the configured routing method.

Configure health checks and alerts by navigating to the "Settings" pane of your Traffic Manager profile and selecting "Monitoring". Here, you can specify parameters such as the protocol (HTTP, HTTPS, or TCP), port, and the path to be monitored. Additionally, alert rules can be created to receive notifications about endpoint health and performance anomalies.

Traffic Manager enhances the fault tolerance, performance, and user experience of distributed applications by providing efficient traffic distribution, intelligent routing, and robust monitoring capabilities.

4.10 Azure Front Door

Azure Front Door is a scalable and secure entry point for web applications, enabling efficient content delivery and improved user experience by intelligently routing requests to the closest backend server. It provides multiple features such as load balancing, SSL offloading, web application firewall (WAF) integration, and dynamic site acceleration.

Load Balancing and Traffic Routing: Azure Front Door offers advanced load balancing and traffic routing capabilities. By utilizing the Domain Name System (DNS), HTTP(S) content-based routing, and global anycast network, it ensures high availability and low latency for the application.

The routing methods include:

- **Priority-based Routing:** Requests are routed to the primary backend until it becomes unavailable, then traffic is rerouted to secondary backends.
- **Weighted Round-Robin Distribution:** Distributes traffic based on assigned weights, proportionally directing requests to different backends to achieve load balancing.
- **Latency-based Routing:** Routes user requests to the backend with the lowest latency to improve responsiveness.
- **Session Affinity:** Ensures that requests from the same client are consistently routed to the same backend, maintaining stateful sessions.

SSL Offloading: SSL offloading refers to decrypting incoming SSL/TLS traffic at the Front Door edge locations, reducing the load on the backend servers and speeding up content delivery. Front Door supports HTTP/2 and TLS 1.3, ensuring secure and optimized connections.

To configure SSL offloading, one can upload a certificate to Azure, and configure the Front Door to use that certificate. Below is an example of command lines for configuring SSL certificates using Azure CLI:

```
# Upload an SSL certificate to Azure Front Door
az network front-door frontend-endpoint update \
--front-door-name <FrontDoorName> \
--name <FrontendEndpointName> \
--ssl-cert-name <CertificateName> \
--certificate-file <PathToCertificateFile> \
--certificate-password <CertificatePassword>
```

Web Application Firewall (WAF) Integration: Azure Front Door integrates seamlessly with WAF policies to protect web applications from common threats, such as SQL injection, cross-site scripting, and DDoS attacks. WAF policies can be customized with predefined and custom rulesets.

A typical WAF policy creation involves defining a set of rules and associating them with the front door frontend endpoints. Here's an example of Azure CLI commands for creating a WAF policy and associating it with Front Door:

```
# Create a WAF policy
az network front-door waf-policy create \
--name <PolicyName> \
--resource-group <ResourceGroupName>

# Add a managed rule set
az network front-door waf-policy managed-rules add \
--policy-name <PolicyName> \
--resource-group <ResourceGroupName> \
--type Microsoft_BotManagerRuleSet \
--version 0.1

# Associate the policy with Front Door
az network front-door update \
--name <FrontDoorName> \
--resource-group <ResourceGroupName> \
--waf-policy <PolicyName>
```

Dynamic Site Acceleration: With dynamic site acceleration, Azure Front Door optimizes the delivery of dynamic content by reducing latency and improving throughput. It leverages techniques such as TCP/UDP optimization and protocol agnostic routing to expedite content delivery to end-users.

URL Path-Based Routing: Azure Front Door also offers URL path-based routing to direct incoming requests to different backend pools based on the URL path. This feature is especially beneficial for complex applications with multiple services hosted under different paths.

An example of URL path-based routing configuration using Azure CLI is illustrated below:

```
# Create a routing rule with path-based routing
az network front-door routing-rule create \
--front-door-name <FrontDoorName> \
--resource-group <ResourceGroupName> \
--name <RoutingRuleName> \
--frontend-endpoints <FrontendEndpointName> \
--route-type Forward \
--backend-pool <BackendPoolName> \
--patterns-to-match '/path1/* /path2/*'
```

Global Reach and High Availability: Azure Front Door provides global reach and high availability by utilizing Microsoft's global network infrastructure. It employs built-in measures for automatic failover and health checks to continuously monitor backend health and switch traffic accordingly to minimize downtime.

Monitoring and Logging: Azure Front Door integrates with Azure Monitor, providing detailed metrics and logging capabilities to track performance and diagnose issues. Metrics such as latency, requests per second, and error counts can be monitored.

Example of enabling diagnostic settings:

```
# Enable diagnostic settings for Azure Front Door
az monitor diagnostic-settings create \
--name <DiagnosticSettingName> \
--resource <FrontDoorResourceID> \
--logs '[{"category":"FrontDoorAccessLog","enabled":true},{"category":"
    FrontDoorWebApplicationFirewallLog","enabled":true}]' \
--metrics '[{"category":"AllMetrics","enabled":true}]' \
--workspace <LogAnalyticsWorkspaceID>
```

4.11 Configuring Azure Firewall

Azure Firewall is a cloud-native and intelligent network security service that provides threat protection for your entire virtual network infrastructure. It is a fully stateful firewall as a service, offering both east-west and north-south traffic inspection. Configuring Azure Firewall involves several steps, including deployment, rule configuration, logging, and performance monitoring.

Azure Firewall supports both application and network level filtering rules and is integrated with Azure Monitor for logging and analytics. This section provides a comprehensive guide to setting up and managing Azure Firewall within your Azure environment.

The primary steps to configure Azure Firewall are as follows:

- Deploying Azure Firewall
- Configuring Azure Firewall rules
- Enabling diagnostics and logging
- Monitoring and managing Azure Firewall

Deploying Azure Firewall:

To deploy Azure Firewall, you need an existing Azure Virtual Network. Azure Firewall requires a dedicated subnet named AzureFirewallSubnet. Here is a sample deployment using the Azure CLI:

```
# Create a resource group
```

```
az group create --name MyResourceGroup --location eastus

# Create the virtual network
az network vnet create --name MyVNet --resource-group MyResourceGroup --location
    eastus --address-prefix 10.0.0.0/16 --subnet-name MySubnet --subnet-prefix
    10.0.1.0/24

# Create the AzureFirewallSubnet
az network vnet subnet create --name AzureFirewallSubnet --resource-group
    MyResourceGroup --vnet-name MyVNet --address-prefix 10.0.2.0/24

# Create a public IP for the firewall
az network public-ip create --name MyFirewallPublicIP --resource-group
    MyResourceGroup --sku Standard --location eastus

# Deploy the Azure Firewall
az network firewall create --name MyFirewall --resource-group MyResourceGroup --
    location eastus

# Attach the public IP to the firewall
az network firewall ip-config create --name MyFirewallConfig --firewall-name
    MyFirewall --resource-group MyResourceGroup --public-ip-address
    MyFirewallPublicIP --vnet-name MyVNet
```

Configuring Azure Firewall Rules:

Azure Firewall allows you to create application rules and network rules to control outbound and inbound traffic.

Application Rules:

Application rules define Fully Qualified Domain Names (FQDNs) that can be accessed from a subnet. Below is an example of creating an application rule collection:

```
az network firewall policy rule-collection-group collection-rule add --policy-name
    MyFirewallPolicy --resource-group MyResourceGroup --rule-collection-group-name
    MyRuleCollectionGroup --rule-collection-type ApplicationRuleCollection --name
    AppRuleCollection --priority 100 --rule-name AllowAppRule --protocols Http=80
    Https=443 --source-addresses '*' --target-fqdns www.microsoft.com --action Allow
```

Network Rules:

Network rules define rules to allow or deny network traffic based on source and destination IP address, protocol, and port. Here is an example of creating a network rule collection:

```
az network firewall policy rule-collection-group collection-rule add --policy-name
    MyFirewallPolicy --resource-group MyResourceGroup --rule-collection-group-name
    MyRuleCollectionGroup --rule-collection-type NetworkRuleCollection --name
    NetworkRuleCollection --priority 200 --rule-name AllowNetworkRule --protocols
    TCP --source-addresses 10.0.1.0/24 --destination-addresses 20.0.0.0/24 --
    destination-ports 22 --action Allow
```

Enabling Diagnostics and Logging:

Azure Firewall integrates with Azure Monitor to provide diagnostic logging. This feature logs traffic processed by the firewall and can be used for troubleshooting and analysis.

```
az monitor diagnostic-settings create --resource MyFirewall --resource-group
    MyResourceGroup --workspace MyLogAnalyticsWorkspace --name
    MyDiagnosticSetting --logs '[{"category": "AzureFirewallApplicationRule","
    enabled": true},{"category": "AzureFirewallNetworkRule","enabled": true},{"
    category": "AzureFirewallDnsProxy","enabled": true}]'
```

Logs can be reviewed in Azure Log Analytics, and you can set up alerts and automated responses based on log data.

Monitoring and Managing Azure Firewall:

Effective management of Azure Firewall involves regular monitoring of firewall logs and performance metrics. Azure Monitor provides a comprehensive suite of tools for monitoring the health, performance, and utilization of Azure Firewall.

```
# Viewing metrics
az monitor metrics list --resource MyFirewall --resource-group MyResourceGroup --
    metric-names All --start-time 2023-01-01T00:00:00Z --end-time 2023-01-31T23
    :59:59Z
```

Metrics such as *CPU utilization*, *Throughput*, and *Network rule evaluation* can be monitored to optimize firewall performance.

```
Metric     Value     Timestamp
CPU        75%       2023-01-15T08:00:00Z
Throughput 500Mbps 2023-01-15T08:00:00Z
Network rule evaluation 12000 2023-01-15T08:00:00Z
```

Additionally, compliance with organizational policies should be continuously verified by auditing firewall rules and configurations. Regular updates and patches should be applied to ensure security controls remain effective against evolving threats. Active management enables the firewall to adapt to changes in the network architecture and security landscape.

Azure Firewall provides a powerful set of features for securing complex networks, and understanding its configurations empowers administrators to create robust security postures.

4.12 Monitoring and Troubleshooting Network Performance

Monitoring and troubleshooting network performance within Azure is critical for maintaining optimal service operation and ensuring high availability and reliability. Azure provides a comprehensive suite of tools and services to facilitate these tasks. Understanding and effectively utilizing these tools allows for the proactive identification and resolution of network-related issues, ensuring minimal disruption to services.

Azure Network Watcher is a key service that assists in monitoring and diagnosing network issues. It enables several functionalities such as Network Performance Monitor, connection troubleshooting, packet capture, VPN diagnostics, and Next Hop analysis.

Network Performance Monitor (NPM) is a cloud-based network monitoring solution that helps in the monitoring of network performance between various Azure resources and hybrid environments. NPM provides end-to-end visibility into network topology, latency, and packet loss.

To initialize NPM, navigate to the Azure portal and search for Network Performance Monitor. Create a new NPM solution by specifying resource details and configuring agents on target VMs.

```
Install-Script -Name Install-NPM -Force
Install-NPM -WorkspaceId '<WorkspaceId>' -Key '<PrimaryKey>'
```

Network monitor solutions require configuration of monitoring rules between the source and destination. These rules define the scope and performance metrics to be gathered.

Setting up packet capture enables the detailed inspection of packets traveling to and from a virtual machine. This is crucial for identifying anomalies and assessing network security and performance.

```
New-AzNetworkWatcherPacketCapture -NetworkWatcherName 'NetworkWatcher_rg' `
                                  -ResourceGroupName 'ResourceGroupName' `
                                  -TargetVirtualMachineId '/subscriptions/sub-id/
                                        resourceGroups/rg-name/providers/Microsoft.
                                        Compute/virtualMachines/vm-name' `
                                  -TimeLimitInSeconds 300
```

Once initiated, network packets are captured according to the defined parameters and stored in a storage account or local file on the VM. Use tools such as Wireshark to analyze captured packets.

Connection Troubleshoot evaluates the connectivity between a source and destination, identifying configuration issues affecting network communication. This tool requires the definition of endpoints, and it tests the connectivity by simulating the network path.

```
az network watcher test-connectivity --source-resource /subscriptions/sub-id/
    resourceGroups/rg-name/providers/Microsoft.Compute/virtualMachines/vm-name
    `
                                    --dest-address www.example.com `
                                    --dest-port 80
```

The command returns detailed information about hops traversed, latency, and potential network issues which are instrumental for troubleshooting.

Next Hop analysis helps determine the next hop for packets destined for a specific IP address from a given virtual machine. It is particularly useful in diagnosing routing issues within a virtual network.

```
az network watcher show-next-hop --resource-group 'resourceGroup' `
                                --network-watcher-name 'watcher' `
                                --vm 'vmName' --source-ip '10.0.0.4' `
                                --dest-ip '10.0.0.10'
```

VPN Diagnostics is essential for resolving issues related to Azure VPN Gateway and Site-to-Site VPN connections. This functionality analyzes the configuration and operational status of the VPN to identify failures or misconfigurations.

```
az network watcher vpn-diagnostic --resource-group 'resourceGroup' `
                                 --gateway-name 'vpnGateway' `
                                 --output-directory '/path/to/output'
```

Executing this command results in a detailed diagnostic report highlighting statuses, possible issues, and recommendations for resolution.

Metrics and Alerts are central to proactive monitoring. Azure Monitor provides extensive capabilities for setting up custom alerts based on metrics and log data. Azure Monitor integrates seamlessly with Network Watcher, enabling the setup of rules to trigger alerts on specific conditions such as increased latency, packet loss, or network downtime.

Log Analytics allows for deep insights into network activity. By collecting diagnostic logs and metrics into a centralized workspace, it provides the ability to run advanced queries, visualize data, and generate reports. Log Analytics can be tailored to specific requirements using the powerful Kusto Query Language (KQL).

```
AzureDiagnostics
| where ResourceType == "NETWORKSECURITYGROUPS"
| summarize count() by bin(TimeGenerated, 5m)
| render timechart
```

This query summarizes network security group logs over five-minute intervals and renders the results as a time chart for visual analysis.

Effective utilization of these tools and techniques ensures robust consistency in network performance, enabling rapid identification and resolution of network issues. Comprehensive monitoring and diagnostics contribute significantly to maintaining Azure environments' operational excellence.

Chapter 5

Azure Storage Solutions

This chapter examines the various storage options available in Azure, including Blob, File, Disk, Queue, and Table Storage. It provides guidance on managing storage accounts, ensuring scalability and performance, and implementing access control and security. The chapter also introduces Azure Storage Explorer, discusses Azure Data Lake, and covers best practices for monitoring and troubleshooting storage solutions.

5.1 Introduction to Azure Storage

Azure Storage is a robust, scalable, and secure cloud storage solution provided by Microsoft. It is designed to meet diverse storage requirements, offering different storage types suitable for various applications and use cases. Azure Storage ensures high availability, durability, and redundancy, making it an integral component of modern cloud-based infrastructures.

Azure Storage services can be broadly categorized into five primary types: Blob Storage, File Storage, Disk Storage, Queue Storage, and Table Storage. Each type is tailored to specific data storage and processing needs, enhancing the versatility and functionality of Azure's storage offerings.

Blob Storage is optimized for storing unstructured data such as text, images, videos, and backups. It supports three types of blobs: Block blobs, Append blobs, and Page blobs. Block blobs are ideal for storing text and binary data, Append blobs are optimized for append operations, making them suitable for logging, and Page blobs are used for scenarios requiring random access to large amounts of data, such as VHD files used by Azure Virtual Machines.

File Storage provides fully managed file shares in the cloud that can be accessed via the Server Message Block (SMB) protocol, enabling seamless integration with on-premises systems. This service is particularly beneficial for legacy applications that rely on traditional file shares.

Disk Storage offers persistent, durable disk storage for Azure Virtual Machines, supporting both solid-state drives (SSD) and hard disk drives (HDD). It ensures high performance and low latency for mission-critical applications, with options for Standard and Premium managed disks.

Queue Storage enables reliable messaging between application components, facilitating decoupled and distributed application architectures. It supports asynchronous communication, improving application scalability and performance by allowing tasks to be processed independently.

Table Storage, a NoSQL key-value datastore, provides fast and cost-effective storage for large volumes of structured data. It is suitable for a wide range of scenarios, including web applications, IoT data, and user logs, where rapid read/write operations are essential.

Azure Storage automatically replicates data to ensure high availability and durability. The redundancy options include Locally Redundant Storage (LRS), Zone-Redundant Storage (ZRS), Geo-Redundant Storage (GRS), and Read-Access Geo-Redundant Storage (RA-GRS). Each option offers varying levels of replication within or across regions, catering to different disaster recovery and compliance requirements.

To interact with Azure Storage, developers and administrators have various tools at their disposal. The Azure portal provides a user-friendly interface for managing storage accounts, configuring settings, and monitoring usage. Additionally, the Azure Storage Explorer is a standalone application that simplifies data operations such as uploading, downloading, and organizing files and containers.

Azure Storage also supports a range of APIs and SDKs, enabling seamless integration with applications developed in various programming languages, including .NET, Java, Python, and JavaScript. These APIs facilitate programmatic access to Azure Storage services, streamlining workflows and enhancing automation capabilities.

Security is a top priority in Azure Storage. Features such as encryption at rest and in transit, advanced threat protection, and identity-based access controls ensure that data remains protected against unauthorized access and breaches. Azure Storage integrates seamlessly with Azure Active Directory (Azure AD) and provides granular permissions management through shared access signatures (SAS) and role-based access control (RBAC).

In terms of scalability, Azure Storage is designed to handle extensive data workloads, supporting virtually unlimited capacity. It adapts to varying usage patterns, automatically scaling resources to maintain optimal performance and cost-efficiency. Monitoring and diagnostic tools such as Azure Monitor and Azure Storage Analytics provide insights into storage operations, facilitating proactive management and troubleshooting.

As organizations increasingly migrate to cloud-based environments, Azure Storage plays a critical role in data management strategies. Its comprehensive offerings address diverse storage needs while ensuring reliability, security, and ease of use. By leveraging Azure Storage, businesses can enhance their operational efficiency, reduce infrastructure costs, and focus on innovation without worrying about underlying storage complexities. Azure Storage's offerings provide a robust foundation for building resilient and scalable applications and services, meeting the demands of modern cloud computing.

5.2 Azure Blob Storage

Azure Blob Storage is a scalable object storage service for unstructured data. It is optimized for storing large amounts of data that do not adhere to a fixed schema, such as documents, videos, images, and backups. This storage option is ideal for scenarios where the data needs to be accessed from multiple locations and devices, integrating seamlessly with other Azure services.

Azure Blob Storage offers three types of blobs: block blobs, append blobs, and page blobs. Block blobs are optimized for efficient upload and storage of large blobs, typically used for files such as videos and images. Append blobs are ideal for scenarios where data needs to be appended frequently, such as logging information. Page blobs are designed for random read/write access and are used primarily as the underlying storage mechanism for VHD files in virtual machines.

To create and manage blob storage, you must first establish a storage account in Azure. A storage account provides a unique namespace within Azure for your data, accessible via HTTP or HTTPS. The storage account is the highest level of the namespace and contains all your blobs, files, queues, tables, and disks.

Once the storage account is created, you can create a container within that account. Containers help organize blobs and provide a security boundary for data. Each container can store an unlimited number of blobs. Below is an example illustrating how to create a storage account, container, and upload a blob using Azure CLI:

```
# Create a resource group
az group create --name myResourceGroup --location eastus

# Create a storage account
az storage account create --name mystorageaccount --resource-group myResourceGroup
    --location eastus --sku Standard_LRS

# Get the storage account key
ACCOUNT_KEY=$(az storage account keys list --resource-group myResourceGroup --
    account-name mystorageaccount --query "[0].value" --output tsv)

# Create a container
az storage container create --name mycontainer --account-name mystorageaccount --
    account-key $ACCOUNT_KEY

# Upload a file to the container
az storage blob upload --container-name mycontainer --file myfile.txt --name myfile.txt
    --account-name mystorageaccount --account-key $ACCOUNT_KEY
```

The example above demonstrates using Azure CLI to perform common tasks, including creating a resource group, creating a storage account, retrieving the storage account key, creating a container, and uploading a file. For authentication, the ACCOUNT_KEY is retrieved and used in subsequent commands to interact with the storage account.

Azure Blob Storage supports multiple access tiers to optimize storage costs based on data access patterns. The access tiers include Hot, Cool, and Archive:

- The **Hot** access tier is optimized for data that is accessed frequently. It provides low-latency access and ensures high availability, but it incurs higher storage costs.

- The **Cool** access tier is suited for data that is infrequently accessed and stored for at least 30 days. It offers lower storage costs compared to the Hot tier but has higher access costs.

- The **Archive** access tier is designed for data that is rarely accessed and held for extended periods. This tier provides the lowest storage costs but the highest access latency and retrieval costs.

Here's an example demonstrating how to set the access tier of a blob using Azure CLI:

```
# Set an existing blob to the cool access tier
az storage blob set-tier --container-name mycontainer --name myfile.txt --tier Cool --
    account-name mystorageaccount --account-key $ACCOUNT_KEY
```

In scenarios where large amounts of data need to be migrated to Azure Blob Storage, Azure Storage offers features like AzCopy and Azure Data Box. AzCopy is a command-line utility designed for data transfer, providing a simple way to move data to and from Azure Storage. Azure Data Box is a physical appliance that helps transfer large volumes of data to Azure when network constraints make transfers over the internet impractical.

Azure Blob Storage supports advanced security features, including shared access signatures (SAS) and Azure Active Directory (Azure AD) integration. Shared access signatures allow fine-grained control over access to your data by generating tokens that specify permissions and duration of access.

Azure Blob Storage also integrates with Azure Data Lake Storage, providing capabilities essential for big data analytics. It enables hierarchical namespace support, enhancing performance and management for data analytics workloads.

Advanced features such as soft delete and point-in-time restore protect data from accidental deletion or corruption. Soft delete retains deleted blobs in a soft-deleted state for a specified retention period, after which they are permanently deleted. Point-in-time restore enables the restoration of containers to a previous state at a specified time.

In the context of scalability, Azure Blob Storage scales automatically to handle massive amounts of data and high request rates. It provides consistent low-latency access to data stored in geographically dispersed data centers.

Monitoring and troubleshooting Azure Blob Storage is accomplished using Azure Storage Analytics, Azure Monitor, and diagnostic logging. These tools provide insights into storage operations, performance metrics, and enable proactive management of storage resources. Azure

Storage Analytics logs detailed operational data, including successful requests, failed requests, and throttling events, facilitating comprehensive storage performance analysis.

The implementation of these features ensures that Azure Blob Storage provides a robust, flexible, and secure solution for a wide range of storage needs, making it an essential component of modern cloud-based architectures.

5.3 Azure File Storage

Azure File Storage is a fully managed file share service provided by Microsoft Azure. It offers a simpler and more scalable alternative to traditional on-premises file servers, and is designed to cater to scenarios where applications need to share content or need persistent storage. The file shares are accessible using the Server Message Block (SMB) protocol and can be mounted concurrently by cloud or on-premises deployments of Windows, Linux, and macOS. This section delves into the core aspects of Azure File Storage, including its architecture, use cases, and how to deploy and manage it.

Azure File Storage enables seamless file sharing across multiple virtual machines (VMs) and services. Each file share created in Azure File Storage can be accessed by multiple VMs, allowing users to centralize their files in a shared location. This is particularly useful for scenarios such as shared application settings, user profiles, or any other shared data needs. Additionally, Azure File Storage ensures high availability and redundancy, offering peace of mind that the data remains accessible even in the case of hardware failures.

The core components of Azure File Storage include:

- **Storage Accounts:** A storage account is required to house one or more file shares. It serves as the top-level namespace for the file shares and provides the unique namespace required by the system. Storage accounts also enable features such as access tiers, replication, and authentication.

- **File Shares:** These are the fundamental units of Azure File Storage. File shares are created within a storage account and are accessed via their Uniform Resource Identifier (URI). Each file share can store an unlimited number of directories and files.

- **Directories:** Directories within a file share allow users to organize files in a hierarchical structure, similar to traditional file systems. Both directories and files within Azure File Storage follow a standard POSIX-compliant structure, enabling compatibility with various applications.

- **Files:** The actual data objects stored in the directories. Files in Azure File Storage can range in size from kilobytes to terabytes, and are accessed using standard file access protocols.

Accessing Azure File Storage requires the following steps. Assume you have already created a storage account named mystorageaccount.

First, create a file share using the Azure Portal:

```
# Navigate to your storage account in the Azure Portal
# Select the "File shares" option on the left-hand menu
# Click on the "+ File share" button to create a new file share
# Provide a name for the file share, e.g., "myfileshare"
# Specify the quota for the file share in GiB
# Click "Create" to complete the process
```

Once the file share is created, it can be mounted from within a VM. For example, in a Windows environment:

```
# Open Command Prompt as Administrator
net use Z: \\mystorageaccount.file.core.windows.net\myfileshare /u:mystorageaccount
    <storage-account-key>
```

The above command maps the file share to a drive letter (Z:) on the local machine. For Linux, the file share can be mounted using the CIFS protocol:

```
sudo apt-get install cifs-utils
sudo mount -t cifs //mystorageaccount.file.core.windows.net/myfileshare /mnt/
    myfileshare -o vers=3.0,username=mystorageaccount,password=<storage-account-
    key>,dir_mode=0777,file_mode=0777
```

To manage permissions and access control, Azure File Storage leverages both Azure Active Directory (Azure AD) and shared access signatures (SAS). These mechanisms ensure that access to the file shares is controlled and secure. Azure AD provides identity-based authentication, which can be integrated into organizational policies with role-based access control (RBAC). SAS tokens, on the other hand, offer a URL-based method to grant time-limited access to the file shares, allowing for granular control over who can access the data and for how long. An example of generating an SAS token via Azure CLI is shown below:

```
az storage share generate-sas --account-name mystorageaccount --name myfileshare --
    permissions rl --expiry 2023-12-31T00:00:00Z
```

The token generated can then be appended to the file share URI to grant temporary access. Monitoring and maintaining Azure File Storage is essential for ensuring optimal performance and security. Azure provides built-in tools such as Azure Monitor and Azure Storage Analytics to help administrators keep track of storage usage, performance metrics, and access logs. These tools allow for proactive monitoring and alerting, facilitating prompt responses to potential issues.

Incorporating Azure File Storage into your infrastructure offers numerous benefits beyond just scalability and ease of access. It integrates seamlessly with other Azure services, ensuring that data workflows are consistent and efficient across the spectrum of cloud solutions. Furthermore, with options for geo-redundant storage and advanced threat protection, it meets stringent compliance and security standards required by various industries.

This section has highlighted the key components and procedures pertinent to effective utilization of Azure File Storage. With this foundation, organizations can leverage Azure's robust and flexible file storage capabilities to meet diverse range of storage needs.

5.4 Azure Disk Storage

Azure Disk Storage is designed to provide high-performance, highly durable block storage that can be used with Azure Virtual Machines (VMs). This section will explore the types of Azure Disk Storage, provisioning and managing disks, and key features that ensure scalability, performance, and security.

Azure Disk Storage offers three distinct disk types: Ultra Disks, Premium SSDs, Standard SSDs, and Standard HDDs. Each disk type targets specific performance and cost needs:

- Ultra Disks cater to data-intensive workloads that require low latency and high throughput. They provide configurable attributes such as IOPS and throughput, offering the most flexibility for performance requirements.
- Premium SSDs are ideal for production workloads requiring consistent low latency and high IOPS. They are suitable

for databases, transaction-heavy applications, and high-performance workloads.

- Standard SSDs provide a balance between performance and cost, fitting for web servers, lightly used enterprise applications, and dev/test environments.

- Standard HDDs are the most economical storage option, designed for non-critical workloads and bulk storage needs where performance is not a primary concern.

Managing Azure Disks involves creating, attaching, resizing, and snapshotting disks. Below is an example of PowerShell commands for disk management:

```
# Create a managed disk
$diskConfig = New-AzDiskConfig -SkuName 'Premium_LRS' -Location 'EastUS' -
    CreateOption Empty -DiskSizeGB 128
$disk = New-AzDisk -ResourceGroupName 'myResourceGroup' -DiskName 'myDisk' -
    Disk $diskConfig

# Attach the managed disk to a VM
$vm = Get-AzVM -ResourceGroupName 'myResourceGroup' -VMName 'myVM'
$vm = Add-AzVMDataDisk -VM $vm -Name 'myDisk' -CreateOption Attach -
    ManagedDiskId $disk.Id -Lun 1
Update-AzVM -ResourceGroupName 'myResourceGroup' -VM $vm

# Resize the managed disk
$disk = Get-AzDisk -ResourceGroupName 'myResourceGroup' -DiskName 'myDisk'
Update-AzDisk -ResourceGroupName 'myResourceGroup' -DiskName 'myDisk' -
    DiskSizeGB 256

# Create a snapshot of the disk
$snapshotConfig = New-AzSnapshotConfig -SkuName 'Premium_LRS' -Location '
    EastUS' -CreateOption Copy -SourceUri $disk.Id
$snapshot = New-AzSnapshot -ResourceGroupName 'myResourceGroup' -
    SnapshotName 'mySnapshot' -Snapshot $snapshotConfig
```

Azure provides several features to ensure the resiliency and performance of disk storage:

Disk Encryption ensures the security of data at rest. Azure allows for customer-managed keys in Azure Key Vault, providing full control over encryption keys:

```
# Enable encryption using customer-managed keys
$disk = Get-AzDisk -ResourceGroupName 'myResourceGroup' -DiskName 'myDisk'
$keyVault = Get-AzKeyVault -ResourceGroupName 'myResourceGroup' -VaultName '
    myKeyVault'
$key = Get-AzKeyVaultKey -VaultName $keyVault.VaultName -KeyName 'myKey'
Update-AzDisk -Disk $disk -EncryptionSettingsEnabled $true -DiskEncryptionKeyUri
    $key.Id -KeyVaultId $keyVault.ResourceId
```

Disk Snapshots allow point-in-time recovery and data protection. Snapshots can be used for backups, disaster recovery, and migrating workloads.

Availability Zones increase resiliency by replicating data across multiple data centers within a region. This ensures high availability even if one data center experiences a failure.

Shared Disks allow for greater flexibility in designing cluster-based applications. This feature supports Azure's high-availability solutions, permitting multiple VMs to attach simultaneously to a single disk for clustered applications.

```
# Create a shared disk
$diskConfig = New-AzDiskConfig -SkuName 'Premium_LRS' -Location 'EastUS' -
    CreateOption Empty -DiskSizeGB 1024 -MaxShares 2
$sharedDisk = New-AzDisk -ResourceGroupName 'myResourceGroup' -DiskName '
    mySharedDisk' -Disk $diskConfig

# Attach shared disk to VMs
$vm1 = Get-AzVM -ResourceGroupName 'myResourceGroup' -VMName 'vm1'
$vm1 = Add-AzVMDataDisk -VM $vm1 -Name 'mySharedDisk' -CreateOption Attach -
    ManagedDiskId $sharedDisk.Id -Lun 0
Update-AzVM -ResourceGroupName 'myResourceGroup' -VM $vm1

$vm2 = Get-AzVM -ResourceGroupName 'myResourceGroup' -VMName 'vm2'
$vm2 = Add-AzVMDataDisk -VM $vm2 -Name 'mySharedDisk' -CreateOption Attach -
    ManagedDiskId $sharedDisk.Id -Lun 0
Update-AzVM -ResourceGroupName 'myResourceGroup' -VM $vm2
```

Performance Tiers allow for dynamic changing of premium SSD performance characteristics without downtime or manual migration. This flexibility helps manage costs and performance as the workload changes.

For monitoring Azure Disk Storage, Azure Monitor and Azure Metrics provide real-time insights into disk performance, helping detect and mitigate issues swiftly:

```
# Create a disk metric alert for high IOPS
Add-AzMetricAlertRule -Name 'HighIOPSAlert' -ResourceGroupName '
    myResourceGroup' -TargetResourceId $disk.Id -MetricName '
    DiskWriteOperations/Sec' -Operator GreaterThan -Threshold 5000 -WindowSize
    00:15:00 -EvaluationPeriods 1 -MetricNamespace 'Microsoft.Compute/disks'
```

This section detailed Azure Disk Storage's types, management techniques, and features enhancing performance, security, and monitoring, offering insights necessary for harnessing the full potential of Azure's disk storage capabilities.

5.5 Azure Queue Storage

Azure Queue Storage is a service for storing large numbers of messages that can be accessed asynchronously from anywhere in the world via authenticated calls using HTTP or HTTPS. It is particularly useful for decoupling parts of a cloud application or for creating a buffer to save data in transient fault handling scenarios. This section delves into the architecture, operations, and practical applications of Queue Storage, enabling a robust understanding of its capability within Azure's comprehensive storage solutions.

Queue Storage provides a cloud-based messaging system that can be scaled up or down as the demand fluctuates. Each queue maintains a collection of messages which can be up to 64 KB in size. The total capacity of a single storage account is 500 TB, and one can create an unlimited number of queues within that limit.

A queue message typically contains two parts:

- **Message Text**: The actual content of the message that adheres to a 64 KB limit. It is stored in UTF-8 format.
- **Message Metadata**: Includes properties such as insertion time, expiration time, and dequeue count.

To start working with Azure Queue Storage, one must utilize storage accounts to organize the storage and administrative boundaries. Each Queue has a URL that adopts the following format:

$$\text{https://}\langle\text{storage-account-name}\rangle\text{.queue.core.windows.net/}\langle\text{queue-name}\rangle$$

Operations on Queue Storage can be performed using REST APIs or client libraries available for various programming languages like .NET, Java, Python, and Node.js. Below is an example demonstrating how to perform basic operations such as creating a queue, inserting a message, peeking messages, and deleting a message in Python using Azure SDK.

```
from azure.storage.queue import QueueServiceClient, QueueClient, QueueMessage

# Creating a Queue Service Client
queue_service_client = QueueServiceClient(account_url="https://<storage-account-
      name>.queue.core.windows.net",
                                          credential=<storage-account-key>)
```

```
# Creating a new queue
queue_client = queue_service_client.get_queue_client(queue="myqueue")
queue_client.create_queue()

# Inserting a message into the queue
queue_client.send_message("Hello, Azure Queue!")

# Peeking a message from the queue
peeked_messages = queue_client.peek_messages(max_messages=5)
for peeked_message in peeked_messages:
    print("Message: ", peeked_message.content)

# Receiving and deleting a message from the queue
messages = queue_client.receive_messages()
for msg in messages:
    print("Message: ", msg.content)
    queue_client.delete_message(msg)
```

The insert operation involves adding a new message to the end of the queue. The peek operation allows viewing the message without removing it from the queue, ensuring it remains available for other consumers. On the other hand, the receive operation entails retrieving the message and marking it invisible to other consumers temporarily until deletion.

Queue Storage's architecture ensures high availability and durability through replication. Azure automatically keeps three copies of the data within a single region (locally redundant storage) or can replicate across regions (geo-redundant storage) for compliance and disaster recovery purposes.

Proper authentication and access control mechanisms are essential for maintaining security. Shared Access Signatures (SAS) provide a secured method to grant granular control over permissions to clients without sharing the account key. For example, generating an SAS token in Python looks like this:

```
from azure.storage.queue import generate_queue_sas, QueueSasPermissions
from datetime import datetime, timedelta

sas_token = generate_queue_sas(account_name="<storage-account-name>",
                               queue_name="myqueue",
                               account_key="<account-key>",
                               permission=QueueSasPermissions(read=True, add=True,
                                          update=True, process=True),
                               expiry=datetime.utcnow() + timedelta(hours=1))

print("Generated SAS Token: ", sas_token)
```

Utilizing such tokens, temporary and narrowly-scoped permissions can be handed out to different components of an application, boosting security.

Monitoring and troubleshooting Azure Queue Storage can be efficiently managed using Azure Monitor. Metrics such as message count, ingress and egress rates, and latency can be tracked to ensure that the Queue performance aligns with application requirements. Alerts can be configured to notify administrators of any threshold breaches, facilitating prompt corrective actions.

Azure Queue Storage thus provides a scalable, secure, and efficient solution for managing asynchronous message processing in cloud-based applications. The ability to decouple components and introduce elasticity in workflow management makes it a significant asset in building resilient and streamlined cloud solutions.

5.6 Azure Table Storage

Azure Table Storage is a NoSQL datastore that provides a key/attribute store with a schema-less design, making it ideal for applications that need to store large amounts of structured, non-relational data. It is highly scalable, allowing developers to store petabytes of data and use it on-demand without having to worry about the underlying infrastructure.

Azure Table Storage stores data as a collection of entities, where each entity is a set of key-value pairs. The entities are organized into tables; however, unlike traditional relational tables, Azure Table Storage tables do not enforce a schema. This flexibility allows developers to change their data models without costly and time-consuming database migrations.

Entities and Properties in Azure Table Storage

Entities in Azure Table Storage are analogous to rows in a traditional database table. Each entity has a collection of properties, which are the key-value pairs storing the data. Each property is defined by a name, a value, and a data type. Supported data types include:

- String
- Int32
- Int64
- Double
- Boolean

- DateTime
- GUID
- Binary

Each entity has three system properties that uniquely identify it within a table:

- PartitionKey: This property is used to segment the table into different partitions. Entities with the same PartitionKey are stored together and can be queried more efficiently.
- RowKey: This property is unique within a partition and, combined with the PartitionKey, serves as the primary key for an entity.
- Timestamp: This property is managed by the server and stores the last modification date and time of the entity.

Creating and Managing Tables and Entities

Managing tables and entities in Azure Table Storage can be performed using the Azure Storage SDKs, REST API, or Azure Portal.

Example in C#:

```
using Microsoft.Azure.Cosmos.Table;

// Create the storage account
CloudStorageAccount storageAccount = CloudStorageAccount.Parse(connectionString);

// Create the table client
CloudTableClient tableClient = storageAccount.CreateCloudTableClient(new
    TableClientConfiguration());

// Retrieve a reference to a table named "customers"
CloudTable table = tableClient.GetTableReference("customers");

// Create the table if it doesn't exist
await table.CreateIfNotExistsAsync();

// Define a new customer entity
public class CustomerEntity : TableEntity
{
    public CustomerEntity(string lastName, string firstName)
    {
        PartitionKey = lastName;
        RowKey = firstName;
    }

    public CustomerEntity() { }

    public string Email { get; set; }
    public string PhoneNumber { get; set; }
}
```

```
// Create a new customer entity
CustomerEntity customer = new CustomerEntity("Smith", "John")
{
    Email = "john.smith@example.com",
    PhoneNumber = "123-456-7890"
};

// Create the TableOperation that inserts the customer entity
TableOperation insertOperation = TableOperation.Insert(customer);

// Execute the insert operation
await table.ExecuteAsync(insertOperation);
```

This code snippet demonstrates how to create a table and insert a new entity using the Azure Table Storage SDK for .NET.

Querying Data in Azure Table Storage

Querying data in Azure Table Storage can be done using the TableQuery class, which provides a flexible interface for constructing complex queries. Queries are expressed using the OData protocol.

Example in C#:

```
// Define the query, filtering by PartitionKey and selecting specific columns
TableQuery<CustomerEntity> query = new TableQuery<CustomerEntity>()
                                    .Where(TableQuery.GenerateFilterCondition("
                                        PartitionKey", QueryComparisons.Equal, "
                                        Smith"))
                                    .Select(new List<string> {"Email", "PhoneNumber"
                                        });

// Iterate through the results
foreach (CustomerEntity customer in table.ExecuteQuery(query))
{
    Console.WriteLine($"Email: {customer.Email}, Phone: {customer.PhoneNumber}");
}
```

Designing for Scalability and Performance

To achieve optimal performance and scalability with Azure Table Storage, consider the following best practices:

- **Partitioning**: Design your PartitionKey to balance the load evenly across partitions. Avoid hot partitions by distributing entities evenly.
- **Batched Operations**: Use batched operations to reduce the number of transactions and improve throughput. Batch transactions must be on entities with the same PartitionKey.
- **Indexing**: Leverage PartitionKey and RowKey to maximize the performance of queries. All queries should ideally include the

PartitionKey.

- **Data Model**: Design your data model to minimize the need for updates. Azure Table Storage is optimized for insert and read operations.

Azure Table Storage is a robust and flexible option for storing structured, non-relational data. Its scalability and performance characteristics make it suitable for a wide range of applications, from simple logs and counters to complex event data and metadata. The schema-less design allows developers to adapt their applications as requirements change, making Azure Table Storage an essential component of modern cloud data solutions.

5.7 Managing Storage Accounts

A fundamental aspect of using Azure Storage is the effective management of storage accounts. A storage account is an Azure resource that provides a unique namespace within Azure to store and manage data objects. Storage accounts provide a range of storage services including Blob, File, Disk, Queue, and Table storage, each serving different use cases and performance requirements.

Creating a Storage Account

Creating a new storage account is the first step in utilizing Azure Storage. This operation can be performed through the Azure portal, Azure CLI, or PowerShell. Below are the steps to create a storage account using the Azure CLI:

```
# Create a resource group
az group create --name myResourceGroup --location eastus

# Create a storage account
az storage account create --name mystorageaccount \
    --resource-group myResourceGroup \
    --location eastus \
    --sku Standard_LRS
```

The command above creates a new storage account named mystorageaccount in the myResourceGroup resource group, located in the East US region. The –sku parameter specifies the performance tier and replication strategy, in this case, Standard Locally-Redundant Storage (LRS).

Configuring Storage Account Settings

Once a storage account is created, several configuration settings can be adjusted to match specific requirements. Common settings include replication, access tiers, and networking configurations.

Replication Options

Azure Storage offers several redundancy options to ensure data durability and availability. These options include:

- **Locally Redundant Storage (LRS)**: Keeps multiple copies of data within a single datacenter.
- **Zone-Redundant Storage (ZRS)**: Spreads data across multiple datacenters within a single region.
- **Geo-Redundant Storage (GRS)**: Replicates data to a secondary region for disaster recovery.
- **Read-Access Geo-Redundant Storage (RA-GRS)**: Similar to GRS but allows read access to the secondary region.

Replication settings can be managed through the Azure portal or programmatically. For example, to enable Geo-Redundant Storage using Azure CLI:

```
az storage account update --name mystorageaccount \
    --resource-group myResourceGroup \
    --sku Standard_GRS
```

Managing Access Tiers

Azure Blob Storage supports different access tiers to balance cost and performance:

- **Hot Tier**: Optimized for data that is accessed frequently.
- **Cool Tier**: For data that is infrequently accessed and stored for at least 30 days.
- **Archive Tier**: For long-term storage of infrequently accessed data.

Access tiers can be set at both the blob and account level. To set the default access tier for a storage account:

```
az storage account blob-service-properties update \
    --account-name mystorageaccount \
    --resource-group myResourceGroup \
    --default-service-version 2019-07-07 \
    --set properties.defaultServiceVersion=Hot
```

Networking Configurations

Storage accounts can be configured with various network settings to control access:

- **Virtual Networks and Subnets**: Limit access to specified virtual networks and subnets.
- **IP Address Ranges**: Restrict access to specified IP address ranges.
- **Service Endpoints**: Extend private network reachability for Azure services.

To restrict access to a specific IP range:

```
az storage account update --name mystorageaccount \
    --resource-group myResourceGroup \
    --set networkRuleSet.ipRules[0].action=Allow \
        networkRuleSet.ipRules[0].value=23.45.67.89/32
```

Monitoring and Auditing Storage Accounts

Monitoring storage accounts is critical for maintaining performance and security. Azure provides several tools for this purpose:

- **Azure Monitor**: Collects and analyzes telemetry data.
- **Diagnostic Logs**: Capture detailed information about requests and errors.
- **Metrics**: Provide insights into usage patterns and performance.

Enabling diagnostic logs using Azure CLI:

```
az storage account management-policy create \
    --account-name mystorageaccount \
    --resource-group myResourceGroup \
    --policy @policy.json
```

In the example above, policy.json contains the configuration for diagnostic logging.

Managing Storage Account Keys and Shared Access Signatures (SAS)

Access to storage accounts is managed through primary and secondary keys, as well as Shared Access Signatures (SAS) for fine-grained control. Rotating keys periodically enhances security.

```
# Regenerate primary key
az storage account keys renew --account-name mystorageaccount \
    --resource-group myResourceGroup --key primary
```

Generating a SAS token for read access to a container:

```
az storage container generate-sas --account-name mystorageaccount \
    --name mycontainer --permissions r --expiry 2023-12-31T23:59:00Z
```

The generated SAS token can be appended to storage account URIs to grant limited access without exposing the primary keys.

By effectively managing storage accounts, users can ensure their data is stored securely, accessed efficiently, and remains cost-effective, while also leveraging the rich features offered by Microsoft Azure Storage.

5.8 Scalability and Performance in Azure Storage

Azure Storage is designed to handle large volumes of data and provide high-performance access to that data. To achieve this, Azure Storage offers several features and capabilities that ensure both scalability and performance. Understanding how to leverage these features effectively is critical for any system architect or developer utilizing Azure Storage.

Scalability:

Azure Storage is built to scale through methods such as partitioning and replication.

- **Partitioning:** Azure Storage automatically partitions tables, blobs, and queues as the volume of data increases. Partitioning involves dividing the data into smaller, manageable segments called partitions. Each partition can be stored on different storage nodes, allowing for parallel access and distribution across servers. This horizontal scaling ensures that the storage service can handle increased workloads and larger data sets without performance degradation.
- **Replication:** Azure Storage uses replication to ensure data durability and high availability. The service offers different replication strategies:

  - **Locally Redundant Storage (LRS):** Copies data three times within a single datacenter.
  - **Zone-Redundant Storage (ZRS):** Copies data across three Azure availability zones, ensuring data resilience to zone failures.
  - **Geo-Redundant Storage (GRS) and Read-Access Geo-Redundant Storage (RA-GRS):** Copies data to a secondary region hundreds of miles away from the primary location, providing disaster recovery capabilities.

- **Scalability Targets:** Azure Storage aims to handle a high volume of transactions and concurrently large numbers of requests. Some targets include:

  - Up to 20,000 requests per second for a single blob container.
  - Tens of gigabytes of data throughput.
  - Up to millions of messages per second in a queue.

Performance:

To achieve optimal performance in Azure Storage, several best practices and features should be considered:

- **Data Layout:** Designing a proper data layout is fundamental for performance. This involves leveraging partition keys in Table storage and blob indexing appropriately. Effective partitioning ensures that requests can be routed and processed efficiently. Avoid hotspots by distributing the workload evenly across partitions.

- **Access Patterns:** Understanding and optimizing access patterns can enhance performance. For example, when dealing with Blob Storage, use block blobs for large objects which support efficient uploading and downloading, and append blobs for scenarios where data is sequentially appended.

- **Concurrency and Asynchrony:** Azure Storage can handle a high level of concurrent operations. Utilize asynchronous programming models and parallelism in your applications to fully leverage Azure's scalability. This allows for better resource utilization and faster completion times for bulk operations.

```
from azure.storage.blob.aio import BlobServiceClient

# Initialize BlobServiceClient
blob_service_client = BlobServiceClient.from_connection_string('
    your_connection_string')

async def upload_file(container_name, blob_name, file_path):
    container_client = blob_service_client.get_container_client(
        container_name)
    async with container_client.get_blob_client(blob_name) as blob_client:
        with open(file_path, 'rb') as data:
            await blob_client.upload_blob(data)

# Event loop to run async functions
import asyncio
asyncio.run(upload_file('mycontainer', 'myfile.txt', 'localfile.txt'))
```

- **Caching:** Azure offers several caching mechanisms to improve performance. Blob Storage can utilize Azure Content Delivery Network (CDN) to cache blobs globally, reducing latency for end-users. Caching frequently accessed data can significantly enhance read performance.

- **Network Considerations:** Optimizing network configurations and choosing appropriate network tiers can influence performance. Use Azure Premium Storage when higher IOPS and low latency are required. Additionally, consider virtual network service endpoints and ExpressRoute for secure and high-throughput connections directly to Azure Storage.

Monitoring and Tuning:

Ongoing monitoring and performance tuning are essential to maintain the desired level of service.

- **Azure Monitor:** Utilize Azure Monitor for comprehensive insights into storage accounts' performance and health. Collect metrics like transaction metrics, availability, latency, and more. Set up alerts for critical performance thresholds.

- **Azure Storage Analytics:** Enable Azure Storage Analytics to collect detailed logs and metrics regarding Blob, Table, Queue, and File services. Analyze this data to identify performance bottlenecks and optimize access patterns.

```
from azure.storage.blob import BlobServiceClient

# Initialize BlobServiceClient
blob_service_client = BlobServiceClient.from_connection_string('
    your_connection_string')
```

```
# Enable logging and metrics
service_properties = {
    'analytics_logging': {
        'read': True,
        'write': True,
        'delete': True,
        'retention_policy': {
            'days': 7,
            'enabled': True
        }
    },
    'hour_metrics': {
        'enabled': True,
        'include_apis': True,
        'retention_policy': {
            'days': 7,
            'enabled': True
        }
    }
}
blob_service_client.set_service_properties(**service_properties)
```

- **Storage Access Tiers:** Optimize costs and performance by leveraging the appropriate access tier for storage needs:
  - **Hot Tier:** Suitable for data that is frequently accessed.
  - **Cool Tier:** Designed for infrequently accessed data with lower storage costs but higher access costs.
  - **Archive Tier:** Intended for long-term storage of data that is rarely accessed.

Scalability and performance in Azure Storage require strategic planning and continuous evaluation. By understanding the core principles and utilizing Azure's built-in features efficiently, one can build a robust and performant storage solution.

5.9 Access Control and Security in Azure Storage

Azure Storage offers robust mechanisms to ensure access control and security for data. Properly implemented security measures help in protecting data from unauthorized access and ensure compliance with regulatory standards. This section provides a detailed exploration of the various options and best practices for securing Azure Storage.

At the core of Azure Storage security are authentication and authorization mechanisms. Azure supports several methods for securing access to storage resources, including Shared Key, Shared Access Signatures (SAS), Azure Active Directory (Azure AD), and Role-Based Access Control (RBAC).

Shared Key Authentication utilizes an account key to secure access. Each storage account has two account keys to ensure continuous access while rotating keys for added security. Use the primary key as the main access key and the secondary key as a backup. Example code to access Azure Blob Storage using the account key is as follows:

```
from azure.storage.blob import BlobServiceClient

account_name = 'your_account_name'
account_key = 'your_account_key'

connection_string = f"DefaultEndpointsProtocol=https;AccountName={account_name
    };AccountKey={account_key};EndpointSuffix=core.windows.net"
blob_service_client = BlobServiceClient.from_connection_string(connection_string)
```

Shared Access Signatures (SAS) provide more granular control. They allow temporary and restricted access to storage resources without exposing account keys. SAS tokens can be scoped to specific permissions, expiry times, and IP addresses. Below is an example of generating a SAS token:

```
from azure.storage.blob import generate_blob_sas, BlobClient
from datetime import datetime, timedelta

account_name = 'your_account_name'
account_key = 'your_account_key'
container_name = 'your_container_name'
blob_name = 'your_blob_name'

sas_token = generate_blob_sas(
    account_name=account_name,
    container_name=container_name,
    blob_name=blob_name,
    account_key=account_key,
    permission='r', # Read permission
    expiry=datetime.utcnow() + timedelta(hours=1) # Token validity
)

blob_url_with_sas = f"https://{account_name}.blob.core.windows.net/{
    container_name}/{blob_name}?{sas_token}"
blob_client = BlobClient(blob_url_with_sas)
```

Azure Active Directory (Azure AD) offers identity-based authentication for Azure services. Using Azure AD, you can manage access to your Azure Storage account with Azure AD user accounts, groups, or managed identities. It integrates seamlessly with Azure RBAC, allowing you to define roles and manage user permissions effectively. Below is an example of configuring Azure AD for Azure Blob Storage:

```
from azure.identity import DefaultAzureCredential
from azure.storage.blob import BlobServiceClient

account_url = 'https://your_account_name.blob.core.windows.net'
credential = DefaultAzureCredential()
blob_service_client = BlobServiceClient(account_url=account_url, credential=
    credential)
```

Role-Based Access Control (RBAC) allows for the assignment of roles to Azure AD users, groups, and service principals at various scopes such as the subscription, resource group, or specific resources. Different roles, such as 'Storage Blob Data Reader' or 'Storage Blob Data Contributor', offer nuances in granted permissions. Role assignments can be managed via the Azure portal, CLI, or PowerShell.

To manage RBAC via Azure CLI:

```
# Assign 'Storage Blob Data Contributor' role to a user at resource group scope
az role assignment create --assignee user@example.com --role "Storage Blob Data
    Contributor" --resource-group your_resource_group
```

Encryption is another critical component of Azure Storage security. Azure Storage automatically provides encryption at rest using server-side encryption (SSE) with Azure-managed keys or customer-managed keys. To use customer-managed keys, integrate Azure Key Vault or specify the key via the Blob storage settings.

Below is an example of configuring a storage account to use a customer-managed key from Azure Key Vault:

```
# Create a Key Vault
az keyvault create --name yourKeyVaultName --resource-group yourResourceGroup --
    location yourLocation

# Add an access policy to the Key Vault
az keyvault set-policy --name yourKeyVaultName --object-id $userObjectId --
    permissions keys=get,list

# Create a key in the Key Vault
az keyvault key create --vault-name yourKeyVaultName --name yourKeyName --
    protection software

# Set the storage account to use the Key Vault key
az storage account update --name yourStorageAccountName --resource-group
    yourResourceGroup --encryption-key-source Microsoft.Keyvault --encryption-key-
    name yourKeyName --encryption-key-vault yourKeyVaultId
```

Network Security aspects include the ability to restrict access to storage account resources via Virtual Network (VNet) rules, firewall settings, and private endpoints. Configuring these settings helps prevent unauthorized access and ensures that traffic between services remains within the Azure backbone.

```
# Add a virtual network rule to a storage account
az storage account network-rule add --resource-group yourResourceGroup --account-
    name yourStorageAccountName --vnet yourVnetName --subnet yourSubnetName
```

Azure Storage further supports **advanced threat detection** by integrating with Azure Security Center to provide security alerts. It identifies unusual and potentially harmful attempts to access or exploit your storage account.

Collectively, implementing these comprehensive access control and security mechanisms ensures that Azure Storage resources are secure and compliant with industry standards.

5.10 Azure Storage Explorer

Azure Storage Explorer serves as a valuable tool for managing and interacting with Azure Storage accounts. The utility supports Azure Blob Storage, Azure File Storage, Azure Queue Storage, and Azure Table Storage. It simplifies tasks such as uploading, downloading, and managing storage entities through a graphical user interface (GUI). This section explores the functionalities and usage of Azure Storage Explorer in detail to provide an exhaustive understanding of its application and benefits.

Azure Storage Explorer is a cross-platform application available on Windows, macOS, and Linux. To install Azure Storage Explorer, navigate to the official Microsoft documentation website, download the installer for your operating system, and follow the installation instructions.

After installation, launching Azure Storage Explorer presents a GUI that facilitates the connection to Azure Storage accounts. The steps to connect to a storage account are outlined below:

```
1. Open Azure Storage Explorer.
2. Click on the 'Add an account' or 'Connect to Azure Storage' button.
3. Choose from the connection options:
   a) Add an Azure Account
   b) Use a connection string or shared access signature (SAS)
   c) Attach to a local emulator (if applicable)
4. Follow the prompts based on your selection:
   a) For Azure Account, sign in using your Azure credentials.
   b) For connection string or SAS, enter the provided connection details.
   c) For local emulator, configure the appropriate settings.
```

Once connected, Azure Storage Explorer displays a hierarchical view of your storage resources. The main window is divided into several panes, including the **Tree View**, which shows the storage accounts and their containers, and the **Properties Pane**, which displays metadata and properties of selected items.

Blob Storage Management: To manage Azure Blob Storage, navigate to Blob Containers within the Tree View. You can create new containers, upload files, and set container access levels. The following example demonstrates how to upload a file to a blob container:

```
1. Right-click on the desired blob container.
2. Select 'Upload' from the context menu.
3. Choose 'Upload Files' or 'Upload Folder' based on the requirement.
4. Browse and select the file(s) or folder to upload.
5. Click 'Upload' to initiate the transfer.
```

File Storage Management: Azure Storage Explorer allows you to handle Azure File Storage similarly to a local file system. You can create directories, upload/download files, and generate share snapshots for backup purposes. The following steps illustrate the process of downloading a file from Azure File Storage:

```
1. Navigate to the chosen file share within the Tree View.
2. Right-click on the file to be downloaded.
3. Select 'Download' from the context menu.
4. Specify the local destination path for the file.
5. Click 'Save' to complete the download.
```

Queue Storage Management: Queue Storage can be managed by accessing the Queues section in the Tree View. You can view messages, add new messages, and clear queues. Here's an example of adding a message to a queue:

```
1. Locate and right-click on the target queue.
2. Choose 'Add Message' from the context menu.
3. Type the message content in the provided input box.
4. Click 'OK' to post the message to the queue.
```

Table Storage Management: Managing Azure Table Storage in Azure Storage Explorer includes operations such as inserting entities, querying tables, and editing rows. The following instructions demonstrate querying data in a table:

```
1. Open the desired table by double-clicking it in the Tree View.
2. Click on the 'Query' tab in the Table Editor window.
3. Enter the OData query to filter the data (e.g., 'PartitionKey eq 'partition1'').
4. Click 'Run Query' to execute and view the results.
```

Security Features: Azure Storage Explorer also supports security management features such as setting stored access policies and generating SAS tokens. These features allow fine-grained control over access to storage resources. To generate a SAS token:

```
1. Right-click on the targeted resource (e.g., blob container, queue).
2. Select 'Get Shared Access Signature...' from the context menu.
3. Configure the permissions and expiry time for the SAS token.
4. Click 'Create' to generate the SAS token.
5. Copy the generated SAS token for secure access to the resource.
```

Azure Storage Explorer CLI: In addition to the GUI, Azure Storage Explorer provides a command-line interface (CLI) for automation of storage operations. This feature is useful for scripting routine tasks and can be integrated into Continuous Integration/Continuous Deployment (CI/CD) pipelines.

Finally, users can customize their experience in Azure Storage Explorer by utilizing settings for caching, proxy configuration, and telemetry preferences. Access these settings by selecting 'Edit' -> 'Settings' from the menu bar. The application also supports numerous language preferences and can be tailored to suit regional formats and conventions.

The utility provided by Azure Storage Explorer significantly enhances productivity by offering an intuitive, user-friendly interface for storage management, thereby facilitating efficient cloud storage operations on the Azure platform.

5.11 Introduction to Azure Data Lake

Azure Data Lake is designed to handle large volumes of data, providing a comprehensive solution for big data analytics. It integrates seamlessly with various Azure services, offering a scalable and secure environment for data storage and processing. This section explores the key components, architecture, and functionalities of Azure Data Lake, illustrating how it can be leveraged for efficient data management and analytics.

Azure Data Lake Storage (ADLS) is a core component, offering high throughput and low latency for diverse data types, regardless of size or format. It supports hierarchical namespace, enabling organized and efficient data access. Here's an overview of its key features:

- **Scalability:** ADLS can scale dynamically, accommodating petabytes of data and thousands of concurrent operations.
- **Security:** Built-in security features ensure data is protected. This

includes encryption at rest and in transit, fine-grained access control using Azure Active Directory (AAD), and role-based access control (RBAC).

- **Cost Efficiency:** ADLS offers a pay-as-you-go pricing model, minimizing costs by only charging for the storage and operational capacity utilized.
- **Integration:** ADLS integrates with various Azure analytics services like Azure HDInsight, Azure Databricks, and Azure Synapse Analytics, facilitating complex data analysis and machine learning workflows.

A crucial aspect of Azure Data Lake is its hierarchical namespace. This enables a file-system-like structure that optimizes data management operations such as moving, renaming, or deleting files. The hierarchical namespace is essential for fine-grained security controls and efficient data access patterns, which are critical for big data environments.

```
from azure.identity import DefaultAzureCredential
from azure.mgmt.storage import StorageManagementClient

subscription_id = 'your-subscription-id'
resource_group_name = 'your-resource-group'
account_name = 'your-datalake-storage-account'

credential = DefaultAzureCredential()
storage_client = StorageManagementClient(credential, subscription_id)

storage_client.storage_accounts.create(
    resource_group_name,
    account_name,
    {
        'location': 'eastus2',
        'sku': {
            'name': 'Standard_LRS'
        },
        'kind': 'StorageV2',
        'properties': {
            'isHnsEnabled': True
        }
    }
)
```

The above Python code demonstrates creating a Data Lake Storage Gen2 account using the Azure SDK. This account supports the hierarchical namespace essential for organizing data efficiently.

Data ingestion into Azure Data Lake can be achieved through various methods such as Azure Data Factory, Azure Databricks, and direct APIs. Here's how to upload a file to ADLS using Azure CLI:

```
az storage fs file upload --account-name <adls-account-name> --file-system <file-
    system-name> --source <local-file-path> --path <destination-path>
```

Once data is ingested, it can be processed using different services. For instance, Azure HDInsight can run Apache Hadoop, Spark, and other big data frameworks directly interfacing with ADLS. This provides a streamlined approach to performing tasks like data transformation, cleaning, and advanced analytics.


```
{
  "totalFiles": 2300,
  "totalDirectories": 100,
  "storageUsage": "2.4TB"
}
```


The JSON output above represents a summary of the data stored within an Azure Data Lake, showcasing its capability to handle extensive datasets. This aggregation of information is vital for monitoring and optimizing storage utilization.

For monitoring and troubleshooting, Azure Data Lake provides integration with Azure Monitor and Azure Log Analytics. These services collect and analyze telemetry data, offering insights into the performance and health of the data lake. Implementing such practices ensures that operations run smoothly and any potential issues are preemptively identified and resolved.

Azure Data Lake's robust architecture and seamless integration with other Azure services make it an indispensable tool for enterprises aiming to gain insights from their data. Its design principles revolve around scalability, security, and cost-efficiency, making it suitable for various big data use cases, from batch processing to real-time analytics.

5.12 Monitoring and Troubleshooting Azure Storage

Monitoring and troubleshooting are integral components of managing any storage solution, and Azure Storage is no exception. Effective monitoring helps maintain the performance, availability, and reliability of storage services, while troubleshooting ensures that issues are identified and resolved promptly. This section delves into the tools and techniques available within Azure for monitoring and troubleshooting storage solutions, ensuring an optimized and resilient storage environment.

Azure provides a suite of monitoring and diagnostic tools, including Azure Monitor, Azure Storage Analytics, Log Analytics, and Application Insights. Each tool offers distinct functionalities helping to address various aspects of monitoring and troubleshooting.

Azure Monitor:

Azure Monitor provides comprehensive monitoring capabilities across all Azure services. It collects and analyzes telemetry data, allowing users to gain insights into the performance and health of their applications. For Azure Storage, it helps monitor key storage metrics like capacity, transactions, ingress and egress data, and latency.

There are several key metrics to monitor in Azure Storage:

- **Capacity**: Tracks the amount of data stored in the storage account.
- **Transactions**: Measures the number of requests made to the storage account.
- **Ingress and Egress**: Indicates the amount of data being read from and written to the storage account.
- **Latency**: Represents the response times for storage operations.

To configure these metrics, navigate to the Azure portal, select the storage account, and click on *Metrics* under the *Monitoring* section. From here, you can add charts to visualize these metrics, create alerts, and configure automated actions based on specific conditions.

Azure Storage Analytics:

Azure Storage Analytics provides logging and metric data for a storage account. This includes detailed information about read, write, and delete operations against blobs, queues, tables, and files. Storage Analytics can be enabled through the Azure portal or via Azure PowerShell.

To enable Storage Analytics using Azure PowerShell, execute the following command:

```
Set-AzStorageServiceLoggingProperty -ServiceType Blob -LoggingOperations "Read,
    Write,Delete" -RetentionDays 10
```

This command enables logging for read, write, and delete operations on the Blob service, retaining the logs for 10 days.

Log Analytics:

Log Analytics allows you to collect and analyze logs from Azure resources. It can be integrated with Azure Monitor to create a unified platform for monitoring and diagnostics. Log queries enable advanced data exploration and can be written using Kusto query language (KQL).

An example of a KQL query to analyze read operations on blobs is:

```
AzureDiagnostics
| where ResourceType == "STORAGEACCOUNTS" and OperationName == "
    GetBlob"
```

This query filters the logs to show only read operations on blobs, providing insights into access patterns and potential bottlenecks.

Application Insights:

While primarily geared towards application monitoring, Application Insights can be utilized to monitor client-side interactions with Azure Storage. It enables you to track dependencies, response times, and failures, offering a comprehensive view of how storage performance impacts application behavior.

To instrument Application Insights in your application, you can use the following code snippet in an ASP.NET application:

```
using Microsoft.ApplicationInsights;
using Microsoft.ApplicationInsights.Extensibility;

var telemetryClient = new TelemetryClient();
telemetryClient.TrackDependency("AzureBlob", "GetBlob", timestamp, duration,
    success);
```

This example demonstrates logging a dependency call to Azure Blob Storage, capturing the timestamp, duration, and success status of the operation.

Effective troubleshooting requires identifying the root cause of issues and addressing them appropriately. Common storage-related issues include high latency, operation failures, and capacity limits. Leveraging the collected logs and metrics is crucial in pinpointing the exact cause.

Consider a scenario where you notice increased latency in read operations. Using Azure Storage Analytics, you can identify if this is due to a high number of concurrent operations, network issues, or suboptimal configuration settings. By analyzing the logs and metrics, you can determine whether to scale out your storage, adjust network configurations, or optimize application code.

To further illustrate, if Storage Analytics logs reveal frequent operation failures, you might use Log Analytics to correlate these failures with specific error codes, times, or even specific API calls. This targeted investigation helps in applying accurate fixes, such as retry logic in applications or configuration changes in the storage account.

Integrating Azure Monitor alerts can proactively notify you of potential issues. For instance, setting up an alert for high latency or unusual transaction patterns ensures that you can respond swiftly to anomalies:

```
Add-AzMetricAlertRule -ResourceGroupName "ResourceGroup" -Name "
    HighLatencyAlert" -Location "East US" -TargetResourceId "/subscriptions/0000/
    resourceGroups/ResourceGroup/providers/Microsoft.Storage/storageAccounts/
    StorageAccount" -TargetNamespace "Microsoft.Storage" -TargetMetricName "
    BlobGetRequest" -TargetMetricAggregation "Average" -TargetConditionOperator
    "GreaterThan" -TargetConditionThreshold 200 -TargetConditionWindowSize 5 -
    ActionGroupId "/subscriptions/0000/resourceGroups/ResourceGroup/providers/
    Microsoft.Insights/actionGroups/ActionGroup"
```

This PowerShell command creates an alert rule for average Blob Get request latency exceeding 200 milliseconds over a five-minute window, triggering an action group for notifications.

In sum, monitoring and troubleshooting Azure Storage is about leveraging the right tools to gain visibility into storage operations, understanding the metrics and logs generated, and using this data to maintain optimal performance and rectify issues promptly. Proper monitoring not only ensures efficient storage management but also leads to a robust and resilient storage infrastructure critical for enterprise applications.

Chapter 6

Azure Security and Compliance

This chapter addresses the key aspects of securing Azure environments and ensuring compliance with industry standards. It covers Azure Security Center, Key Vault, and Active Directory security features. Additionally, it discusses network security, policy management with Azure Policy and Blueprints, and data encryption methods. The chapter includes information on Azure Sentinel for threat detection, identity protection, privileged identity management, and auditing security practices to maintain robust security posture and compliance.

6.1 Overview of Azure Security

Securing Microsoft Azure environments involves a comprehensive approach, leveraging an array of built-in tools and services to protect data, applications, and infrastructure. Azure's security offerings are designed to cater to the diverse needs of organizations, providing mechanisms to safeguard against threats, manage identities and access, and ensure compliance with regulatory standards.

Defense in Depth Strategy

Azure utilizes a defense in depth strategy, which layers multiple security measures to protect against various threats. This approach ensures that if one security control fails, additional controls are in place to maintain security. The primary layers include:

- **Physical Security:** Ensures data centers are protected from unauthorized physical access. Measures include surveillance, access controls, and environmental safeguards.
- **Network Security:** Protects the network infrastructure through virtual network peering, network security groups (NSGs), and Azure Firewall.
- **Perimeter Security:** Utilizes distributed denial of service (DDoS) protection and perimeter firewalls to defend against large-scale attacks.
- **Identity and Access Management:** Manages and secures access to resources using Azure Active Directory (Azure AD) and Multi-Factor Authentication (MFA).
- **Application Security:** Involves code analysis, security testing, and application firewall to secure applications deployed in Azure.
- **Data Security:** Employs encryption (both in-transit and at-rest), access controls, and data masking to protect sensitive information.
- **Monitoring and Compliance:** Includes continuous monitoring, logging, and auditing to ensure compliance and detect anomalies.

Azure Security Center

Azure Security Center plays a pivotal role in protecting resources hosted in Azure and on-premises environments. Key features include:

- Continuous Monitoring and Threat Detection: Provides real-time insights into the security state of resources, identifying vulnerabilities and prioritizing security recommendations.
- Advanced Threat Protection: Uses machine learning and threat intelligence to detect and respond to potential threats proactively.
- Security Score: Offers an aggregated score to help organizations evaluate their security posture and take remedial actions.

Azure Key Vault

Azure Key Vault helps safeguard cryptographic keys, secrets, and certificates used by cloud applications and services. Features include:

- Centralized Key Management: Simplifies management of encryption keys and secrets.
- Secure By Design: Keys are protected using hardware security modules (HSMs) and software-based encryption methods.
- Auditing and Logging: Tracks access and usage for audit and compliance purposes.

Azure Active Directory (Azure AD)

Azure AD offers comprehensive identity management and access control capabilities. Key components include:

- User Authentication and Authorization: Manages user identities and secure access to resources.
- Conditional Access Policies: Enforces policies based on user location, device state, and risk level.
- Identity Protection: Utilizes machine learning to detect suspicious activities and mitigate identity-related risks.

Network Security in Azure

Azure's network security leverages several mechanisms to ensure secure communication and data transfer:

- Virtual Networks (VNets): Isolate and control network traffic.
- Network Security Groups (NSGs): Define inbound and outbound traffic rules.
- Azure Firewall: Provides comprehensive network security with high availability and scalability.
- DDoS Protection: Defends against large-scale network attacks, ensuring service availability.

Azure Policy and Blueprints

To maintain adherence to organizational standards and regulatory requirements, Azure Policy and Blueprints are extensively utilized:

- Azure Policy: Automates enforcement and compliance through policy definitions and assignments.
- Azure Blueprints: Facilitates the deployment of compliant environments using pre-defined artifacts.

Compliance in Azure

Azure supports various compliance needs by offering a variety of certifications and attestations. Key points include:

- Compliance Certifications: Includes ISO 27001, SOC 1/2/3, HIPAA, and GDPR among others.
- Regulatory Compliance: Provides tools and features to support compliance with regional and industry-specific regulations.
- Trust Center: Acts as a repository for compliance documentation and resources.

Data Encryption in Azure

Data encryption is an essential aspect of Azure security, ensuring data confidentiality and integrity:

- Encryption at Rest: Uses Azure Storage Service Encryption (SSE) and Transparent Data Encryption (TDE).
- Encryption in Transit: Enforces TLS/SSL to protect data moving between systems.
- Customer-managed Keys: Utilize Azure Key Vault for customer-controlled key management.

Azure Sentinel

Azure Sentinel is Microsoft's cloud-native security information and event management (SIEM) system providing:

- Intelligent Security Analytics: Collects, detects, and investigates security threats across the enterprise.

- Automated Response: Facilitates automatic responses to detected threats using playbooks.
- Customizable Dashboards: Provides visibility into security posture through user-defined dashboards.

Identity Protection and Privileged Identity Management

These Azure services mitigate risks associated with identity-based attacks:

- Identity Protection: Continuously monitors and mitigates potential identity risks.
- Privileged Identity Management (PIM): Manages, controls, and monitors privileged access within Azure AD.

Securing Applications in Azure

Application security in Azure focuses on ensuring that applications are resistant to threats and vulnerabilities through:

- Secure Development Lifecycle (SDL): Integrates security practices into the software development lifecycle.
- Static and Dynamic Analysis: Employs testing methodologies to identify vulnerabilities in the code.
- Web Application Firewalls (WAF): Protects web applications from common threats like SQL injection and cross-site scripting (XSS).

Monitoring and Auditing Security in Azure

Continuous monitoring and auditing are critical for maintaining a robust security posture:

- Azure Monitor: Tracks the performance and health of resources.
- Azure Log Analytics: Collects, correlates, and analyzes log data from various sources.
- Security Center: Provides a unified security management and threat protection system.

TexImage security is about layering safeguards to manage identity and access, protect data, and comply with regulations effectively.

6.2 Azure Security Center

Azure Security Center (ASC) is a comprehensive security management system that handles the detection, prevention, and response to security threats in an Azure environment. It integrates numerous Azure services to provide a cohesive security posture and allows for centralized visibility across Azure resources. Understanding its core components and functionalities is crucial for maintaining robust security within a cloud infrastructure.

Azure Security Center is divided into several key areas that contribute to its overall function: security posture management, advanced threat protection, and adaptive application controls.

Security Posture Management is the process of evaluating the security strength of the cloud infrastructure. ASC aids in this by continuously assessing the configuration of Azure resources. It provides recommendations to improve the security posture based on the Azure Security Benchmark, which is aligned with established industry standards. The ASC evaluates resources against security best practices, and its findings can be viewed within the *Security Center Dashboard*.

```
security_resources
| summarize count()
  by Category, RecommendationName
  | top 10 by count_
```

The output of the Azure Security Center compliance check query might look like this:

```
Category          RecommendationName            count_
------------    --------------------    ------
Networking        Enable Network Security Groups    85
Data & Storage    Enable Encryption for Data        45
Computing         Apply Disk Encryption             30
```

Advanced Threat Protection involves leveraging machine learning, behavioral analytics, and anomaly detection to identify and mitigate potential threats. Security Center provides built-in support for analyzing activities across various levels of the Azure infrastructure. These protections can automatically apply patches, restrict access, and implement security best practices to protect against advanced threats without user intervention.

```
SecurityAlert
| where TimeGenerated > ago(1d)
  and AlertSeverirty == "High"
| summarize count() by AlertName, CompromisedEntity
```

The sample output for this advanced threat detection query could be:

```
AlertName          CompromisedEntity       count_
-----------------  ---------------------   ------
RDP Brute Force     VM1-WEB-EAST              5
Malware Threat      VM2-DB-SOUTH              2
```

Adaptive Application Controls in ASC enable organizations to define rules and application whitelisting to control the applications running on VMs. By analyzing the processes and applications executed on these VMs, ASC recommends a set of allowed applications, enhancing security by preventing unauthorized programs from being executed.

```
let allowedApps = dynamic(["app1.exe", "app2.exe", "app3.exe"]);
VMProcessEvents
| where Executable in (allowedApps)
| summarize by Category, Count
```

The output for defining application control rules might be interpreted as:

```
Category          Count
--------------    -----
Allowed Apps         50
```

Security Center extends its functionalities through integration with other Azure services like Azure Policy, Azure Sentinel, and Azure Arc, allowing for governance and auditing, security analytics, and managing resources outside of Azure respectively. **Azure Policy** ensures environments remain compliant through policy definitions that can be applied to resources to assess their compliance state automatically. Policies can automatically remediate non-compliant resources.

```
policyAssignment=$(az policy assignment create --policy {policyId}
  --scope "/subscriptions/{subscriptionId}/resourceGroups/{resourceGroup}")
```

Azure Sentinel integrates seamlessly with ASC to provide a broader scope of threat intelligence and analytics. Sentinel uses the telemetry from ASC to build deeper insights into security events and issues, offering an added layer of security operations.

In summary, Azure Security Center provides a holistic approach to security, guiding users in establishing a secure, compliant, and well-monitored Azure environment. Progressing through understanding and applying ASC's principles ensures that security best practices are ingrained within the organizational cloud infrastructure strategy, mitigating risks and maintaining an elevated security posture.

6.3 Azure Key Vault

Azure Key Vault provides a secure storage solution for secrets, keys, and certificates. This service is integral to maintaining the confidentiality and integrity of sensitive information in an Azure environment. It helps manage access and meets compliance requirements for various industry standards.

Azure Key Vault offers two primary functionalities: secret management and key management. Secret management allows for the secure storage and handling of sensitive data such as passwords, connection strings, and API keys. Key management, on the other hand, is used for the creation and control of encryption keys.

Azure Key Vault can also manage SSL/TLS certificates, which can be provisioned and renewed automatically with certain Certificate Authorities. This automatic handling of certificates mitigates the risk of service outages due to expired certificates.

Secret Management:

Secrets in Azure Key Vault are pieces of sensitive information, such as passwords, that need to be tightly controlled. The primary operations associated with secrets are:

- Storing secrets.
- Retrieving secrets.
- Deleting secrets.
- Listing secrets and their versions.

To store a secret in Azure Key Vault, the following command can be used via Azure CLI:

```
az keyvault secret set --vault-name <vault-name> --name <secret-name> --value <
    secret-value>
```

To retrieve a stored secret, the command is:

```
az keyvault secret show --vault-name <vault-name> --name <secret-name>
```

The retrieval command returns the secret in the following format:

```
{
  "value": "<retrieved-secret-value>"
}
```

Key Management:

Azure Key Vault's key management capabilities support the creation, storage, and management of cryptographic keys. The keys can be asymmetric or symmetric and can be used for encryption, decryption, signing, and verification. Supported algorithms include RSA, RSA-HSM (Hardware Security Module), and elliptic curve algorithms.

To create a new RSA key in Azure Key Vault using Azure CLI:

```
az keyvault key create --vault-name <vault-name> --name <key-name> --kty RSA --
    size 2048
```

To retrieve an existing key:

```
az keyvault key show --vault-name <vault-name> --name <key-name>
```

The output will look like this:

```
{
  "key": {
    "kid": "<key-identifier>",
    ...
  }
}
```

Access Policies and Security:

Access to Azure Key Vault is controlled using Azure Active Directory (Azure AD) and access policies. These policies determine who can perform various operations on the vault and its contents. Fine-grained access control can be configured using Azure Role-Based Access Control (RBAC) or access policies directly defined in the Key Vault.

An access policy can grant permissions such as get, list, set, delete for secrets, and other relevant permissions for keys and certificates. This level of control helps ensure that only authorized applications or users have access to sensitive data.

The command to set an access policy that grants a user permission to list and retrieve secrets:

```
az keyvault set-policy --name <vault-name> --upn <user-principal-name> --secret-
    permissions get list
```

Compliance and Regulatory Inputs:

Azure Key Vault helps organizations adhere to compliance and regulatory requirements by providing secure key management that supports standards such as FIPS 140-2. Organizations can leverage the built-in security features and access logging to demonstrate compliance with various data protection regulations.

The service integrates seamlessly with various Azure security services, such as Azure Security Center, for monitoring and alerting, ensuring that an organization's security posture is maintained.

Integration with Azure Services:

Azure Key Vault integrates with many other Azure services, providing a centralized key management system. For instance, Azure Storage and SQL Database can use keys stored in Key Vault for encryption. Azure DevOps services can retrieve secrets for use in build and release pipelines.

To employ an encryption key from Azure Key Vault for an Azure Storage account:

```
az storage account update --name <storage-account-name> --resource-group <resource-group-name> --encryption-key-source Microsoft.Keyvault --encryption-key-vault <keyvault-id> --encryption-key-name <key-name>
```

This involvement with an extensive range of Azure services highlights the crucial role that Azure Key Vault plays in a secure and compliant cloud architecture.

Azure Key Vault is a fundamental component for protecting and managing secrets and encryption keys in Azure environments, assisting in compliance and elevating an organization's security constructs.

6.4 Azure Active Directory (Azure AD) Security

Azure Active Directory (Azure AD) is Microsoft's cloud-based identity and access management service, which helps employees sign in and access resources. Given the critical role that identity management plays in securing modern IT environments, Azure AD provides a comprehensive set of capabilities to protect identities, manage governance, and ensure compliance with industry standards.

Azure AD offers several advanced security features that include multi-factor authentication, conditional access policies, identity protection, and the management of hybrid environments. These mechanisms ensure that only authorized users have access to organizational resources, which is crucial for maintaining security.

1. Multi-Factor Authentication (MFA)

Multi-Factor Authentication (MFA) is a security feature that requires more than one method of authentication to verify a user's identity. This helps to protect organizations from identity theft and other malicious activities involving compromised credentials. In Azure AD, MFA can be configured using a range of methods including:

- SMS and phone calls
- Mobile app notifications and verification codes
- Hardware tokens
- FIDO2 security keys

The configuration of MFA can be enforced at the user level or via conditional access policies to ensure compliance with security requirements while reducing friction for end-users.

2. Conditional Access Policies

Conditional access policies in Azure AD allow administrators to define specific conditions under which users can access resources. These policies create a layer of security by granting access based on factors such as:

- User's location
- Device compliance status
- Application sensitivity
- Sign-in risk level

For example, access might be granted only if the user is signing in from a trusted location or using a compliant device. Implementing conditional access policies helps to mitigate risks associated with unauthorized access and protect sensitive information.

3. Identity Protection

Azure AD Identity Protection employs machine learning and behavioral analytics to detect and respond to suspicious activities. It provides risk-based conditional access and alerts administrators to potential issues such as unusual sign-in behaviors or compromised credentials. Identity Protection includes the following capabilities:

- Risk detection: Identifies risks such as anonymous IP address usage, atypical travel, and known leaked credentials.
- Risk remediation: Allows for automatic or manual remediation actions, like prompting users to reset their passwords.
- Reports and notifications: Provides security insights and alerts to take immediate action on detected threats.

These functionalities contribute to a more secure authentication process and help maintain the integrity of the identity infrastructure.

4. Hybrid Identity Management

Many organizations operate in hybrid environments where on-premises directories coexist with cloud-based services. Azure AD supports hybrid identity management through Azure AD Connect, allowing seamless integration and synchronization between on-premises Active Directory and Azure AD. This integration offers several advantages:

- Single sign-on (SSO): Users can access both on-premises and cloud resources with a single set of credentials.
- Password hash synchronization: Synchronizes password hashes from on-premises Active Directory to Azure AD for consistent password policies.
- Pass-through authentication: Provides a more secure authentication method by validating passwords directly against on-premises Active Directory.

Hybrid identity solutions enhance the flexibility and control organizations have over their identity environments while leveraging the robust security features of Azure AD.

5. Privileged Identity Management (PIM)

Azure AD Privileged Identity Management (PIM) is a feature that improves control over privileged roles in Azure AD, Azure, and other Microsoft Online Services. With PIM, organizations can:

- Assign time-bound privileged roles.
- Require approval to activate privileged roles.
- Enforce just-in-time (JIT) access for elevated roles.

- Conduct access reviews for privileged roles.
- Receive alerts about privileged access and review the access history.

PIM helps minimize the risk of excessive, unnecessary, or misused access to sensitive resources, enhancing the overall security posture of the organization.

In an evolving threat landscape, Azure Active Directory ensures that robust identity protection and management are central to an organization's security strategy. Through multi-factor authentication, conditional access policies, identity protection, hybrid identity management, and privileged identity management, Azure AD provides comprehensive safeguards against unauthorized access and identity-related threats.

6.5 Network Security in Azure

Azure provides a comprehensive suite of network security features designed to protect resources and ensure compliance. Effective network security in Azure involves creating secure network boundaries, managing access control, monitoring traffic, and utilizing advanced threat detection mechanisms.

Virtual Networks (VNets)

Azure Virtual Network (VNet) is the fundamental building block for network security. VNets enable users to create isolated network environments where Azure resources, such as Virtual Machines (VMs) and storage accounts, can securely communicate with each other. Within a VNet, one can define subnets, apply network security groups (NSGs), and define routing rules.

Network Security Groups (NSGs)

Network Security Groups are the primary mechanism to control network traffic to and from network interfaces (NICs), VMs, and subnets. NSGs contain security rules that allow or deny inbound and outbound traffic based on source and destination IP addresses, ports, and protocols.

Here is an example of creating an NSG and defining rules using Azure CLI:

```
# Create a Network Security Group
az network nsg create --resource-group MyResourceGroup --name MyNSG
```

```
# Create an inbound security rule that allows HTTP traffic on port 80
az network nsg rule create --resource-group MyResourceGroup --nsg-name MyNSG \
  --name AllowHTTP --priority 100 \
  --destination-port-ranges 80 --protocol Tcp --access Allow --direction Inbound

# Create an outbound rule that denies all traffic to the Internet
az network nsg rule create --resource-group MyResourceGroup --nsg-name MyNSG \
  --name DenyInternetOutbound --priority 200 \
  --destination-address-prefixes Internet --protocol '*' --access Deny --direction
      Outbound
```

Azure Firewall

Azure Firewall is a managed, cloud-based network security service that provides protection for resources within VNets. It supports high availability and scaling automatically based on traffic. It allows inbound and outbound filtering rules, supports threat intelligence, and integrates with Azure Monitor for sophisticated logging capabilities.

Setting up Azure Firewall involves creating a firewall instance and setting rules. Example using Azure CLI:

```
# Create a virtual network
az network vnet create --name MyVnet --resource-group MyResourceGroup --address-
    prefix 10.0.0.0/16 --subnet-name AzureFirewallSubnet --subnet-prefix 10.0.1.0/24

# Create a public IP for the firewall
az network public-ip create --resource-group MyResourceGroup --name
    MyFirewallPublicIP

# Create the firewall
az network firewall create --name MyFirewall --resource-group MyResourceGroup --
    location eastus

# Configure the firewall's IP configuration
az network firewall ip-config create --firewall-name MyFirewall --name
    MyFirewallConfig --public-ip-address MyFirewallPublicIP --vnet-name MyVnet

# Create application rule collection
az network firewall application-rule create --resource-group MyResourceGroup --firewall-
    name MyFirewall --collection-name AppRuleCollection --action Allow --priority
    100 --rule-name AllowWeb --protocols Http=80 Https=443 --source-addresses
    10.0.1.0/24 --target-fqdns '*.microsoft.com'
```

Azure DDoS Protection

Distributed Denial of Service (DDoS) protection is crucial for safeguarding online services from overwhelming traffic that can disrupt operations. Azure DDoS Protection provides active monitoring and mitigation services, identifying and responding to threat patterns to protect resources.

Azure offers two tiers:

- **Basic:** Integrated with Azure platform at no cost. Automatically enabled for all Azure services.

- **Standard:** Provides additional mitigation capabilities against larger and more sophisticated attacks. Requires configuration.

Example enabling DDoS Protection Standard:

```
# Enable DDoS Protection on an existing virtual network
az network vnet update --resource-group MyResourceGroup --name MyVnet --ddos-
    protection true --ddos-protection-plan /subscriptions/{subscription-id}/
    resourceGroups/{resource-group-name}/providers/Microsoft.Network/
    ddosProtectionPlans/{ddos-protection-plan-name}
```

Azure Bastion

Azure Bastion provides secure and seamless RDP/SSH connectivity to virtual machines directly through the Azure portal. It eliminates the need to expose VMs to the public internet, reducing the attack surface.

To create an Azure Bastion service:

```
# Create a virtual network
az network vnet create --name MyVnet --resource-group MyResourceGroup --address-
    prefix 10.0.0.0/16 --subnet-name AzureBastionSubnet --subnet-prefix 10.0.0.0/24

# Create an Azure Bastion host
az network bastion create --name MyBastionHost --resource-group MyResourceGroup --
    vnet-name MyVnet --public-ip-address MyBastionPublicIP --location eastus
```

Network Watcher

Azure Network Watcher is a network performance monitoring, diagnostic, and analytics service. It provides capabilities such as packet capture, connection monitoring, and IP flow verification. Network Watcher enables deep visibility into network operations and aids in troubleshooting network issues.

Enable Network Watcher in a region:

```
# Enable Network Watcher in a specific region
az network watcher configure --resource-group NetworkWatcherRG --locations eastus --
    enabled true
```

Azure Private Link and Endpoints

Azure Private Link enables private connectivity from a virtual network to Azure platform services, customer-owned services, and Microsoft partner services. It extends the virtual network capabilities with service endpoints, allowing private access to services without exposing them to the public internet.

Example of setting up a private endpoint:

```
# Create a private endpoint
az network private-endpoint create --name MyPrivateEndpoint --resource-group
    MyResourceGroup --vnet-name MyVnet --subnet MySubnet --private-connection-
    resource-id /subscriptions/{subscription-id}/resourceGroups/{resource-group-
    name}/providers/Microsoft.Storage/storageAccounts/{storage-account-name} --
    group-ids blob --connection-name myConnection
```

By utilizing Azure's rich set of network security tools, organizations can build a robust and secure network infrastructure that not only safeguards resources against common threats but also ensures compliance with industry standards.

6.6 Azure Policy and Blueprints

Azure Policy and Blueprints are essential components for managing governance and compliance within Microsoft Azure environments. These tools enable organizations to enforce organizational standards and assess compliance at-scale, helping ensure that resources remain compliant with corporate or external standards throughout their lifecycle.

Azure Policy is a governance tool that allows the creation, assignment, and management of policies. These policies enforce different rules and effects over resources, ensuring that those resources remain compliant with corporate standards and service level agreements. Azure Blueprints, on the other hand, are a declarative way to orchestrate the deployment of resource templates and other artifacts such as role assignments, policy assignments, Azure Resource Manager (ARM) templates, and resource groups. Blueprints simplify large-scale deployments by packaging compliance standards and resource provisioning into reusable artifacts.

Understanding these tools deeply involves understanding their capabilities, configurations, and best practices for use in production environments.

Azure Policy

Azure Policy provides a method to create, deploy, and manage policy definitions that enforce resource compliance. Policies are written in JSON and can be assigned to different scopes, such as subscriptions, resource groups, or individual resources. They are evaluated when resources are created or updated, ensuring that the resources adhere to the policies set by the organization.

A policy definition specifies the desired criteria and the effect when those criteria are met. Effects include Deny, which blocks the request, Audit, which logs non-compliance, and Append/Modify, which alters resource properties to meet policy requirements.

Consider the following example policy definition JSON to enforce the use of managed disks:

```
{
  "properties": {
    "displayName": "Enforce managed disks",
    "description": "Ensure that all virtual machines use managed disks.",
    "policyRule": {
      "if": {
        "field": "Microsoft.Compute/disks/accountType",
        "notIn": ["Standard_LRS", "Premium_LRS"]
      },
      "then": {
        "effect": "deny"
      }
    }
  }
}
```

Once a policy is defined, it can be assigned to a scope using assignments. Here is an example command to create a policy assignment using Azure CLI:

```
az policy assignment create --policy EnforceManagedDisks --scope /subscriptions/{
    subscriptionId}/resourceGroups/{resourceGroupName} --name
    enforceManagedDisksAssignment
```

Azure Blueprints

Azure Blueprints enable the automation of environment setup that adheres to organizational or regulatory requirements. Blueprints can encompass multiple artifacts, which can include:

- Resource Manager Templates
- Policy assignments
- Role assignments
- Resource Group creations

A blueprint consists of artifacts and can be shared, versioned, and applied across multiple subscriptions. This feature makes managing complex deployments easier by ensuring that each deployed instance meets the predefined blueprint standards.

Creating and publishing a blueprint involves several steps: defining a blueprint, adding artifacts, publishing, and assigning the blueprint to a subscription or resource group. Here is an example of defining and publishing a blueprint using Azure Portal:

- Navigate to the Blueprint service within the Azure Portal.
- Select Create blueprint, then define its properties.
- Add artifacts, such as ARM templates and policies.
- Publish the blueprint, setting a version.
- Assign the blueprint to apply it to a specific scope.

The following code snippet demonstrates a simplified ARM template artifact:

```
{
  "$schema": "https://schema.management.azure.com/schemas/2019-04-01/
      blueprintTemplate.json#",
  "contentVersion": "1.0.0.0",
  "resources": [
    {
      "type": "Microsoft.Resources/resourceGroups",
      "apiVersion": "2020-10-01",
      "location": "[parameter('location')]",
      "properties": {}
    },
    {
      "type": "Microsoft.Network/virtualNetworks",
      "apiVersion": "2019-11-01",
      "location": "[resourceGroup().location]",
      "properties": {
        "addressSpace": {
          "addressPrefixes": [
            "10.0.0.0/16"
          ]
        }
      }
    }
  ]
}
```

Combining both Azure Policy and Azure Blueprints ensures continuous compliance and governance. While Azure Policy enforces rules and regulations continuously, Blueprints streamline the deployment process, ensuring that environments are set up correctly from the beginning. Together, they provide a robust framework for maintaining compliance and governance across all Azure resources.

6.7 Compliance in Azure

Compliance in Microsoft Azure is achieved through a combination of dedicated services, robust policies, and adherence to industry standards. The management of compliance involves ensuring that applications, infrastructures, and services within Azure meet regulatory and organizational requirements. This section elaborates on the mechanisms and tools provided by Azure to maintain and monitor compliance.

Compliance in Azure is facilitated through several key tools and features:

- **Azure Policy**: Azure Policy enables you to enforce organizational standards and assess compliance at scale. It allows for the creation, assignment, and management of policies to ensure the resources stay compliant with corporate standards.
- **Azure Blueprints**: Azure Blueprints streamline the deployment and development of environments while ensuring compliance with organizational policies and regulatory requirements.
- **Compliance Manager**: It helps in managing compliance controls aligned with various standard frameworks. Compliance Manager offers a centralized view of compliance status, provides actionable insights, and facilitates the management of audit controls.

Azure Policy is a service in Azure that you use to create, assign, and manage policies. These policies enforce different rules and effects over your resources, so those resources stay compliant with your corporate standards and service level agreements.

```
az policy definition create --name "RequireTag" \
  --rules '{
    "if": {
    "field": "tags",
    "exists": "false"
    },
    "then": {
    "effect": "deny"
    }
  }' \
  --description "Deny resources without tags" \
  --mode All
```

With **Azure Blueprints**, users can define a repeatable set of Azure resources that implement and adhere to standards, patterns, and requirements. This may include resource groups, policies, role assignments, and resource manager templates. Blueprints provide the assurance and governance controls to manage and scale environments in a compliant manner from the start.

```
{
  "properties": {
    "displayName": "{blueprintName}",
    "description": "{blueprintDescription}",
    "targetScope": "subscription",
    "parameters":{
      "roleAssignments": {
        "type": "object"
      },
      "policies": {
        "type": "object"
      }
    },
    "resourceGroups": {
      "myRg": {
        "tags": {
          "displayName": "My New Resource Group"
        },
        "location": "eastus"
      }
    }
  }
}
```

Compliance Manager offers a detailed and centralized compliance dashboard to manage certifications and audits. The dashboard aligns with numerous regulatory frameworks including GDPR, ISO 27001, HIPAA, etc. It helps in tracking and documenting compliance activities, providing insights into areas requiring attention.

```
Compliance Manager Dashboard
-----------------------------
- Certifications
  - ISO 27001: Compliant
  - GDPR: Compliant
  - HIPAA: Review Required

- Actions Needed
  - Review HIPAA Compliance: Due 05/20/2023
  - Update ISO Documentation: Due 06/15/2023
```

Regular monitoring, auditing, and maintaining compliance in Azure requires a responsive approach to identify non-compliant resources and remediating them promptly. Azure Policy Definitions are instrumental in these activities. Example policies might include ensuring that virtual machines are backed up, only certain SKUs are allowed within a region, or specific tags are applied to cost centers.

Beyond these Azure-specific tools, Azure provides extensive documentation and third-party auditing to certify its compliant operations. This includes adherence to standards like SOC, PCI DSS, and others. The

Azure Trust Center offers resources like audit reports, whitepapers, and compliance roadmaps to help users understand and maintain compliance within the Azure environment.

Lastly, to streamline audits, Azure offers the **Azure Security and Compliance Blueprints** which are pre-built sets of Azure resources that align with numerous industry standards. These blueprints help organizations expedite their compliance postures by deploying environments tailored to specific regulatory requirements.

To ensure ongoing compliance, adopting a proactive compliance management strategy leveraging Azure's comprehensive suite of tools and services is essential. This enables organizations to maintain a robust security posture and meet regulatory obligations efficiently.

6.8 Data Encryption in Azure

Data encryption in Microsoft Azure is fundamental for protecting sensitive information, ensuring data confidentiality, and meeting regulatory compliance requirements. Azure offers a comprehensive suite of encryption technologies that safeguard both data at rest and in transit. This section delves into the diverse encryption mechanisms available in Azure, including Azure Storage encryption, SQL Database encryption, Virtual Machine (VM) disk encryption, and the use of Azure Key Vault for key management and secure key storage.

Azure Storage encryption is an essential feature that protects data stored in Azure Blob Storage, Azure Files, and other Azure storage services. Encryption for data at rest in Azure Storage is implemented using server-side encryption (SSE), which automatically encrypts data before it is written to storage and decrypts it before retrieval. This encryption helps prevent unauthorized access to the data when physical media is accessed or in scenarios of unauthorized transmission.

Azure provides multiple options for encryption keys used in SSE. By default, Microsoft manages these encryption keys, but customers can also choose to manage their keys using Azure Key Vault, known as customer-managed keys (CMKs). To configure Azure Storage encryption with CMKs, use the following Azure CLI commands:

```
# Create a Key Vault
az keyvault create --name <KeyVaultName> --resource-group <ResourceGroup> --
    location <Location>

# Create a key in Key Vault
```

```
az keyvault key create --vault-name <KeyVaultName> --name <KeyName> --
    protection software

# Set the Key Vault key to be used for Storage Account encryption
az storage account update --name <StorageAccountName> --resource-group <
    ResourceGroup> \
  --encryption-key-source Microsoft.Keyvault --encryption-key-vault <KeyVaultUri> \
  --encryption-key-name <KeyName>
```

The SQL Database offering in Azure also supports transparent data encryption (TDE), which transparently encrypts data file storage, ensuring that only encrypted data is written to disk. TDE protects databases against unauthorized third parties gaining access to storage media. To enable TDE on an Azure SQL Database, execute the following T-SQL commands:

```
-- Enable TDE on a SQL Database at the server level
ALTER DATABASE [YourDatabaseName] SET ENCRYPTION ON;
```

To further enhance security, keys used for TDE can be stored and managed in Azure Key Vault, leveraging the advantages of HSM-backed keys for maximum security.

Another critical area of focus is the encryption of VM disks. Azure offers Azure Disk Encryption (ADE), which leverages BitLocker for Windows VMs and the dm-crypt feature for Linux VMs to provide volume-level encryption for OS and data disks. ADE seamlessly integrates with Azure Key Vault for encryption key and secret management. The following PowerShell script demonstrates how to enable ADE on a VM:

```
# Define variables
$vmName = "<VMName>"
$resourceGroup = "<ResourceGroup>"
$keyVaultName = "<KeyVaultName>"
$keyName = "<KeyName>"

# Update the VM to use the Azure Disk Encryption extension
Set-AzVMDiskEncryptionExtension -ResourceGroupName $resourceGroup -VMName
    $vmName -DiskEncryptionKeyVaultUrl $(az keyvault show --name
    $keyVaultName --query 'properties.vaultUri' -o tsv) -DiskEncryptionKeyVaultId $
    (az keyvault show --name $keyVaultName --query 'id' -o tsv) -
    KeyEncryptionKeyUrl $(az keyvault key show --vault-name $keyVaultName --
    name $keyName --query 'key.kid' -o tsv)
```

Ensuring data protection during transmission is equally essential. Azure employs several measures to safeguard data in transit, utilizing industry-standard encryption protocols such as TLS (Transport Layer Security). TLS encrypts the data as it travels between clients and Azure services, thus protecting it against interception and tampering. Azure's networking components, including Virtual Networks (VNets),

VPN Gateways, Application Gateways, and Azure Front Door, support end-to-end encryption to ensure secure data transfer.

Azure Key Vault is paramount in managing and safeguarding cryptographic keys and secrets used for encryption. Key Vault can store keys, passwords, certificates, and other secrets securely and can be used to manage access and permissions through Azure Role-Based Access Control (RBAC) and policies. Here is an example of creating a secret in Key Vault using the Azure CLI:

```
# Store a secret in Key Vault
az keyvault secret set --name MySecret --value <SecretValue> --vault-name <
    KeyVaultName>
```

To ensure robust access controls, Azure integrates Key Vault further with Azure Active Directory (Azure AD) to manage identities and control access to vault resources through RBAC and managed identities.

Azure endeavors to continuously improve and enhance its encryption and data protection mechanisms. Therefore, best practices and configurations evolve as new features and compliance requirements are introduced. Leveraging Azure's encryption offerings, coupled with comprehensive key management and access control provided by Azure Key Vault, ensures that sensitive data remains secure, complies with regulations, and is protected against unauthorized access across Azure's diverse services and infrastructure.

6.9 Azure Sentinel

Azure Sentinel is a scalable, cloud-native security information and event management (SIEM) and security orchestration automated response (SOAR) solution. It delivers intelligent security analytics and threat intelligence across the enterprise, providing a single solution for alert detection, threat visibility, proactive hunting, and threat response. Unlike traditional SIEM systems, Azure Sentinel benefits from the scalability and power of the Azure cloud, enabling rapid deployment and flexibility that align with dynamic IT environments.

Azure Sentinel leverages the following features:

- **Integration with Existing Tools:** Azure Sentinel integrates with various Microsoft services such as Office 365, Azure Active Directory, and Microsoft Defender. Additionally, it supports diverse non-Microsoft services and devices, improving its adaptability in heterogeneous environments.

- **Data Collection:** Data ingestion in Azure Sentinel involves collecting data from multiple sources, such as users, applications, servers, and devices, running on-premises or in any cloud. This is achieved through connectors, which are natively available within Azure Sentinel or can be custom-built using Logstash extensions, REST API, and other methods.
- **Advanced Analytics and AI:** Sentinel utilizes advanced machine learning models and artificial intelligence to proactively hunt for security incidents. This analytics power helps in detecting known and unknown threats in real-time, reducing the alert fatigue by correlating signals into meaningful insights.
- **Investigation:** Sentinel offers powerful tools to investigate threats, allowing security teams to seamlessly navigate through data, visualize attack timelines, and infer the root cause of security incidents.
- **Automation and Orchestration:** Sentinel provides built-in playbooks powered by Azure Logic Apps, enabling automated responses to detected threats. These playbooks can perform actions such as isolating infected machines, disabling compromised accounts, or running scripts to collect further forensic data.

Creating and Managing Workspaces

To use Azure Sentinel, a workspace in Azure Log Analytics must be created. This workspace acts as the fundamental unit to collect and analyze data. Workspaces can be easily created via the Azure portal. After setting up the workspace, data connectors are used to stream data from different sources to Sentinel.

```
# Sample PowerShell script to create a Log Analytics workspace
# Resource Group and Location variables
$resourceGroupName = "MyResourceGroup"
$location = "eastus"

# Define the workspace name
$workspaceName = "MyWorkspace"

# Create the Log Analytics workspace
New-AzOperationalInsightsWorkspace -ResourceGroupName $resourceGroupName `
    -Name $workspaceName -Location $location `
    -Sku Standard
```

Once the workspace is set up, data connectors help integrate various data sources:

```
# Python SDK example to link Azure Active Directory Diagnostics to Sentinel
from azure.mgmt.loganalytics import LogAnalyticsManagementClient
from azure.common.credentials import ServicePrincipalCredentials

# Define client details
client_id = 'your_client_id'
client_secret = 'your_client_secret'
tenant_id = 'your_tenant_id'
subscription_id = 'your_subscription_id'

# Get credentials and create client
credentials = ServicePrincipalCredentials(
    client_id=client_id,
    secret=client_secret,
    tenant=tenant_id
)
log_analytics_client = LogAnalyticsManagementClient(credentials, subscription_id)

# Define linkage source and destination
resource_id = "/subscriptions/{}/resourceGroups/{}/providers/Microsoft.
      OperationalInsights/workspaces/{}".format(subscription_id, "MyResourceGroup"
      , "MyWorkspace")
aad_diagnostic_settings = {
    'logs': [
        {
            'category': 'SignInLogs',
            'enabled': True
        }
    ]
}

# Create linkage
log_analytics_client.data_sources.create_or_update(
    resource_id=resource_id,
    parameters=aad_diagnostic_settings
)
```

Creating and Managing Analytics Rules

Analytics rules in Sentinel are based on various templated or custom detection rules that identify suspicious activities. These rules can be easily authored using the Kusto Query Language (KQL).

```
SecurityEvent
| where EventID == 4625 and LogonType == 2
| summarize FailedLogins = count() by AccountName
| where FailedLogins >= 5
| project AccountName, FailedLogins
```

This query detects multiple failed login attempts by users, indicating potentially suspicious behavior. Once configured, such rules can be customized with automated playbooks to respond to these detections.

Proactive Threat Hunting

Azure Sentinel allows security analysts to conduct proactive threat hunting using collected data and built-in hunting queries. Hunting queries use the same KQL language and can uncover hidden threats not detected by automated rules.

```
let timeframe = 1d;
SecurityEvent
| where TimeGenerated >= ago(timeframe)
| where EventID == 4688
| summarize ExecutionCount = count() by ProcessName
| order by ExecutionCount desc
| limit 10
```

This query identifies the most frequently executed processes over the past day, allowing security analysts to spot unusual processes that may indicate malicious behavior.

Visualization and Reporting

Sentinel includes capabilities for creating comprehensive dashboards and reports, using data from the connected sources. Pre-built dashboards can be customized to focus on specific security concerns, such as identity protection or network security, providing actionable insights and situational awareness.

Azure Sentinel is instrumental in building a robust cybersecurity posture within Azure and hybrid environments. Its comprehensive capabilities, including integration, analytics, proactive hunting, and automated response, make it a crucial tool for modern security operations centers seeking to manage and mitigate threats effectively.

6.10 Identity Protection and Privileged Identity Management

Azure Active Directory (Azure AD) provides comprehensive identity management services, enabling organizations to safeguard user identities and control access to sensitive resources. This involves both identity protection and privileged identity management, crucial elements for maintaining a secure environment.

Identity protection in Azure revolves around detecting, mitigating, and preventing identity-related threats. Azure AD Identity Protection utilizes advanced machine learning algorithms and heuristics to detect anomalies in real-time, providing actionable insights to IT administrators. This proactive approach helps to secure user sign-ins and the activities associated with critical accounts.

Azure AD's risk-based conditional access policies are fundamental in identity protection. These policies evaluate the risk level associated with each sign-in attempt and enforce controls such as Multi-Factor Authentication (MFA) or block access altogether. To illustrate, the following LaTeX code snippet showcases how to configure a risk-based conditional access policy using Azure PowerShell:

```
# Connect to Azure AD
Connect-AzureAD

# Create a Conditional Access Policy
$policy = New-AzureADMSConditionalAccessPolicy -DisplayName "Risky Sign-In
    Policy" -State "enabled" `
  -GrantControls @{"builtInControls" = @("mfa")} `
  -Conditions @{"signInRiskLevels" = @("high")} `
  -Assignments @{"users" = @{"include" = @("all")} `
  "excludeGroups" = @()} `
  "applications" = @{"includeApplications" = @("all")}
```

The New-AzureADMSConditionalAccessPolicy cmdlet helps create a policy that mandates MFA for high-risk sign-in attempts. The policy applies to all users, ensuring comprehensive protection.

Alongside identity protection, Privileged Identity Management (PIM) is essential for controlling access to high-privilege roles. Azure AD PIM manages, controls, and monitors access within Azure AD, Azure, and other Microsoft Online Services.

PIM allows you to enforce just-in-time (JIT) access, reducing the window during which privileged roles are active. This minimizes the risk of misused credentials or privilege escalation. To accomplish JIT access through PIM, admins can set up policies that require approval workflows. Below is an example of enabling and configuring PIM for a subscription using Azure PowerShell:

```
# Connect to Azure AD
Connect-AzureAD

# Enable PIM for a subscription
$roleAssignment = New-AzureADMSPrivilegedRoleAssignmentRequest -
    RoleDefinitionId "<roleDefinitionId>" `
  -PrincipalId "<principalId>" `
  -ResourceScope "<resourceScope>" `
  -AssignmentState "Eligible"
```

In the above script, roleDefinitionId specifies the role to configure, while principalId identifies the user or group for the PIM assignment, and resourceScope determines the scope of the role. This setup ensures that privileged roles are only available when necessary, enhancing security.

PIM also supports auditing and reporting capabilities. Administrators can review privileged role assignments and activations to identify potential security incidents. Using PIM, you can generate audit logs and reports to analyze privileged activities. Here is an example using Azure PowerShell to generate an activity log:

```
# Retrieve PIM activities
$activities = Get-AzureADMSPrivilegedRoleAssignmentRequest `
    -Filter "status eq 'Completed' and assignedDateTime ge 2021-01-01"

# Output activity details
$activities | Format-Table id, principalDisplayName, roleDefinitionDisplayName,
      roleAssignmentId, status
```

The Get-AzureADMSPrivilegedRoleAssignmentRequest cmdlet fetches completed role assignment requests since a specified date, providing insight into PIM activities. This information is crucial for compliance and auditing purposes.

By combining Identity Protection and Privileged Identity Management, Azure AD provides a robust framework for securing and controlling access in Azure environments. The effectiveness of these tools lies in their ability to adapt to evolving threats, ensuring that organizations can detect, prevent, and respond to identity-related incidents promptly. This layered security approach helps maintain a secure and compliant environment, essential for modern cloud operations.

6.11 Securing Applications in Azure

Securing applications in Azure involves implementing various strategies and tools that span multiple aspects of the application lifecycle. It is essential to ensure that security measures are applied consistently across development, deployment, and runtime. This section discusses best practices and tools to secure applications within the Azure ecosystem effectively.

Identifying security risks during the development phase is crucial. Utilizing Microsoft's Security Development Lifecycle (SDL) can aid in embedding security into the development process. Applying the SDL includes practices such as threat modeling, security testing, and secure coding principles. Ensure all dependencies are managed properly by regularly updating libraries and frameworks to mitigate vulnerabilities.

Azure provides several services and features to enhance the security of applications:

Azure App Service Security: Azure App Service allows developers to build and host web applications, RESTful APIs, and mobile backends. It supports multiple programming languages and frameworks. To secure apps hosted on Azure App Service, consider the following:

- **Authentication and Authorization**: Use Azure Active Directory (Azure AD) for authentication. Azure App Service integrates with Azure AD to provide a secure authentication mechanism. Implement Role-Based Access Control (RBAC) to ensure users have the appropriate level of access.

- **Managed Certificates**: Leverage Azure App Service Managed Certificates to handle SSL/TLS termination, ensuring encrypted communication between clients and your application.

- **Application Secrets Management**: Use Azure Key Vault to store and manage application secrets, keys, and certificates securely. Integrate Key Vault with App Service to avoid hardcoding sensitive information.

- **Continuous Monitoring and Alerting**: Enable Application Insights to monitor the application's health and performance. Set up alerts for anomalous activities or performance degradation.

Container and Kubernetes Security:

For applications deployed as containers using Azure Kubernetes Service (AKS), security best practices include:

- **Network Policies**: Define network policies to control the traffic between pods. Use the Azure Network Policy Manager for fine-grained control over pod communication.

- **Pod Security Policies**: Implement pod security policies to enforce security configurations such as non-root containers, privilege escalations, and volume usage restrictions.

- **Secrets Management**: Use Kubernetes secrets to manage sensitive data. Integrate with Azure Key Vault to retrieve secrets dynamically.

- **Image Vulnerability Scanning**: Regularly scan container images for vulnerabilities before deployment. Azure Security Center can be configured to scan images within Azure Container Registry (ACR).

Serverless Application Security: Azure Functions provides a platform for building serverless applications. To secure serverless applications:

- **Function-Level Authentication**: Use functions-specific keys or Azure AD to secure function endpoints.
- **Application Secrets and Configuration**: Leverage Azure Key Vault and Azure App Configuration to manage secrets and configuration settings securely.
- **Logging and Monitoring**: Use Application Insights for end-to-end monitoring and to track function execution and performance issues.

API Management and Security: Azure API Management helps safeguard APIs by providing a centralized endpoint for managing, securing, and monitoring API traffic. Key features include:

- **Authentication and Authorization**: Implement OAuth 2.0, OpenID Connect, or Azure AD integration to secure API calls.
- **Rate Limiting and Throttling**: Configure policies to rate limit and throttle API requests, protecting against denial of service (DoS) attacks.
- **Request and Response Validation**: Validate requests and responses to ensure they meet expected formats and constraints, reducing the risk of injection attacks.
- **Monitoring and Logging**: Utilize Azure Monitor and Log Analytics to capture usage metrics, logs, and notifications on API usage and potential security threats.

Code Security and DevSecOps:

Embedding security in the CI/CD pipeline is fundamental for modern application security, often referred to as DevSecOps.

- **Static Code Analysis**: Integrate static code analysis tools such as SonarQube into your build pipeline to identify vulnerabilities early in the development process.

- **Dynamic Application Security Testing (DAST)**: Automate DAST tools in the CI/CD workflow to find runtime vulnerabilities by monitoring application behavior.

- **Infrastructure as Code (IaC) Security**: Secure IaC templates (e.g., ARM templates) by using tools such as Terraform with Azure Policies to enforce compliant configurations and detect drifts.

- **Continuous Compliance**: Enforce compliance checks throughout the CI/CD pipeline using Azure Policy to ensure deployments meet security and compliance requirements continuously.

Application Gateway and Web Application Firewall (WAF): For web applications, using Application Gateway with WAF provides an additional layer of security.

- **Web Application Firewall (WAF)**: WAF provides protection against common threats and vulnerabilities by filtering and monitoring HTTP requests. It helps to protect applications from SQL injection, cross-site scripting (XSS), and other OWASP top 10 vulnerabilities.

- **SSL Termination**: Manage SSL termination at the gateway level, simplifying certificate management and ensuring secure communication.

- **URL-Based Routing**: Use URL path-based routing to manage traffic more efficiently and securely direct requests to backend pools.

The combination of these practices ensures applications deployed in Azure remain secure throughout their lifecycle. Implementation of security measures at every stage from development, deployment to runtime forms a robust security posture ensuring protection against potential vulnerabilities and threats.

6.12 Monitoring and Auditing Security in Azure

Monitoring and auditing are critical components in maintaining a secure and compliant Azure environment. They provide visibility into the operational status, security posture, and policy compliance of resources within Azure. These processes involve the continuous collection, analysis, and reporting of data to detect potential security threats, anomalies, and compliance violations.

Azure offers several services and tools to monitor and audit security, which include Azure Monitor, Azure Security Center, Azure Log Analytics, and Azure Advisor.

Azure Monitor is a comprehensive solution for collecting, analyzing, and acting on telemetry from your cloud and on-premises environments. By providing full-stack monitoring, it helps to maximize the availability and performance of applications and services.

```
# Create Azure Resource Group
az group create --name MonitoringResourceGroup --location eastus

# Create Log Analytics Workspace
az monitor log-analytics workspace create --resource-group MonitoringResourceGroup --
    workspace-name MyWorkspace

# Configure Diagnostic Settings to send data to Log Analytics
az monitor diagnostic-settings create --resource-group MonitoringResourceGroup --
    workspace MyWorkspace --name MyDiagnosticSetting \
  --logs '[{"category": "AllCategories", "enabled": true}]'
```

Azure Security Center enhances Azure Monitor by providing advanced threat protection across your hybrid workloads in the cloud—whether they're in Azure, on-premises, or in other clouds. Security Center automatically collects, evaluates, and analyzes security data, and offers a unified security management system and advanced threat protection. Additionally, it includes integration with Azure Defender, which protects against security vulnerabilities and threats.

Azure Log Analytics, a core component of Azure Monitor, is specifically designed to analyze large volumes of data across all your IT assets. It allows for detailed query capabilities using the Kusto Query Language (KQL) to slice and dice data quickly to identify trends, insights, and correlations.

```
// Query to summarize count of failed logins over time
SecurityEvent
| where EventID == 4625
```

```
| summarize count() by bin(TimeGenerated, 1h)
| order by TimeGenerated asc
```

Azure Advisor provides proactive, actionable, and personalized best practices recommendations. For security, it integrates with Azure Security Center to deliver recommendations based on the best practices for security configuration and encourage best-in-class security hygiene.

Auditing security involves tracking changes, configuration updates, and administrative actions in the Azure environment. Azure provides robust auditing capabilities through Azure Activity Logs and Azure Resource Logs.

Azure Activity Log is a subscription-level log that provides insight into subscription-level events in Azure. It records actions such as resource creation, modification, and deletion.

```
# Retrieve the Azure Activity Log
az monitor activity-log list --resource-group MonitoringResourceGroup --start-time
    2022-01-01T00:00:00Z --end-time 2022-01-31T23:59:59Z
```

Azure Resource Logs provide insights at the individual resource level, offering granularity to understand and audit resource-specific operations. This is crucial for compliance and forensic investigations to locate the source of an issue or breach.

To facilitate comprehensive auditing, you can enable Azure Monitor to collect and route Activity Logs, Resource Logs, and Diagnostic Settings data to a Log Analytics workspace. This integration allows you to leverage Log Analytics' robust querying and alerting capabilities to monitor critical activities and configurations continuously.

```
{
    "properties": {
        "storageAccountId": "/subscriptions/{subscription-id}/resourceGroups/{
            resource-group}/providers/Microsoft.Storage/storageAccounts/{storage-
            account}",
        "workspaceId": "/subscriptions/{subscription-id}/resourceGroups/{resource-
            group}/providers/Microsoft.OperationalInsights/workspaces/{workspace}",

        "logs": [
            {
                "category": "Administrative",
                "enabled": true,
                "retentionPolicy": {
                    "enabled": true,
                    "days": 365
                }
            },
            {
                "category": "Audit",
                "enabled": true,
                "retentionPolicy": {
```

```
                "enabled": true,
                "days": 365
            }
        }
    ]
  }
}
```

Ensuring security in Azure requires continuous vigilance and the use of comprehensive monitoring and auditing tools provided by the platform. By leveraging these services, administrators can effectively maintain a secure environment, swiftly detect and respond to potential threats, and ensure compliance with organizational and regulatory standards.

Chapter 7

Azure Identity and Access Management

This chapter explores identity and access management within Azure, focusing on Azure Active Directory (Azure AD). It covers user and group management, multi-factor authentication, conditional access, and hybrid identity with Azure AD Connect. The chapter also discusses role-based access control (RBAC), managed identities, and securing applications using Azure AD. Additionally, it provides insights on monitoring, reporting, and implementing identity governance and policies to enhance security and compliance.

7.1 Introduction to Identity and Access Management

Identity and Access Management (IAM) forms the cornerstone of securing digital resources and ensuring that the appropriate entities have the right access to those resources. IAM encompasses an array of technologies and policies used to secure, manage, and control access to systems, applications, and data. It provides a framework for managing digital identities and their corresponding access rights.

In Microsoft Azure, IAM is primarily managed through Azure Active Directory (Azure AD). Azure AD is a cloud-based identity and access management service that combines core directory services, application access management, and advanced identity protection.

The IAM lifecycle includes several key components:

- **Identity Management** involves the creation, maintenance, and deletion of identities. It includes the registration of a new identity within a system, updating its attributes, and removing access when it is no longer required.
- **Authentication** verifies the identity of a user or entity attempting to access a system. Techniques like passwords, Multi-Factor Authentication (MFA), and biometric verification are common approaches.
- **Authorization** determines what resources an authenticated entity can access and what operations they are permitted to perform. Role-Based Access Control (RBAC) is a prevalent authorization mechanism.
- **Access Control** implements policies to ensure entities access only the resources they are permitted to and nothing more.
- **Audit and Reporting** provide mechanisms to record, monitor, and analyze access to resources, ensuring compliance with regulatory requirements and aiding in the detection of unauthorized access.

Azure AD leverages these IAM components to offer a comprehensive solution for managing and safeguarding access to resources. Here are several concepts essential to understanding IAM within Azure:

- **Identities**: Represent users, applications, or other services that require access to resources. In Azure AD, identities can be users from the organization, guests, or service principals.
- **Azure AD Tenants**: A tenant is a dedicated instance of Azure AD that an organization receives when they sign up for a Microsoft cloud service. Tenants act as a boundary for identity and access management.
- **Roles**: Azure AD uses RBAC to manage access to resources. Roles define the level of access and capabilities of an identity within the Azure environment.

- **Groups**: Collections of identities can be grouped together, allowing administrators to assign permissions to a group, thereby simplifying access management.
- **Resource Principals**: Objects that represent a resource (like a virtual machine or an application) to which access can be granted.

Authentication plays a vital role in IAM. Azure AD supports various forms of authentication, including:

- **Password-based Authentication**: The most common form, though it presents security risks if not managed properly.
- **Multi-Factor Authentication (MFA)**: Significantly enhances security by requiring additional verification methods, such as a mobile phone or biometric data.
- **Certificate-based Authentication**: Relies on digital certificates to authenticate an identity, often used for device or service authentication.
- **Token-based Authentication**: Utilizes tokens, such as JSON Web Tokens (JWT), to verify and represent the authenticated user's access rights.

Authorization in Azure AD is facilitated by RBAC, which assigns predefined roles to users or groups, specifying their permissions within the Azure environment. Custom roles can also be created to address specific requirements.

To implement access control effectively, Azure AD employs:

- **Conditional Access Policies**: These policies allow administrators to set rules and conditions for accessing applications and data. They can enforce MFA, restrict access based on location, device compliance, and user risk.
- **Access Reviews**: Help in maintaining appropriate access by regularly reviewing and ensuring that users only have the permissions they need.
- **Privileged Identity Management (PIM)**: Enables just-in-time privileged access, reducing the risk of excessive, unnecessary, or misused permissions.

Auditing and reporting are critical for ensuring compliance and detecting potential security incidents. Azure AD provides logging capabilities and integrated tools like Azure Monitor, Azure Security Center, and Azure Sentinel to achieve robust monitoring and reporting.

Understanding these foundational concepts primes the reader for a deeper dive into more specialized areas of identity and access management within Azure, as covered in subsequent sections of this chapter.

7.2 Overview of Azure Active Directory (Azure AD)

Azure Active Directory (Azure AD) is a comprehensive cloud-based identity and access management (IAM) solution provided by Microsoft. Azure AD enables organizations to manage identities, secure access to applications, and ensure compliance with organizational policies. This section delves into the architecture, features, and functionalities of Azure AD, providing a robust understanding of its capabilities.

Azure AD operates as the backbone of Microsoft's cloud-based identity services. It provides a centralized platform for managing user authentication, authorizations, and permissions across various cloud and on-premises applications. Key components and concepts associated with Azure AD include tenants, identities, applications, and roles.

An **Azure AD tenant** represents a dedicated instance of the Azure AD service that an organization receives when subscribing to Microsoft cloud services such as Azure, Microsoft 365, or Dynamics 365. Each tenant is a unique and isolated directory that contains a specific collection of users, groups, and applications.

Identities within Azure AD are digital representations of users, devices, services, and applications. These identities can be sourced from multiple directories, databases, or other systems, ensuring seamless integration within an organization's ecosystem. Azure AD distinguishes between *user identities* and *service identities*, each serving distinct roles. User identities represent individual users, while service identities are used for applications or services needing to authenticate as themselves.

Azure AD supports three main authentication protocols:

- *OAuth 2.0*: An open standard protocol for authorization, enabling applications to access resources on behalf of users without exposing user credentials.

- *OpenID Connect (OIDC)*: An identity layer built on top of OAuth 2.0, allowing applications to verify the identity of users based on the authentication performed by an authorization server.
- *Security Assertion Markup Language (SAML)*: An XML-based protocol used for single sign-on (SSO), facilitating secure authentication and authorization for applications.

Authentication in Azure AD can be enhanced using various methods, ranging from passwords to multifactor authentication (MFA) mechanisms. Password policies, including complexity requirements, expiration rules, and self-service password reset (SSPR), can be enforced to strengthen security.

Authorization in Azure AD revolves around *role-based access control* (RBAC) and *app roles*. RBAC allows administrators to assign specific permissions to users or groups based on their roles within the organization. Azure AD defines a set of built-in roles, such as *Global Administrator*, *User Administrator*, and *Application Administrator*, each granting different levels of access to Azure resources. Custom roles can also be created to fine-tune access controls as needed.

```
# Assign the Global Administrator role to a user
$role = Get-AzureADDirectoryRole | Where-Object {$_.DisplayName -eq "Global
    Administrator"}
Add-AzureADDirectoryRoleMember -ObjectId $role.ObjectId -RefObjectId <user-
    object-id>
```

Applications integrated with Azure AD can be classified as *enterprise applications* or *registered applications*. Enterprise applications refer to those provided by third-party vendors or developed in-house that rely on Azure AD for authentication. Registered applications, on the other hand, are those that have been explicitly registered within an Azure AD tenant, enabling them to use Azure AD for identity and access management.

Application registrations involve defining specific properties such as reply URLs, API permissions, and certificates or secrets used for authentication. The process is facilitated through the Azure portal, following these steps:

- Navigate to the *Azure Active Directory* blade.
- Select *App registrations*, then click *New registration*.

- Provide the required application details, including name, supported account types, and redirect URIs.
- Configure API permissions to specify the resources the application needs to access.
- Obtain the client ID, tenant ID, and secret or certificate necessary for application authentication.

```
az ad app create --display-name "Example App" --identifier-uris "http://example.com"
    --password "example-password"
```

Azure AD supports *conditional access* policies, allowing administrators to enforce access controls based on contextual factors such as user location, device state, and application sensitivity. Conditional access enhances security by applying real-time risk assessments and enforcing adaptive authentication requirements.

Monitoring and reporting are essential components of Azure AD, providing insights into directory activities and potential security risks. Administrators can leverage built-in reports and integrate Azure AD logs with external monitoring solutions like Azure Monitor or third-party security information and event management (SIEM) systems.

Lastly, Azure AD's integration with *identity governance* tools ensures compliance with organizational policies and regulatory requirements. Features such as access reviews, privileged identity management (PIM), and terms of use (TOU) enable organizations to maintain control over access permissions and mitigate risks associated with elevated privileges.

Through its comprehensive suite of features, Azure AD serves as a foundational element of Microsoft's cloud security strategy, facilitating secure and efficient identity and access management.

7.3 Managing Users and Groups in Azure AD

Organizations leveraging Azure Active Directory (Azure AD) require efficient and secure management of users and groups to ensure seamless identity and access management. This section delves into the intricacies of managing users and groups within Azure AD, encompassing user creation, group configuration, role assignments, and intricacies of policy enforcement.

User Management

Managing users in Azure AD involves several key tasks including user creation, updating user attributes, and managing user lifecycles.

Creating a User A new user can be created through the Azure portal, Azure AD PowerShell, or using the Azure CLI. Each method provides a unique set of capabilities suited for different scenarios.

Via Azure Portal:

- Navigate to the *Azure Active Directory* service.
- Select *Users*, then *New user*.
- Fill in the required fields such as *Name*, *User name*, and *Password*.
- Click *Create*.

```
Connect-AzureAD
New-AzureADUser -DisplayName "John Doe" -UserPrincipalName "
    johndoe@yourdomain.com" -UsageLocation "US" -MailNickname "johndoe" -
    PasswordProfile $passwordProfile -AccountEnabled $true
```

```
az ad user create --display-name "John Doe" --user-principal-name "
    johndoe@yourdomain.com" --password "StrongPassword123"
```

Updating User Attributes To modify user attributes, administrators can use the Azure portal or programmatically via Azure AD PowerShell and CLI.

Example updating a user's display name:

```
Set-AzureADUser -ObjectId "user_object_id" -DisplayName "New Display Name"
```

```
az ad user update --id "user_object_id" --display-name "New Display Name"
```

Managing User Lifecycle Managing user lifecycles involves handling creation, updates, and deletion of user accounts. This includes adhering to organizational policies for onboarding and offboarding processes. Automating these processes can enhance efficiency and security.

Group Management

Groups in Azure AD facilitate managing access permissions for multiple users collectively, simplifying the administration and enforcement of security policies.

Creating a Group Groups can be created similarly to users using the Azure portal, Azure AD PowerShell, or Azure CLI.

Via Azure Portal:

- Navigate to the *Azure Active Directory* service.
- Select *Groups*, then *New group*.
- Choose the group type (Security or Microsoft 365), provide a *Group name* and *Group description*.
- Specify *Membership type* (Assigned, Dynamic User, Dynamic Device).
- Click *Create*.

```
New-AzureADGroup -DisplayName "Engineering Team" -MailNickname "
    engineeringteam" -SecurityEnabled $true -MailEnabled $false
```

```
az ad group create --display-name "Engineering Team" --mail-nickname "
    engineeringteam"
```

Adding Members to a Group Adding users to groups can be managed through the Azure portal or via scripting.

Via Azure Portal:

- Navigate to the group within the *Groups* section.
- Select *Members*, then *Add members*.
- Search for and select the users to be added.
- Click *Select*.

```
Add-AzureADGroupMember -ObjectId "group_object_id" -RefObjectId "
    user_object_id"
```

```
az ad group member add --group "Engineering Team" --member-id "user_object_id"
```

Dynamic Group Membership Azure AD supports dynamic group memberships, which allows for automatic group membership assignment based on user attributes. This is particularly useful for large organizations.

Example rule for dynamic membership based on department attribute:

```
user.department -eq "Engineering"
```

Group-Based Licensing Azure AD allows licenses to be assigned to users through group membership. This streamlines the management of licenses for subscriptions like Office 365.

```
$licenseAssignment = @{
  AccountSkuId = "yourtenant:O365_BUSINESS"
  SkuPartNumber = "O365_BUSINESS"
}
Set-AzureADGroupLicense -ObjectId "group_object_id" -AddLicenses @(
    $licenseAssignment)
```

Role Assignments

Roles in Azure AD define a set of permissions. Assigning roles to users or groups determines what administrative tasks they can perform.

Assigning Roles Roles can be assigned through the Azure portal, PowerShell, or CLI.

Via Azure Portal:

- Navigate to the *Role assignments* section.
- Select + *Add*.
- Choose the role and assign it to a user or group.
- Click *Save*.

```
Add-AzureADDirectoryRoleMember -ObjectId "role_object_id" -RefObjectId "
    user_object_id"
```

```
az role assignment create --role "User Access Administrator" --assignee "user_object_id
    "
```

Effectively managing users and groups in Azure AD involves a detailed understanding of the capabilities provided by the platform, along with leveraging automation and scripting for efficiency. This contributes significantly to maintaining the security and manageability of an organization's identity and access management framework.

7.4 Azure AD Multi-Factor Authentication

Azure AD Multi-Factor Authentication (MFA) is a security feature that ensures users perform a multi-step verification process to establish their identity. This involves providing more than one form of identification when logging into a service or application. By leveraging MFA, organizations can significantly reduce the risk of compromised credentials and unauthorized access.

Azure AD MFA operates on the concepts of *something the user knows* (like a password), *something the user possesses* (such as a mobile device), and *something inherent to the user* (e.g., biometric characteristics like fingerprints). Implementing MFA in Azure AD requires proper configuration and adherence to best practices, which we will delineate in this section.

Key Components and Mechanisms

- **Authentication Methods:** Azure AD MFA supports various authentication methods:
- **Phone Call:** Users receive an automated voice call and are prompted to press a key to confirm their identity.
- **Text Message (SMS):** A one-time passcode is sent to the user's registered mobile number. The user must enter this code on the sign-in interface.
- **Mobile App Notification:** Push notifications through applications such as Microsoft Authenticator enable users to approve or deny access with a simple tap.
- **Mobile App Verification Code:** The mobile app generates a verification code the user must enter during sign-in.
- **OATH Hardware Tokens:** Physical tokens generate verification codes to be entered manually.
- **Biometrics:** Some scenarios may involve biometric verification like fingerprints or facial recognition.

- **Configuration Steps:**
- Enable MFA: Administrators must navigate to the Azure portal and activate MFA at the organizational level or per-user basis.
- Define Authentication Methods: Configure which methods are available for the users.
- User Registration: Guide users through registering their authentication methods, ensuring they are properly set up to use MFA.
- Policies and Procedures: Establish policies for when MFA is required, such as during specific access attempts or under certain conditions.
- Monitoring and Reporting: Continuously monitor MFA activity and produce reports to track usage and detect potential issues.

Example of Enabling MFA:

The following example demonstrates how to enable MFA for a user using PowerShell.

```
Install-Module -Name MSOnline
Connect-MsolService
$st = New-Object -TypeName Microsoft.Online.Administration.
    StrongAuthenticationRequirement
$st.RelyingParty = "*"
$st.State = "Enabled"
Set-MsolUser -UserPrincipalName <user-email> -StrongAuthenticationRequirements @
    ($st)
```

MFA Policies:

- **Conditional Access:** MFA can be enforced through conditional access policies. Administrators can configure conditions under which MFA is required, such as when accessing certain applications or from specific locations.
- **User Risk:** Policies can be set to trigger MFA if the user's sign-in behavior is deemed risky, e.g., logging in from an unusual location.

Example of Creating a Conditional Access Policy:

The following example configures a conditional access policy focusing on requiring MFA for accessing specific applications.

```
Connect-AzureAD
$policy = New-AzureADMSConditionalAccessPolicy -DisplayName "Require MFA for
    Salesforce" `
  -State "Enabled" `
  -Conditions @{
      "Users" = @{
          "IncludeRoles" = @("All")
      }
      "Applications" = @{
          "IncludeApplications" = @("00000000-0000-0000-0000-000000000000")
      }
  } `
  -GrantControls @{
      "BuiltInControls" = @("Mfa")
  }
New-AzureADMSConditionalAccessPolicy -InputObject $policy
```

User Experience:

Once MFA is enabled, the first time users attempt to log in, they will be prompted to set up the second form of validation. For instance, for authentication via the Microsoft Authenticator app:

- Users will be guided to download and install the Microsoft Authenticator app on their mobile devices.
- Users will complete the setup by linking the app to their Azure AD account through a provided QR code.
- During subsequent sign-in attempts, users will receive a notification in the app to approve or deny the access request.

The system's response and user feedback confirm the effectiveness and smooth operation of MFA.

```
Authentication request has been approved.
Welcome, user@example.com!
```

Troubleshooting and Support:

- **Failed MFA Attempts:** Analyze logs and reports to understand why users are experiencing failed MFA attempts. Ensure they have registered the correct information and are following the MFA steps properly.
- **Device Issues:** In cases where users face issues with registered devices, guide them through registering an alternative device or method.

- **Support Tickets:** Set up a support ticketing system for handling MFA-related issues efficiently.

Azure AD MFA is an essential component for strengthening security by enforcing an added layer of verification, thus safeguarding against unauthorized access to organizational resources. The successful implementation of MFA depends upon precise configuration, user training, and continuous monitoring. By integrating these practices, organizations can mitigate security risks and enhance overall compliance with security policies.

7.5 Azure AD Conditional Access

Azure AD Conditional Access leverages various signals to enforce policies that manage how users can access your cloud applications. It provides a significant layer of security by requiring users to meet certain conditions before accessing sensitive resources. This section elaborates on the key components, policy creation, and best practices for employing Conditional Access.

Azure AD Conditional Access policies are created using conditions and access controls. Conditions specify under what circumstances the policy applies, while access controls dictate what must happen for the user to gain access. These policies can be applied to any application registered with Azure AD, allowing fine-grained control over user access.

Conditions

Conditions define which scenarios trigger Conditional Access policies. They are categorized into several types, including:

- User or group membership: Policies can apply to individual users or groups.
- IP Location: Policies can enforce rules based on the user's IP address or geographical location.
- Device Platforms: Policies can target specific operating systems, such as Windows, macOS, iOS, or Android.
- Client Applications: Policies can differentiate between browser-based applications, mobile applications, and desktop clients.

- Sign-in Risk: Integration with Azure AD Identity Protection can enforce policies based on the risk level calculated during sign-in attempts.

Access Controls

Access controls determine the required actions for users to access resources. These include:

- Grant controls: Specify requirements such as multi-factor authentication (MFA), device compliance, or domain-joined device.
- Session controls: Define behaviors like limiting user session persistence or enhancing the monitoring of user actions.

Creating a Conditional Access Policy

Creating Conditional Access policies involves defining user assignments, selecting cloud applications, setting conditions, and configuring access controls. Here's an example of defining a Conditional Access policy using PowerShell:

```
# Connect to Azure AD
Connect-AzureAD

# Create a new Conditional Access policy
\$policy = New-Object -TypeName Microsoft.Open.MSGraph.Model.PolicyObject

# Set the conditions for the Conditional Access policy
\$policy.Conditions = New-Object -TypeName Microsoft.Open.MSGraph.Model.
    ConditionsData
\$policy.Conditions.Users = New-Object -TypeName Microsoft.Open.MSGraph.Model.
    UserCondition
\$policy.Conditions.Users.IncludeUsers = @("All")
\$policy.Conditions.Platforms = New-Object -TypeName Microsoft.Open.MSGraph.
    Model.PlatformCondition
\$policy.Conditions.Platforms.IncludePlatforms = @("Windows", "iOS")

# Define the grant controls for the policy
\$policy.GrantControls = New-Object -TypeName Microsoft.Open.MSGraph.Model.
    GrantControls
\$policy.GrantControls.Operator = "OR"
\$policy.GrantControls.BuiltInControls = @("Mfa", "CompliantDevice")

# Define the session controls for the policy
\$policy.SessionControls = New-Object -TypeName Microsoft.Open.MSGraph.Model.
    SessionControls
\$policy.SessionControls.PersistantBrowser = "Always"

# Set target applications for the Conditional Access policy
\$policy.Targets = New-Object -TypeName Microsoft.Open.MSGraph.Model.
    TargetsData
\$policy.Targets.TargetResources = @("All")

# Create the policy
```

```
\$policy.Id = (New-Guid).Guid
New-AzureADMSConditionalAccessPolicy -Policy \$policy
```

It is essential to test policies in report-only mode before enforcing them. This mode allows administrators to see what the impact of the policy would be without actually enforcing it. Here's how to enable report-only mode:

```
# Enable report-only mode for a Conditional Access policy
Set-AzureADMSConditionalAccessPolicy -Id <PolicyId> -State "ReportOnly"
```

Testing policies in report-only mode helps ensure they do not inadvertently block legitimate users or necessary services.

Best Practices for Conditional Access

Implementing Conditional Access requires following best practices to achieve optimal security:

- Start with a baseline policy: Use Azure AD's built-in security baseline policies as a starting point for your configurations.
- Leverage multiple conditions: Combine several conditions to create more precise policies and reduce false positives.
- Gradually roll out policies: Begin with a small group of users or a single application to assess the impact before broader deployment.
- Continuously review and adjust: Regularly analyze policy impact using Azure AD logs and adjust the settings as necessary.
- Educate users: Ensure that end users understand the requirements and process for actions like multi-factor authentication.

Conditional Access Policies play a vital role in securing your environment by ensuring that only authorized users under compliant conditions access your resources. The strategic application of these policies can significantly enhance your organization's security posture.

7.6 Azure AD Connect and Hybrid Identity

Azure AD Connect is a pivotal tool for organizations aiming to achieve hybrid identity. This section delves into the intricacies of connecting your on-premises directory with Azure Active Directory (Azure AD). Understanding the integration methodologies and functionalities of Azure AD Connect is crucial for preserving a seamless experience for users and maintaining robust security protocols.

Azure AD Connect is a Microsoft-designed synchronization service that facilitates the cohesion of on-premises directories with Azure AD. By integrating on-premises Active Directory (AD) with Azure AD, organizations can provide a unified identity for users to access both on-premises and cloud resources.

Central to Azure AD Connect is the synchronization of on-premises user accounts, groups, and credential management information with Azure AD. This assures that identities are consistent across various platforms, allowing for a hybrid identity that serves as the fundamental layer of a more extensive identity solution.

Installation and Configuration

To install Azure AD Connect, follow the steps below, ensuring prerequisites such as having the appropriate permissions and domain administrator rights:

```
1. Download Azure AD Connect from the Microsoft website.
2. Run the installer and select the desired installation type.
3. Provide the credentials for connecting to Azure AD.
4. Configure the integration options (e.g., password hash synchronization or pass-
     through authentication).
5. Confirm and complete the setup.
```

Once Azure AD Connect is installed, it can be configured to sync your on-premises directory to Azure AD.

Synchronization Options

Azure AD Connect offers several synchronization options, including:

- - **Password Hash Synchronization**: Synchronizes a hash of the on-premises Active Directory password to Azure AD. This option allows users to use the same password on-premises and for Azure AD resources.
- - **Pass-through Authentication**: Provides a secure method to validate passwords directly against your on-premises Active Directory.
- - **Federation with AD FS**: Integrates Azure AD with Active Directory Federation Services (AD FS), enabling complex single sign-on (SSO) scenarios.

The chosen synchronization option must align with the security policies and infrastructure of the organization.

To configure synchronization, follow these steps:

```
1. Open Azure AD Connect and click on 'Configure'.
2. Navigate to 'Synchronization Options'.
3. Choose your preferred method of synchronization:
   a. Password Hash Synchronization
   b. Pass-through Authentication
   c. Federation with AD FS
4. Follow the wizard to complete configuration.
```

Synchronization Schedule and Monitoring

By default, Azure AD Connect is set to sync every 30 minutes. To modify this schedule:

```
1. Open a PowerShell window with elevated privileges.
2. Use the 'Set-ADSyncScheduler' cmdlet to modify the interval:

   Set-ADSyncScheduler -CustomizedSyncCycleInterval "hh:mm:ss"

   Example: Set-ADSyncScheduler -CustomizedSyncCycleInterval "01:00:00"
```

Monitoring is essential to ensure synchronization completes successfully. This can be accomplished through 'Azure AD Connect Health', a service that provides monitoring and insights for your synchronization solution. To monitor using Azure AD Connect Health, follow these steps:

- Install Azure AD Connect Health for Sync using the Azure portal.
- Open the 'Azure AD Connect Health' blade from the Azure portal.
- Review alerts, performance metrics, and synchronization errors.

Hybrid Identity Scenarios

Azure AD Connect plays a critical role in various hybrid identity scenarios. These include:

- - **Seamless Single Sign-On (SSO)**: Enables users to authenticate once and access both on-premises and cloud resources without repeated logins.
- - **Hybrid Exchange Deployment**: Facilitates coexistence between on-premises Exchange servers and Exchange Online.
- - **Conditional Access**: Leverages synchronized group memberships and attributes to enforce access policies.

Handling Synchronization Conflicts

Occasionally, synchronization conflicts can occur. Common issues include duplicate attribute conflicts or matching errors. To resolve these:

- Review synchronization logs within Azure AD Connect.
- Identify the object causing the conflict.
- Modify the attribute on either the on-premises AD or Azure AD to resolve the conflict.

Disabling and Enabling Directory Synchronization

There may be circumstances requiring the temporary disabling of directory synchronization. To disable:

- Open a PowerShell window with elevated privileges.
- Execute the following cmdlet:

```
Set-MsolDirSyncEnabled -EnableDirSync $false -Force
```

To enable it again:

- Open a PowerShell window with elevated privileges.
- Execute the following cmdlet:

```
Set-MsolDirSyncEnabled -EnableDirSync $true
```

By comprehensively managing Azure AD Connect and understanding its functionalities and potential issues, administrators can ensure an effective hybrid identity environment, optimizing user experience and maintaining security standards.

7.7 Azure Role-Based Access Control (RBAC)

Azure Role-Based Access Control (RBAC) is a critical feature for managing access to Azure resources. It provides fine-grained access management to Azure resources, allowing users to have specific permissions necessary to perform their jobs. RBAC is essential for implementing the principle of least privilege, which minimizes the exposure of sensitive data and operations.

RBAC in Azure operates based on role assignments, which consist of three primary elements: security principal, role definition, and scope. Let us delve deeply into each of these components.

Security Principal: A security principal is an object that represents a user, group, service principal, or managed identity that needs access to resources in Azure.

- **User** - An individual who has a specific set of login credentials.
- **Group** - A collection of users who can be managed collectively.
- **Service Principal** - An identity used by applications or services to access resources.
- **Managed Identity** - A feature of Azure AD that provides Azure services with an automatically managed identity in Azure AD.

Role Definition: A role definition is a collection of permissions. It can be seen as a job description including the lists of actions that can be performed, like read, write, and delete. Azure provides several built-in roles which are typically categorized as:

- **Owner** - Has full access to all resources and can delegate access to others.
- **Contributor** - Can create and manage all types of Azure resources but can't grant access to others.
- **Reader** - Can view existing Azure resources but not make any changes.
- **Custom Roles** - Specific roles created by the user which can be precisely tailored to the necessary permissions.

Scope: Scope is the set of resources that the access applies to. It can range from a management group level, subscription level, resource group level, or down to an individual resource.

Once these elements are clearly defined, a role assignment can be created to grant access. Here is the command to create a role assignment using Azure CLI:

```
az role assignment create --assignee <Principal-ID> --role <Role-ID> --scope <scope>
```

The output of this command will look like:


```
{
  "canDelegate": null,
  "condition": null,
  "conditionVersion": null,
  "description": null,
  "id": "/subscriptions/<Subscription-ID>/resourceGroups/<Resource-Group>/providers/Microsoft.Authorization/roleAssignments/<Assignment-ID>",
  "name": "<Assignment-ID>",
  "principalId": "<Principal-ID>",
  "principalType": "User",
  "roleDefinitionId": "/subscriptions/<Subscription-ID>/providers/Microsoft.Authorization/roleDefinitions/<Role-ID>",
  "scope": "/subscriptions/<Subscription-ID>/resourceGroups/<Resource-Group>",
  "type": "Microsoft.Authorization/roleAssignments"
}
```


RBAC is enforced through Azure Resource Manager (ARM), the management layer of Azure, which provides a unified way to manage resources via various means like the Azure portal, Azure CLI, Azure PowerShell, and REST APIs.

When a user attempts to access an Azure resource, ARM checks the list of role assignments to determine if the user has the necessary permissions. If there is a match, access is granted; otherwise, it is denied. This process is seamless and typically requires administrative oversight for initial configuration and periodic audits to ensure compliance with organizational policies.

RBAC also integrates seamlessly with Azure AD Privileged Identity Management (PIM) for just-in-time access. PIM allows you to manage, control, and monitor access to important resources within your organization, ensuring users have the right permissions for the required duration.

```
az role assignment list --assignee "<Principal-ID>"
```

The above command retrieves the list of role assignments for a given security principal, providing transparency and ease of management.

Comprehensive monitoring and reporting are supported. Administrators can utilize Azure Monitor and Azure Security Center to track RBAC activities, which include modifications to role assignments. It allows alert configuration for any unusual activity, enhancing security and compliance. With RBAC logging in place, audit trails can be maintained for forensic investigations.

The principle of least privilege, role assignments clarity, and the robust integration of ARM make Azure RBAC an indispensable component of Azure's security framework.

7.8 Azure Managed Identities

Azure Managed Identities provide an automatic and secure way to manage identities for applications running in Azure without requiring explicit credentials. They eliminate the need for developers to manage secrets, such as connection strings and API keys, by providing an identity for applications to use when connecting to resources that support Azure AD authentication. There are two types of managed identities: system-assigned and user-assigned.

A system-assigned managed identity is created for a specific Azure service instance, such as a Virtual Machine or an Azure App Service. When the service instance is deleted, the managed identity is automatically removed. The service instance's identity is managed through the Azure portal, Azure CLI, or Azure PowerShell. To create and assign a system-assigned managed identity, the following Azure CLI command can be used:

```
az vm create --resource-group myResourceGroup --name myVM \
  --image UbuntuLTS --assign-identity
```

This command provisions a new VM in 'myResourceGroup', and an identity is assigned to this virtual machine. After creation, one can retrieve the VM's managed identity information:

```
az vm show --resource-group myResourceGroup --name myVM --query identity
```

To utilize this managed identity to access Azure resources, appropriate role assignments must be configured. For instance, to allow the VM to read from an Azure Storage account, the following command can be employed:

```
storageAccountId=$(az storage account show --name mystorageaccount \
  --resource-group myResourceGroup --query id --output tsv)

az role assignment create --assignee '<managed-identity-client-id>' \
  --role 'Storage Blob Data Reader' --scope $storageAccountId
```

This command assigns the "Storage Blob Data Reader" role to the VM's managed identity on the specified storage account.

A user-assigned managed identity, on the other hand, is independent of the Azure service instances and can be shared across multiple instances. This type provides more flexibility, such as the capability to assign the same identity to several resources, facilitating streamlined access management. To create a user-assigned managed identity via

Azure CLI, the following command can be executed:

```
az identity create --resource-group myResourceGroup --name myIdentity
```

Once created, the identity can be assigned to an Azure VM:

```
identityId=$(az identity show --resource-group myResourceGroup \
  --name myIdentity --query id --output tsv)

az vm identity assign --resource-group myResourceGroup --name myVM \
  --identities $identityId
```

Both system-assigned and user-assigned managed identities are integrated with Azure AD, offering the identical authentication benefits, such as seamless authentication flows and enhanced security. When an application using a managed identity needs to authenticate with a resource, it acquires tokens from the Azure Instance Metadata Service (IMDS). For example, to obtain a token programmatically within a VM using a managed identity, one may use the Azure SDK or directly perform an HTTP request:

```
import requests

endpoint = "http://169.254.169.254/metadata/identity/oauth2/token"
params = {
    'api-version': '2018-02-01',
    'resource': 'https://management.azure.com/'
}

headers = {'Metadata': 'true'}

response = requests.get(endpoint, params=params, headers=headers)
token = response.json()['access_token']
```

In this script, the VM makes a request to the IMDS to fetch an access token to authenticate with Azure Resource Manager. The 'Metadata' header is crucial for security purposes, ensuring that only authorized requests are entertained.

Managed identities simplify credential management and bolster security by leveraging Azure AD authentication for resource access. When combined with Azure's role-based access control (RBAC), they provide fine-grained permissions tailored to specific tasks, reducing the attack surface by adhering to the principle of least privilege. Additionally, managed identities facilitate compliance with security policies by systematically removing the need to store credentials within the codebase or configuration files, thus mitigating risks associated with credential leakage or unauthorized access.

Applications leveraging managed identities can substantially improve security posture while reducing administrative overhead, allowing developers to focus on building robust and scalable solutions.

7.9 Azure AD B2C and B2B

Azure Active Directory (Azure AD) extends its identity and access management solutions with Azure AD B2C (Business-to-Consumer) and Azure AD B2B (Business-to-Business). These services are designed to provide secure and seamless access to applications for both consumers and external partners. The distinction between Azure AD B2C and B2B lies in their target user bases and specific purposes.

Azure AD B2C is tailored for applications that require end-user access, such as customer-facing applications. It allows developers to integrate identity management into applications with social and enterprise accounts as well as local accounts. This enables a wide array of authentication providers and offers customization capabilities for branding and user experiences.

In contrast, Azure AD B2B facilitates collaboration between organizations by allowing external partners to access corporate resources using their own credentials. This integration maintains security and compliance standards, making it easier for organizations to share their internal resources with external parties without complex cross-organization federation agreements.

Both Azure AD B2C and B2B leverage modern authentication protocols such as OAuth 2.0, OpenID Connect, and SAML, adhering to the latest security and interoperability standards.

Azure AD B2C Functionalities

Azure AD B2C supports various authentication methods, including email signup, social accounts (e.g., Facebook, Google), and enterprise accounts through OpenID Connect. Key functionalities include:

- **Custom Policies**: These provide extensive control over the authentication process, enabling complex conditional logic and orchestration of identity experiences.
- **User Flows**: These predefined policies streamline common identity tasks like sign-up, sign-in, profile editing, and password reset. User flows simplify integration by reducing the need for custom development.

- **Branding and Localization**: Developers can customize the appearance and behavior of the Azure AD B2C interfaces to align with their brand guidelines, including localization for different languages and regions.

- **Multi-Factor Authentication (MFA)**: Azure AD B2C can prompt users to provide additional verification, such as an SMS code, enhancing account security without the need for backend integration.

- **Integration with External Providers**: Configuration for integrating with external identity providers is straightforward, encompassing OAuth 2.0, OpenID Connect, and SAML protocols.

A basic configuration of an Azure AD B2C signup and signin policy might use JSON for custom policies or built-in user flows. Below is an example demonstrating how a policy JSON looks:

```
{
  "Id": "B2C_1A_signup_signin",
  "Type": "SignUpOrSignIn",
  "DisplayName": "Sign Up and Sign In",
  "IdentityProviders": [
    "MicrosoftAccount",
    "Facebook"
  ],
  "UserAttributes": [
    "DisplayName",
    "GivenName",
    "Surname",
    "EmailAddress"
  ]
}
```

Azure AD B2B Features

Azure AD B2B extends the identity capabilities of Azure AD to external users, allowing them to use their existing credentials from any organization that supports modern authentication. Notable features include:

- **Guest User Invitations**: Administrators can invite external users to collaborate by sending invitations through the Azure portal or programmatically via APIs.

- **Seamless Integration**: Once invited, external users access resources using their existing identity solutions, without requiring administrators to manage external accounts directly.

- **Conditional Access Policies**: Apply the same security constraints to guest users as internal users, including MFA, device compliance, and location-based controls.

- **Monitoring and Auditing**: Azure AD logs all access attempts, providing visibility into external user activity for security and compliance purposes.

- **Role-Based Access Control (RBAC)**: Admins can assign roles to external users, ensuring they have appropriate permissions within shared resources.

An Azure AD B2B invitation process typically involves sending an email invitation to the guest user. Below is an example of PowerShell script for inviting a guest user:

```
$Email = "example@contoso.com"
$DisplayName = "Contoso Guest"
$InviteRedirectUrl = "https://myapp.contoso.com"
New-AzureADMSInvitation -InvitedUserEmailAddress $Email -InviteRedirectUrl
    $InviteRedirectUrl -InvitedUserDisplayName $DisplayName
```

Use Cases and Best Practices

Practical use cases for Azure AD B2C include consumer-facing applications requiring streamlined and secured user registration, login processes, and customized user experiences. Azure AD B2B is ideal for scenarios where businesses need to collaborate with partners, suppliers, and contractors while maintaining robust security and compliance measures.

Best practices for utilizing Azure AD B2C and B2B involve ensuring policies are up to date with current security recommendations, such as enforcing MFA and regular review of guest access permissions. Moreover, user experiences should be continually refined using Azure AD B2C's customization options to maintain consistency with the brand's look and feel.

Both services enhance the flexibility and security of identity and access management in Azure, providing end-to-end solutions for a multitude of scenarios from consumer applications to business collaborations.

7.10 Securing Applications with Azure AD

Azure Active Directory (Azure AD) offers a comprehensive framework for securing applications by providing a robust identity solution that integrates seamlessly with various application types. Azure AD's suite of security features ensures that users can access applications securely while maintaining organizational compliance and governance. This section elaborates on the mechanisms and best practices for securing applications using Azure AD, focusing on key areas such as application registration, authentication protocols, single sign-on (SSO), and app roles and permissions.

Application registration in Azure AD is the foundational step for securing applications. It involves creating an identity for your application in Azure AD, which facilitates various identity management features. Application registration allows developers to configure how their applications interact with Azure AD. The essential attributes provided during registration include the application ID (client ID), tenant ID, directed URIs (URLs), and client secrets or certificates for credential management.

```
az ad app create \
  --display-name "MyApplication" \
  --password "StrongPassword!" \
  --available-to-other-tenants false \
  --web-redirect-uris "https://myapplication.com/auth-callback"
```

```
Output:
{
  "appId": "12345678-1234-1234-1234-123456789012",
  "displayName": "MyApplication",
  "password": "StrongPassword!",
  "availableToOtherTenants": false,
  "webRedirectUris": ["https://myapplication.com/auth-callback"]
}
```

Authentication protocols play a critical role in ensuring secure access to applications. Azure AD supports several protocols, including OAuth 2.0, OpenID Connect, and SAML 2.0. OAuth 2.0 and OpenID Connect are particularly useful for modern web and mobile applications, providing robust mechanisms for handling token-based authentication and authorization. These protocols enable applications to authenticate users and acquire tokens for accessing protected resources.

OAuth 2.0 and OpenID Connect

OAuth 2.0 is an authorization framework that enables a third-party application to obtain limited access to a HTTP service. OpenID Connect extends OAuth 2.0, adding authenticated user information. In Azure

AD, you can use these protocols to secure your web applications, APIs, and mobile applications.

```
const tenant = "yourTenantID";
const clientId = "yourAppID";
const redirectUri = "https://yourapplication.com/auth-callback";

const authUrl = `https://login.microsoftonline.com/${tenant}/oauth2/v2.0/authorize?
    client_id=${clientId}&response_type=code&redirect_uri=${redirectUri}&
    response_mode=query&scope=openid profile offline_access&state=12345`;
window.location.href = authUrl;
```

Single Sign-On (SSO)

Single Sign-On (SSO) significantly enhances user experience by enabling users to access multiple applications with a single set of credentials. Azure AD supports SSO for both cloud-based and on-premises applications. With SSO, users authenticate once and gain access to multiple applications without re-entering credentials.

To enable SSO for an application:

- Register the application in Azure AD and configure relevant authentication settings.
- Configure the application to trust Azure AD as an Identity Provider (IdP).
- Implement the necessary code or configuration changes in the application to handle SSO.

```
<SSO>
  <ServiceProviderSettings>
    <EntityID>https://yourapplication.com</EntityID>
    <AssertionConsumerService>https://yourapplication.com/sso/acs</
        AssertionConsumerService>
  </ServiceProviderSettings>
  <IdentityProviderSettings>
    <SignOnService>https://login.microsoftonline.com/saml2</SignOnService>
    <SignOffService>https://login.microsoftonline.com/saml2logout</SignOffService>
    <SigningCertificate>MIID...AB</SigningCertificate>
  </IdentityProviderSettings>
</SSO>
```

Azure AD App Roles and Permissions allow administrators to define roles and permissions for applications, ensuring that users have appropriate access levels. These roles can be configured at the application level or for API scopes, enabling fine-grained access control.

Defining App Roles

Roles are defined within the application manifest:

```
"appRoles": [
  {
    "id": "b2cddf02-7d42-4a78-9f65-3d5ec255bd10",
    "allowedMemberTypes": ["User"],
    "description": "Read-only access to the application data",
    "displayName": "Reader",
    "isEnabled": true,
    "value": "Reader"
  },
  {
    "id": "e20bb69e-928a-4b34-b4ee-7e282d3bcf3f",
    "allowedMemberTypes": ["User"],
    "description": "Full access to the application data",
    "displayName": "Admin",
    "isEnabled": true,
    "value": "Admin"
  }
]
```

Permissions can be granted to users or groups through the Azure portal, ensuring that only authorized users have access to specific features and data within the application.

By leveraging Azure AD's capabilities, applications can achieve high security and compliance standards. Application registration, authentication protocols, SSO, and app roles and permissions collectively create a seamless and secure user experience. These mechanisms not only enhance security but also streamline access management, fostering a more productive and secure environment for users and administrators alike.

7.11 Monitoring and Reporting in Azure AD

Effective monitoring and reporting are paramount in maintaining a secure and compliant Azure Active Directory (Azure AD) environment. This section delineates the key components and methodologies for monitoring and reporting within Azure AD, ensuring that administrators can track activities, detect anomalies, and generate comprehensive reports for audits and compliance purposes.

Azure AD Audit Logs

Azure AD provides comprehensive audit logs that capture a variety of directory activities. These logs encompass changes made to resources within Azure AD, including the creation, deletion, and modification of users, groups, applications, and roles. Audit logs offer a detailed historical record and are crucial for tracking administrative actions and policy changes.

Users can view audit logs via the Azure portal by navigating to **Azure Active Directory → Monitoring → Audit logs**. The following example illustrates how to retrieve audit log data programmatically using Azure CLI:

```
# Retrieve Azure AD audit logs for the past 7 days
az ad signin-log list --filter "createdDateTime ge $(date -d '7 days ago' +%Y-%m-%dT
    %H:%M:%S)"
```

Audit logs provide insights into the WHO, WHAT, WHEN, and WHERE of each change, which is indispensable for forensic analysis and compliance reporting. The log details can also be exported to third-party Security Information and Event Management (SIEM) systems for advanced analysis.

Azure AD Sign-In Logs

Sign-in logs capture information about user sign-in activities and are essential for identifying potential security issues such as unauthorized access attempts or login anomalies. These logs include vital details such as the sign-in time, user identity, application accessed, and the client IP address.

Sign-in logs can be accessed in the Azure portal by navigating to **Azure Active Directory → Monitoring → Sign-ins**. Here's an example of retrieving sign-in logs via Microsoft Graph API:

```
import requests
import json

# Define the API endpoint and headers
url = "https://graph.microsoft.com/v1.0/auditLogs/signIns"
headers = {
    "Authorization": "Bearer YOUR_ACCESS_TOKEN",
    "Content-Type": "application/json"
}

# Make the API request
response = requests.get(url, headers=headers)
sign_in_logs = response.json()

# Output the sign-in logs
print(json.dumps(sign_in_logs, indent=4))
```

Administrators can leverage sign-in logs for detecting unusual patterns, such as multiple failed login attempts or logins from unfamiliar locations. This information aids in the early detection of compromised accounts or malicious activities.

Log Analytics and Workbooks

For a more sophisticated analysis of audit and sign-in logs, Azure AD can integrate with Azure Monitor and Log Analytics. This integration enables the aggregation of logs from multiple sources and the creation of custom dashboards and workbooks.

To configure Log Analytics, navigate to **Azure Active Directory → Monitoring → Logs (Log Analytics)**. Queries can be written using the Kusto Query Language (KQL) to analyze log data. Below is an example KQL query to count sign-ins per user over the last 24 hours:

```
SigninLogs
| where TimeGenerated >= ago(24h)
| summarize SignInCount=count() by UserPrincipalName
```

Workbooks in Azure Monitor enable the visualization of log data through customizable charts and graphs. They provide predefined templates for common scenarios, which can be adapted to fit specific monitoring requirements.

Reporting and Alerts

Azure AD facilitates the generation of predefined and custom reports to meet various compliance and operational needs. The reports can be scheduled and exported to different formats such as CSV, Excel, or PDF.

Moreover, setting up alerts is a crucial aspect of operational security. Alerts can be configured for specific events or thresholds in the Azure portal under **Azure Active Directory → Monitoring → Alerts**. For instance, an alert can be configured to notify administrators of sign-in failures exceeding a predefined count within a specific timeframe:

```
az monitor metrics alert create --name "FailedSignInAlert" \
    --resource-group MyResourceGroup --scopes /subscriptions/{subscription-id} \
    --condition "aggregatedValue > 10" --description "Alert for failed sign-ins"
```

Real-time alerts ensure that administrators are promptly informed of potential issues, enabling swift remediation to minimize security risks.

Audit logs, sign-in logs, integration with Log Analytics, and the capability to configure comprehensive reporting and alerting collectively enhance the security posture of Azure AD. These tools empower administrators to maintain visibility into the directory's operations, ensuring that the environment remains secure and compliant.

7.12 Identity Governance and Policies

Identity governance and policies within Azure Active Directory (Azure AD) play a critical role in ensuring that the right users have the right access to the right resources, at the right time. Governance is achieved by implementing policies that define and enforce how identities are managed and regulated. This section focuses on key components such as access reviews, entitlement management, terms of use, and privileged identity management.

Azure AD Identity Governance provides a framework for managing identity lifecycle, privileged access, and access governance. It ensures compliance with organizational regulations and policies while maintaining a security posture aligned with best practices.

Access Reviews

Access reviews help ensure that only the necessary users have access to resources and groups. This process is particularly important for critical applications, ensuring compliance and security by periodically reviewing user access and permissions.

```
# Creating an access review in Azure AD using PowerShell
$description = "Quarterly access review for Finance group"
$reviewer = "admin@contoso.com"
$resourceID = "group_object_id"
Start-AzureADAccessReview -DisplayName "Finance Group Review" -Description
    $description -Reviewer $reviewer -ResourceId $resourceID -FrequencyType
    Quarterly
```

During an access review, reviewers can approve or deny access for users based on their necessity of access for job roles. The review results assist in making informed decisions on maintaining or revoking access.

Entitlement Management

Entitlement management in Azure AD defines how to manage identity governance through access packages. Access packages are collections of resources such as applications, groups, and SharePoint sites that help manage user access based on predefined policies.

```
# Creating an access package
$packageName = "Finance Team Access Package"
$catalogId = "catalog_object_id"
$resourceRole = "group_object_id"

New-AzureADMSAccessPackage -DisplayName $packageName -CatalogId $catalogId -
    ResourceRole $resourceRole
```

Access packages allow organizations to automate the process of granting and managing access, minimizing the risk associated with manual interventions. They support scenarios such as onboarding new employees, granting contractors temporary access, and providing external partners with the requisite access.

Terms of Use

Azure AD Terms of Use (ToU) policy helps organizations present information to end users that they must accept before obtaining access to resources. Terms of Use policies ensure users acknowledge the policy information, which typically includes legal disclaimers or corporate guidelines.

```
# Creating a Terms of Use Policy
$fileNames = "TermsOfUse.pdf"
$displayName = "Contoso ToU Policy"
$requiredToAccept = $true

New-AzureADMSAgreement -DisplayName $displayName -FileLocation $fileNames -
    RequiredToAccept $requiredToAccept
```

By enforcing acceptance of ToU policies, organizations can ensure that users are aware of and agree to terms and conditions before accessing sensitive information or critical applications. These policies can be tailored to meet specific compliance requirements or legal obligations.

Privileged Identity Management (PIM)

Privileged Identity Management (PIM) in Azure AD provides oversight into how administrative privileges are granted and used. It controls and monitors access to ensure that administrators maintain privileges only for as long as necessary.

```
# Activating a privileged role using PIM
$roleObjectId = "role_object_id"
$tenantId = "tenant_id"

Enable-AzureADPrivilegedRoleAssignment -RoleId $roleObjectId -TenantId $tenantId -
    Duration "00:30:00"
```

PIM allows defining policies around role activation, approval requirements, and duration limits to mitigate the risks associated with permanent administrative access. Audit logs and notifications provide visibility into role activation history and approvals.

Implementing a Comprehensive Governance Strategy

A comprehensive identity governance strategy in Azure AD integrates the above elements into a cohesive framework ensuring compliance, security, and efficiency. Organizations can automate and streamline identity lifecycle management, minimize risks associated with unauthorized access, and maintain compliance with internal and external regulations.

Integrating Azure AD Identity Governance into an organization's overall security posture promotes a secure, compliant, and efficient environment, aligning with security best practices and regulatory requirements.

Chapter 8

Azure DevOps and Application Lifecycle Management

This chapter delves into the principles of DevOps and the services provided by Azure DevOps. It covers setting up repositories with Azure Repos, implementing continuous integration and deployment with Azure Pipelines, and managing artifacts. The chapter also explores infrastructure as code, testing, quality assurance, agile planning with Azure Boards, CI/CD best practices, and deploying applications to Azure Kubernetes Service (AKS). Additionally, it emphasizes monitoring and feedback mechanisms essential for successful application lifecycle management.

8.1 Introduction to DevOps

DevOps is a portmanteau of "Development" and "Operations," representing a set of practices that aim to bridge the gap between software development and IT operations. The core objective of DevOps is to shorten the systems development life cycle while delivering features, fixes, and updates frequently in close alignment with business objectives. Furthermore, DevOps fosters a culture of collaboration and shared responsibility between developers and operators.

The fundamental principles of DevOps encompass continuous integration, continuous delivery, automated testing, infrastructure as code, monitoring, and feedback. These principles are engineered to enhance the speed, efficiency, and reliability of software development and deployment processes.

Continuous Integration (CI) refers to the practice of merging all developers' working copies to a shared mainline several times a day. CI aims to detect integration issues early, using automated testing to validate new code after each merge. This practice ensures that the codebase is perpetually in a deployable state, allowing for rapid iteration and reduced integration headaches.

Continuous Delivery (CD) extends the principles of CI by automating the deployment process, enabling code changes to be automatically deployed to a production-like environment. The primary goal is to ensure that the software can be released to production at any time, safely and sustainably. This practice complements continuous integration by pushing the boundaries to include deployment automation and environment consistency.

Automated Testing is integral to ensuring the reliability and stability of software as it evolves. Automated tests are scripts that execute to verify the correctness of code changes. By integrating automated testing within CI/CD pipelines, issues can be detected and resolved early, ensuring higher quality in the final product.

Infrastructure as Code (IaC) is a key DevOps practice whereby infrastructure is provisioned and managed using code and software development techniques. IaC allows for the automation of environment setup, configuration management, and orchestration by defining infrastructure through declarative or imperative models. Common tools for IaC include Terraform, Ansible, and Azure Resource Manager (ARM) templates.

Monitoring and Feedback are critical components in the DevOps lifecycle. Continuous monitoring of applications and infrastructure ensures that any issues are detected early and addressed promptly. Feedback loops from monitoring systems provide data that can drive improvements in process and practices and ensure robustness in deployments.

Implementing DevOps practices requires a transformation in both technical and cultural aspects within an organization. This transformation includes establishing a collaborative culture, adopting toolchains that support automation and integration, and instituting processes that enhance transparency and accountability.

```
trigger:
- main

pool:
  vmImage: 'ubuntu-latest'

steps:
- task: UseDotNet@2
  inputs:
    packageType: 'sdk'
    version: '5.x'

- script: dotnet build --configuration Release
  displayName: 'Build project'

- script: dotnet test
  displayName: 'Run tests'
```

In the example above, an Azure Pipelines configuration file (YAML format) is used to define a simple continuous integration workflow. This workflow is triggered by pushes to the "main" branch, utilizing the latest Ubuntu virtual machine image for execution. The steps involve setting up the .NET SDK, building the project, and running tests.

```
# Output of a sample Azure Pipelines build
Starting: Build project
==============================================================================
Task         : Command line
Description  : Run a command line script using Bash on Linux and macOS and
               cmd.exe on Windows
Version      : 2.182.0
Author       : Microsoft Corporation
Help         : https://docs.microsoft.com/azure/devops/pipelines/tasks/utility/
                 command-line?view=azure-pipelines&tabs=yaml
==============================================================================
Generating script.
Script contents:
dotnet build --configuration Release
[command]/usr/bin/bash --noprofile --norc /___w/_temp/98d87255-aa87-4e41-88f8-9
59ec6b6aefd.sh
Microsoft (R) Build Engine version 16.7.2+be8c7b5e1 for .NET
Copyright (C) Microsoft Corporation. All rights reserved.

Determining projects to restore...
Restored /___w/1/s/sample-app/sample-app.csproj (in 144 ms).
You are using a preview version of .NET. See: https://aka.ms/dotnet-core-preview
  sample-app -> /___w/1/s/sample-app/bin/Release/net5.0/sample-app.dll

Build succeeded.
    0 Warning(s)
    0 Error(s)

# Output truncated for brevity
```

Understanding the intricate details of DevOps practices and their implementation within Azure ensures that organizations can leverage these methodologies efficiently. The structured integration of these principles results in improved collaboration, faster delivery cycles, and a more reliable operational environment.

8.2 Overview of Azure DevOps Services

Azure DevOps is a comprehensive suite of development tools offered by Microsoft for software development teams. These services encompass a wide array of functionalities that streamlines the application lifecycle, enabling continuous integration/continuous deployment (CI/CD), continuous testing, and more. This section explores the core components of Azure DevOps, illustrating how they collectively facilitate efficient and agile development workflows.

Azure DevOps services are comprised of five primary components: Azure Boards, Azure Repos, Azure Pipelines, Azure Test Plans, and Azure Artifacts. Each of these services plays a distinct role in the software development lifecycle, working in conjunction to provide robust support for planning, development, delivery, and operations.

Azure Boards enables agile planning, tracking, and project management through work items, backlogs, team dashboards, and custom reporting. It supports various agile methodologies including Scrum, Kanban, and customized processes.

Azure Repos provides version control with Git repositories or Team Foundation Version Control (TFVC). This allows for collaboration on code through pull requests, code reviews, and branch policies that can enforce quality standards before code is merged.

Azure Pipelines is a CI/CD service that automates the building, testing, and deployment of code. It supports a variety of languages and project types, from simple web apps to complex service-oriented architectures. Pipelines can be configured through YAML files or a visual designer interface.

Azure Test Plans offers manual and exploratory testing, providing stakeholders with tools for defining, managing, and executing test cases. Integrated with Azure Boards and Pipelines, it ensures that every aspect of application quality is covered from requirements to release.

Azure Artifacts manages dependencies used by applications, offering an integrated package management experience for managing your NuGet, npm, Maven, and Python package feeds from public and private sources. This is crucial for consistency and reliability of application dependencies across multiple stages of development.

The following sections delve deeper into each of these components, providing detailed instructions and examples.

```
# Log in to your Azure account
az login

# Create a new Azure DevOps organization
az devops organization create --name MyOrganization --location 'East US'

# Set the default organization for future commands
az devops configure --defaults organization=https://dev.azure.com/MyOrganization
```

Output from the execution of the above command:

```
- Creating organization 'MyOrganization'
- Setting default organization to 'https://dev.azure.com/MyOrganization'
Success: Organization 'MyOrganization' created
```

The integration between these services facilitates not just isolated tasks but a seamless DevOps workflow. Azure Boards provide the foundation for planning and tracking work. Developers check in code to Azure Repos, ensuring versioning and proper code management. This code then flows through Azure Pipelines to automatically build, test, and deploy. Azure Test Plans enables both manual and automated testing throughout the process, while Azure Artifacts ensures all dependencies are correctly resolved and maintained.

Scalability and Flexibility are integral features of Azure DevOps. The system supports a wide range of extensions and integrations, available through the Visual Studio Marketplace, enabling teams to extend their pipelines with additional functionalities such as integrating third-party tools or custom scripts.

The flexibility of Azure Pipelines is particularly noteworthy. It supports build and deployment pipelines across multiple environments and cloud providers. For example, a pipeline can be constructed to deploy applications to Azure, AWS, Google Cloud Platform, or on-premises infrastructure with consistent workflows.

```
trigger:
- main

pool:
  vmImage: 'ubuntu-latest'

steps:
- script: echo Hello, World!
  displayName: 'Run a one-line script'

- script: |
    echo Add other commands here
    echo Use a pipe symbol (|) for multi-line commands
  displayName: 'Run multi-line script'
```

By enabling CI/CD, continuous testing, and comprehensive project management, Azure DevOps not only accelerates the development cycle but also ensures higher quality delivery. Each component's tight integration ensures that teams can move seamlessly from planning to deployment, with continuous improvements derived from feedback and telemetry collected across the lifecycle.

Using Azure DevOps, organizations can adopt DevOps methodologies and practices, leading to enhanced collaboration between development and operations teams and delivering a more efficient and reliable application lifecycle.

8.3 Setting Up Azure Repos

Azure Repos provides version control to manage your code and collaborate with others. It includes both Git, which is distributed version control, and Team Foundation Version Control (TFVC), which is a centralized version control system. Git repositories are recommended due to their flexibility and the support they enjoy within the DevOps community. In this section, we will focus on setting up Git repositories in Azure Repos and cover essential commands and operations.

Creating a New Repository

To create a new repository in Azure Repos, follow these steps:

1. **Navigate to Azure DevOps Portal:** Open your web browser and go to https://dev.azure.com. Sign in with your Azure DevOps credentials.

2. **Select Your Project:** Choose the project where you want to add the repository from the list of projects.

3. **Access Repos:** Click on the Repos tab on the left-hand menu.

4. **Create Repository:** Within the Repos view, click the + New repository button. Fill in the repository name, and select Git as the type of version control. Optionally, initialize the repository with a readme file, .gitignore file, or a license file, depending on your project's needs.

5. **Complete Creation:** Click Create, and your new repository is now available for cloning, pushing, and pulling operations.

Cloning a Repository

Cloning is the process of copying a repository from Azure Repos to your local machine. This operation is performed using Git command-line tools. The following commands demonstrate how to clone a repository:

```
git clone https://dev.azure.com/{organization}/{project}/_git/{repository}
```

- Replace organization with the name of your Azure DevOps organization.
- Replace project with the name of your project.
- Replace repository with the name of your repository.

After executing the command, Git will copy the repository's contents into a new directory on your local machine.

Adding Files and Committing Changes

Once the repository is cloned, you can add new files to it and commit changes. The following sequence of commands illustrates this process:

```
cd {repository}
echo "# Azure Repo" >> README.md
git add README.md
git commit -m "Initial commit with README"
```

- Navigate to the repository directory.
- Create or modify files, in this case, adding a README.md.
- Add the new or changed files to the staging area using git add.
- Commit the changes to the local repository with a descriptive message using git commit.

Pushing Changes to Azure Repos

To reflect local commits in the Azure Repos repository, you need to push the changes. Use the following command:

```
git push origin main
```

This command pushes all committed changes to the remote repository associated with the main branch. The name of the branch may vary depending on your configuration.

Pulling Changes from Azure Repos

To synchronize your local repository with changes made in the Azure Repos repository by other team members, use the following pull command:

```
git pull origin main
```

This updates your local copy with the latest changes from the remote repository.

Branching and Merging

Branching allows multiple developers to work on different features without interfering with each other. To create and switch to a new branch:

```
git checkout -b new-feature
```

Afterward, you can work on your new feature independently. Once your feature is complete, merge it back into the main branch:

```
git checkout main
git merge new-feature
```

To push the merged changes back to Azure Repos:

```
git push origin main
```

Pull Requests in Azure Repos

Pull requests (PRs) facilitate code review and discussion before integrating changes into the main branch. To create a PR:

1. **Push Branch to Remote:** Use git push to push your feature branch to the remote repository.

```
git push origin new-feature
```

2. **Create Pull Request:** In Azure DevOps, navigate to the Repos tab and select Pull requests. Click New pull request, select the source branch (new-feature) and the target branch (main). Add reviewers, a description, and any additional information as needed before clicking Create.

This initiates a pull request workflow, where designated reviewers can evaluate the changes, provide feedback, and approve or request modifications.

Managing Repository Permissions

Access control is crucial for maintaining repository integrity. To manage permissions:

1. **Navigate to Project Settings:** Go to the project settings by selecting Project settings in the sidebar.

2. **Select Repositories:** Under Repos, select Repositories, then select the repository you wish to manage.

3. **Update Permissions:** Click Security, and adjust permissions for users or groups. You can set specific rights, such as read, contribute, or full control.

Implementing Branch Policies

Enforcing branch policies ensures code quality and integration standards. To setup policies:

1. **Navigate to Repositories Settings:** In the Project Settings, select Repositories, then the repository.

2. **Set Up Policies:** Choose Branches, select the branch (e.g., main), and click Branch policies. Configure policies such as requiring a minimum number of reviewers, checking for linked work items, requiring that builds pass before merges, etc.

This ensures that changes meet predefined criteria before becoming part of the main codebase.

```
Repository: main
Minimum number of reviewers: 2
Build validation: Required
Match work items: Enabled
```

The meticulous setup of Azure Repos enables efficient source code management within the Azure DevOps ecosystem. Adhering to these practices fosters collaboration, ensures code quality, and maintains a robust development workflow.

8.4 Continuous Integration with Azure Pipelines

Continuous Integration (CI) is an essential practice within the DevOps methodology, aiming to automate the process of integrating code changes from multiple contributors into a shared repository, ensuring that the new code does not break the existing system. Azure Pipelines, a service provided by Azure DevOps, facilitates this by enabling developers to automatically build, test, and deploy their applications.

The first step in implementing CI with Azure Pipelines is to configure a pipeline for your project. This involves creating a pipeline configuration file, typically named azure-pipelines.yml and placed at the root of your repository. This file defines the build and test steps that are executed whenever new code is committed.

```
trigger:
  branches:
    include:
      - main
      - develop

pool:
  vmImage: 'ubuntu-latest'

jobs:
- job: Build
  steps:
  - task: UseNode@2
    inputs:
      version: '14.x'
  - script: npm install
    displayName: 'Install dependencies'
  - script: npm run build
    displayName: 'Build the project'
  - script: npm test
    displayName: 'Run tests'
```

This sample pipeline configuration file specifies the following:

- trigger: It defines the branches that will trigger the pipeline. In this example, changes to the main and develop branches will start the CI process.
- pool: It sets the virtual machine (VM) image that will be used for the build. Here, ubuntu-latest is specified, indicating that the build will run on the latest Ubuntu image.
- jobs: A job represents a sequence of steps to execute. In this case, there is a single job named Build.
- steps: These are the individual tasks within a job. The steps include setting up the Node.js environment, installing dependencies with npm install, building the project with npm run build, and running tests with npm test.

Once the pipeline configuration file is created, it is necessary to link your Git repository with Azure DevOps and create a new pipeline:

- Navigate to the Azure DevOps portal and select your project.
- Under the **Pipelines** section, click on **New Pipeline**.

- Select **GitHub** (or your version control provider) to authenticate and select the repository.
- Azure DevOps will automatically detect the azure-pipelines.yml file and use its configuration.

Azure Pipelines will now automatically execute the stages defined in the YAML file whenever code is committed to the specified branches. Each step in the pipeline is logged, and outputs from commands such as npm test are displayed in the Azure DevOps interface.

Consider a more complex pipeline that includes multiple stages, such as Build, Test, and Deploy. The following YAML configuration illustrates this:

```
trigger:
  branches:
    include:
      - main

pool:
  vmImage: 'ubuntu-latest'

stages:
- stage: Build
  jobs:
  - job: Build
    steps:
    - task: UseNode@2
      inputs:
        version: '14.x'
    - script: npm install
      displayName: 'Install dependencies'
    - script: npm run build
      displayName: 'Build the project'

- stage: Test
  dependsOn: Build
  jobs:
  - job: Test
    steps:
    - script: npm test
      displayName: 'Run tests'

- stage: Deploy
  dependsOn: Test
  condition: succeeded()
  jobs:
  - job: Deploy
    steps:
    - script: echo Deploying the project...
      displayName: 'Deploy the project'
```

This configuration introduces stages, which are logical groups of jobs. Each stage can depend on the completion of the previous stages. In the example:

- Build: This stage compiles the project. It runs only the build steps.
- Test: This stage runs the tests and depends on the Build stage. This ensures tests are only run if the build succeeds.
- Deploy: This stage can be used to deploy the application. It has a condition to run only if the previous stages succeed (succeeded()).

Azure Pipelines supports a wide range of triggers, tasks, and conditional execution options to cater to various CI requirements. For example, to trigger builds for specific paths or files, the paths filter can be used:

```
trigger:
  branches:
    include:
      - main
  paths:
    include:
      - src/*
      - tests/*
```

This configuration ensures that the pipeline only triggers when changes are made to files within the src or tests directories.

Monitoring the execution of the pipeline is crucial. The Azure DevOps portal provides detailed logs and reports for each run, where you can view the status of each step, including errors and warnings if any. For instance, a successful pipeline run may show:

```
Job Build
  Step: Install dependencies - SUCCESS
  Step: Build the project - SUCCESS
Job Test
  Step: Run tests - SUCCESS
Job Deploy
  Step: Deploy the project - SUCCESS
```

Whereas a failure in the test step would result in:

```
Job Build
  Step: Install dependencies - SUCCESS
  Step: Build the project - SUCCESS
Job Test
  Step: Run tests - FAILURE
```

Integrating CI practices using Azure Pipelines not only ensures code quality through automated testing but also accelerates the development process by providing immediate feedback to developers about the impact of their code changes. This setup forms the backbone of efficient and reliable software development workflows, adapting seamlessly to various project requirements and scaling as needed.

8.5 Continuous Deployment with Azure Pipelines

Continuous Deployment (CD) within Azure Pipelines ensures that every change to your codebase is automatically deployed to a production environment, provided it passes critical stages of testing and validation. This practice strengthens the feedback loop, reduces manual intervention, and fosters a culture of frequent, reliable production releases.

A typical CD pipeline in Azure Pipelines encompasses several key steps: defining deployment stages, setting up release triggers, configuring required approvals, managing deployment environments, and handling potential rollback scenarios. To establish a CD pipeline effectively, we integrate the following elements:

- **Stages** - Logical phases in the deployment process (e.g., development, testing, production).
- **Jobs** - A collection of steps executed by a specific agent during deployment.
- **Steps** - Individual tasks within a job, such as running scripts, copying files, or configuring settings.
- **Environments** - Deployment targets which might include physical servers, virtual machines, or Kubernetes clusters.

Creating a Release Pipeline

To initiate a release pipeline in Azure Pipelines, follow these steps:

1. Navigate to *Pipelines* and select *Releases*. 2. Click on *New pipeline* to create a new release pipeline. 3. Define the artifact sources that will trigger this pipeline. Common artifact sources include Azure Repos, GitHub, or a pipeline build artifact.

```
trigger:
  branches:
    include:
      - main

pool:
  vmImage: 'ubuntu-latest'

stages:
  - stage: Deploy
    jobs:
    - deployment: DeployWeb
```

```
  environment: 'Production'
  strategy:
    runOnce:
      deploy:
        steps:
        - script: echo Deploying to Production...
          displayName: 'Deployment Script'
```

The above YAML code snippet outlines a basic release pipeline configuration that triggers a deployment upon changes to the 'main' branch. It includes a single stage 'Deploy' that executes a deployment job 'DeployWeb' to a 'Production' environment.

Defining Deployment Strategies

Azure Pipelines supports various deployment strategies to facilitate smooth updates:

- **RunOnce**: Executes the deployment job once per stage. Example provided in the above snippet.
- **Rolling**: (Not shown) Deploys new instances in phases to reduce downtime.
- **Canary**: (Not shown) Gradually shifts a portion of traffic to new deployments before full rollout. Useful for minimizing risk.
- **Blue-Green**: (Not shown) Deploys the new version alongside the old version, switching traffic once validation completes.

For example, implementing a rolling deployment strategy to incrementally deploy the application might look like this:

```
stages:
  - stage: Deploy
    jobs:
    - deployment: DeployWeb
      environment: 'Production'
      strategy:
        rolling:
          maxParallel: 2
          preDeploy:
            steps:
            - script: echo Pre-deployment steps...
          deploy:
            steps:
            - script: echo Deploying to Production...
          postDeploy:
            steps:
            - script: echo Post-deployment steps...
```

In this configuration, 'rolling' specifies that at most two instances are updated simultaneously. 'preDeploy', 'deploy', and 'postDeploy' allow for customized actions at different stages of the deployment.

Setting Up Approval Gates

To enhance control over deployments, Azure Pipelines offers approval gates. These gates ensure that deployments proceed only after explicit approval, thus mitigating unplanned disruptions.

- Navigate to the 'Environments' section within the deployment job.
- Add a pre-deployment gate for manual approval:

  Approvals and checks > Add > Approvals.

- Configure the necessary approvers and conditions for the deployment to proceed.

Rolling Back Deployments

Handling failed deployments is critical. Azure Pipelines includes mechanisms to rollback changes and maintain system stability.

- Utilize deployment strategies to safely rollback by defining appropriate conditions.
- Implement rollback scripts or reusable templates to revert to a stable state upon failure.

For instance, a rollback script:

```
steps:
- script: echo Rolling back deployment...
- script: ./scripts/rollback.sh
```

Use the above steps to initiate a rollback process through scripting, ensuring the system reverts correctly to the previous stable state.

Monitoring and Feedback

Continuous monitoring and real-time feedback are paramount to CD's success. Azure Pipelines facilitates integration with monitoring tools like Azure Monitor and Application Insights to track deployment outcomes and performance.

Integrate monitoring tools:

- Within your pipeline, add tasks to send telemetry data:

```
steps:
- task: AzureMonitorMetrics@1
  inputs:
    azureSubscription: 'AzureSubscription'
    resourceGroupName: 'ResourceGroup'
    resourceName: 'Resource'
    timeGrain: 'PT1M'
```

By leveraging Azure Monitor, obtain detailed insights into deployment performance and issues, enabling better decision-making and proactive issue resolution.

Continuous Deployment with Azure Pipelines ensures a streamlined, reliable, and automated approach to deploying applications, critical for maintaining high-quality software in modern development practices.

8.6 Managing Artifacts with Azure Artifacts

Azure Artifacts is a key component of Azure DevOps that facilitates the management of different types of packages used as artifacts in the development lifecycle. It supports the creation, hosting, and sharing of packages, enabling teams to add fully integrated package management to their continuous integration/continuous deployment (CI/CD) pipelines.

Azure Artifacts supports multiple package formats including NuGet, npm, Maven, Python, and Universal Packages, making it a versatile tool for various project needs. Each feed in Azure Artifacts can store multiple packages, manage versions, and control access through permissions. This section will provide a comprehensive technical walkthrough on setting up and managing Azure Artifacts.

Packages in Azure Artifacts are hosted in feeds. A feed is a container for packages that allows you to manage permissions and settings. To create a feed in Azure Artifacts, follow these steps:

- Navigate to the Azure DevOps portal.
- Select your project.
- Click on 'Artifacts' in the sidebar.
- Click 'Create Feed'.

- Enter a name for the feed and choose visibility options (e.g., whether it is accessible within the organization or project).
- Click 'Create'.

After creating a feed, you can publish packages to it using respective package managers. Here is an example of how to publish a NuGet package to an Azure Artifacts feed using the built-in Azure CLI support:

```
# Set variables
$feedName="my-feed"
$projectName="my-project"
$organizationUrl="https://dev.azure.com/my-organization"

# Authenticate with Azure DevOps
az devops login

# Add the feed source to NuGet configuration
nuget sources add -name "My Feed" -source "$organizationUrl/$projectName/
    _packaging/$feedName/nuget/v3/index.json" -username "AzureDevOps" -
    password $(az artifacts universal download-token --organization $organizationUrl
    --project $projectName --feed $feedName --name "my-feed")

# Publish the package
nuget push -source "My Feed" -apikey az .\my-package.nupkg
```

Likewise, you can publish other types of packages (e.g., npm, Maven, Python) following their respective commands. Below is an example of publishing an npm package:

```
# Configure npm to use the Azure Artifacts feed
npm config set registry $organizationUrl/$projectName/_packaging/$feedName/npm/
    registry/

# Authenticate with Azure Artifacts
npm login --registry=$organizationUrl/$projectName/_packaging/$feedName/npm/
    registry/ --scope=@my-scope

# Publish the package
npm publish --registry=$organizationUrl/$projectName/_packaging/$feedName/npm/
    registry/
```

Once packages are published, they can be consumed in CI/CD pipelines by adding the feed as an artifact source. This process involves including the appropriate service connection and configuring the pipeline with the necessary steps to download and use the packages. To include a feed in a YAML pipeline, the following example illustrates how to consume a NuGet package:

```
# azure-pipelines.yml
trigger:
- master

pool:
```

```
  vmImage: 'ubuntu-latest'

steps:
- task: UseDotNet@2
  inputs:
    packageType: 'sdk'
    version: '5.x'

- task: NuGetCommand@2
  inputs:
    command: 'restore'
    feedsToUse: 'select'
    vstsFeed: '<ProjectName>/<FeedName>'
    nugetConfigPath: 'NuGet.config'

- task: DotNetCoreCLI@2
  inputs:
    command: 'build'
    projects: '*.csproj'
    arguments: '--configuration Release'
```

Moreover, Azure Artifacts provides an intuitive interface for package management including version control, deprecating or promoting particular versions, and inspecting historical usage data. Access control is managed through Azure DevOps permissions, allowing team members to restrict or permit access at granular levels.

Azure Artifacts also allows integrating upstream sources, which are external package sources like the public npm registry, NuGet.org, or Maven Central. When set up, upstream sources enable automatic capture of external packages to ensure reproducibility and reduce external dependencies. To configure an upstream source:

- Navigate to the desired feed in Azure DevOps.
- Click 'Use packages from external sources'.
- Select the upstream sources to include.
- Save the configuration.

Finally, Azure Artifacts facilitate dependency management, ensuring package versions are consistent across development and deployment environments. This integrated approach simplifies the development workflow, improves build times by utilizing cached packages, and enhances overall team productivity by ensuring that all developers have access to the latest and consistent sets of dependencies.

Understanding and utilizing Azure Artifacts effectively will ensure that software artifact management is robust, secure, and efficient, further streamlining the CI/CD pipelines within Azure DevOps.

8.7 Infrastructure as Code with Azure DevOps

Infrastructure as Code (IaC) is a critical practice in DevOps, where infrastructure is provisioned and managed using code and software development techniques, such as version control and continuous integration. Azure DevOps facilitates IaC through robust integration with tools like ARM templates, Terraform, and Azure CLI. This section explores how to implement IaC using Azure DevOps, highlights best practices, and provides detailed examples with ARM templates and Terraform.

IaC enables the declarative definition of infrastructure, allowing teams to version control and automate the provisioning of resources. With Azure DevOps, you can integrate these practices into your CI/CD pipelines, ensuring consistent and reproducible environments across different stages of the application lifecycle.

Using ARM Templates in Azure DevOps

Azure Resource Manager (ARM) templates are JSON files that define the infrastructure and configuration for your Azure deployment. They support the deployment of various Azure resources with dependencies, ensuring resources are deployed in the correct order.

To utilize ARM templates with Azure DevOps, follow these steps:

- Create an ARM template: Define the resources and configurations in a JSON template file.
- Commit the template to Azure Repos: Store the template in version control for collaboration and change tracking.
- Configure a release pipeline: Use Azure Pipelines to automate the deployment of resources defined in the ARM template.

Consider the following example of an ARM template that provisions a virtual network and a subnet:

```
{
  "$schema": "https://schema.management.azure.com/schemas/2019-04-01/
       deploymentTemplate.json#",
  "contentVersion": "1.0.0.0",
  "resources": [
    {
      "type": "Microsoft.Network/virtualNetworks",
      "apiVersion": "2020-07-01",
      "name": "myVnet",
```

```
"location": "[resourceGroup().location]",
    "properties": {
      "addressSpace": {
        "addressPrefixes": [
          "10.0.0.0/16"
        ]
      },
      "subnets": [
        {
          "name": "mySubnet",
          "properties": {
            "addressPrefix": "10.0.1.0/24"
          }
        }
      ]
    }
  }
 ]
}
```

After committing this template to Azure Repos, a deployment pipeline can be created with the following steps:

```
trigger:
- main

pool:
  vmImage: 'ubuntu-latest'

steps:
- task: AzureResourceManagerTemplateDeployment@3
  inputs:
    deploymentScope: 'Resource Group'
    azureResourceManagerConnection: 'AzureServiceConnection'
    subscriptionId: '<Your Subscription Id>'
    action: 'Create Or Update Resource Group'
    resourceGroupName: 'MyResourceGroup'
    location: 'East US'
    templateLocation: 'Linked artifact'
    csmFile: '$(System.DefaultWorkingDirectory)/<path-to-your-template>/
      azuredeploy.json'
    csmParametersFile: ''
    deploymentMode: 'Complete'
```

This pipeline triggers on commits to the main branch and uses the AzureResourceManagerTemplateDeployment task to deploy the resources defined in the ARM template.

Using Terraform in Azure DevOps

Terraform is an open-source tool by HashiCorp for building, changing, and versioning infrastructure safely and efficiently. It uses a declarative language to define both cloud and on-premises resources.

Integrating Terraform with Azure DevOps involves the following steps:

- Write Terraform configuration files: Define your infrastructure in

HashiCorp Configuration Language (HCL).

- Store the configuration files in Azure Repos: Keep the Terraform code under version control.
- Create a pipeline for Terraform: Automate the Terraform workflow with Azure Pipelines.

Here is an example Terraform configuration for provisioning an Azure storage account:

```
provider "azurerm" {
  features {}
}

resource "azurerm_resource_group" "example" {
  name = "example-resources"
  location = "East US"
}

resource "azurerm_storage_account" "example" {
  name = "examplestorageacc"
  resource_group_name = azurerm_resource_group.example.name
  location = azurerm_resource_group.example.location
  account_tier = "Standard"
  account_replication_type = "LRS"
}
```

After committing this configuration to Azure Repos, you can create a pipeline as shown below:

```
trigger:
- main

pool:
  vmImage: 'ubuntu-latest'

steps:
- task: TerraformInstaller@0
  inputs:
    terraformVersion: '0.14.9'

- script: terraform init
  displayName: 'Terraform Init'

- script: terraform plan -out=tfplan
  displayName: 'Terraform Plan'

- script: terraform apply tfplan
  displayName: 'Terraform Apply'
```

This pipeline installs Terraform, initializes the configuration, creates a plan, and applies the plan to provision the resources.

Both ARM templates and Terraform offer powerful mechanisms for defining and deploying infrastructure programmatically. Utilizing Azure

DevOps pipelines to manage these deployments ensures consistency, repeatability, and version control, all of which are essential for successful DevOps practices. Employing these IaC practices reduces manual intervention, prevents configuration drift, and enables scalable and predictable infrastructure management.

8.8 Testing and Quality Assurance in Azure DevOps

Testing and Quality Assurance (QA) are integral components of the software development lifecycle, ensuring that applications meet the required standards and function correctly within the defined parameters. In Azure DevOps, several tools and practices facilitate effective testing and quality assurance, ranging from manual and automated testing to continuous testing practices that are inherently integrated into the CI/CD pipelines.

Azure DevOps provides a cohesive framework for implementing testing and QA, promoting early detection of defects and continuous improvement of software quality.

Automated Testing with Azure Pipelines

Automated testing is a crucial practice in the DevOps pipeline, enabling the running of tests automatically upon code commits. Azure Pipelines support various testing frameworks and languages, facilitating the automation of unit tests, integration tests, and acceptance tests.

To get started with automated testing in Azure Pipelines, include the testing tasks within your pipeline YAML file. Below is an example of a YAML configuration for running unit tests with NUnit:

```
trigger:
- main

pool:
  vmImage: 'ubuntu-latest'

steps:
- task: UseDotNet@2
  inputs:
    packageType: 'sdk'
    version: '5.x'
    installationPath: $(Agent.ToolsDirectory)/dotnet

- script: dotnet restore
  displayName: 'Restore dependencies'
```

```
- script: dotnet build --configuration Release
  displayName: 'Build solution'

- script: dotnet test --configuration Release --no-build --verbosity normal
  displayName: 'Run unit tests'
```

This pipeline is triggered by changes to the main branch. It installs the .NET SDK, restores dependencies, builds the solution, and runs the unit tests using NUnit. Automated test results are recorded, and any failures are flagged immediately.

Manual Testing with Azure Test Plans

While automated testing is essential, some scenarios require manual intervention. Azure Test Plans allows teams to author, execute, and track manual tests effectively.

1. **Creating Test Plans and Suites**: Begin by creating a test plan, which can encapsulate multiple test suites and test cases. Navigate to Test Plans in Azure DevOps, select + New Test Plan, and provide the necessary details. 2. **Authoring Test Cases**: Create test cases within your test suites. Define the step-by-step actions and expected results in each test case. 3. **Executing Manual Tests**: Execute tests by navigating to the Execute tab within a test suite. Record outcomes and capture any encountered bugs.

Continuous Testing with Azure DevTest Labs

Azure DevTest Labs provides a environment to test applications continuously. Developers can create VMs quickly, configure environments on-demand, and set recurring tasks for testing.

1. **Creating a Lab**: Set up a lab from the Azure portal by selecting DevTest Labs and configure settings as per project needs. 2. **Provisioning VMs**: Create VMs and install the necessary testing software and agents. 3. **Automating Tests**: Integrate the lab with Azure Pipelines to automate the deployment of the latest build and execution of tests on the provisioned VMs.

Managing Test Artifacts

Azure Artifacts can store test binaries, allowing seamless management and distribution of test results. Publish these artifacts in the pipeline as follows:

```
- task: PublishTestResults@2
  inputs:
    testResultsFiles: '**/TestResults/*.trx'
    testResultsFormat: 'VSTest'
    failTaskOnFailedTests: true
```

```
testRunTitle: 'Unit Tests'
```

This task collects test result files and makes them accessible for analysis in Azure DevOps.

Tracking Quality Metrics

Azure DevOps provides comprehensive reporting capabilities to track quality metrics like test pass rate, code coverage, and defect density. Utilize the built-in widgets and dashboards to visualize these metrics.

- **Test Pass Rate**: Monitors the ratio of passed tests to the total executed tests.
- **Code Coverage**: Measures the percentage of code exercised by the tests, which helps in identifying untested parts of the codebase.
- **Defect Density**: Indicates the number of defects found relative to the size of the software module.

These metrics are vital in assessing the overall health of the application and guiding quality improvements.

Integration with External Test Tools

Azure DevOps supports integration with numerous third-party testing tools, such as Selenium, JUnit, and LoadRunner. Integration can be accomplished via extensions available in the Azure DevOps marketplace or through custom tasks in pipelines.

By leveraging these practices and tools, teams can ensure robust testing and quality assurance processes within Azure DevOps, leading to the delivery of high-quality software products.

8.9 Agile Planning and Tracking with Azure Boards

Azure Boards is a robust, integrated work tracking system that provides agile project management tools to support planning and tracking work within DevOps teams. Leveraging Azure Boards, teams can manage their product backlog, plan sprints, and track work items through various stages. This integration aids in maintaining a smooth workflow and ensures that project milestones are met with reliability.

Azure Boards supports methodologies such as Scrum and Kanban, offering features to accommodate both frameworks effectively. Agile practices, such as defining user stories, prioritizing tasks, and managing project timelines, are seamlessly integrated into Azure Boards, making it easier to maintain an organized and efficient development lifecycle.

To begin with Azure Boards, first, navigate to the Azure DevOps portal and select the project you want to work on. Within the project, select "Boards" from the sidebar menu.

```
https://dev.azure.com/{organization}/{project}/_boards
```

This interface presents several views, including Work Items, Boards (Kanban-style), Backlogs, Sprints, and Queries.

Work Items Management

Work items represent a unit of work within the project. They can be user stories, tasks, bugs, or issues. To create a work item, choose Boards > Work Items from the sidebar. Click the "New Work Item" button and select the type of work item you want to create. Fill in the necessary fields such as Title, Description, and Acceptance Criteria. Tags can be added to enhance filtering and searching capabilities.

```
Title: "Implement user authentication"
Description: "Develop login and registration functionality"
Acceptance Criteria: "Users should be able to register and log in with their email and
    password"
```

Backlog Management

The backlog is a central repository where all product features are documented and prioritized. To access the backlog, navigate to Boards > Backlogs. Here, the backlog items can be dragged and dropped to prioritize them. This list is critical for ensuring that the team works on the most important tasks first. Each item within the backlog can be detailed with additional information, ensuring that development tasks are fully scoped before being worked on.

```
Title: "User Dashboard Development"
Priority: "High"
Effort: "8 Story Points"
```

Sprint Planning

Sprints are iterative time-boxed periods during which specific work has to be completed and made ready for review. In Azure Boards, navigate to Boards > Sprints. Here, the team can plan their sprints effectively by assigning work items to the sprint. Work items from the backlog can be dragged into the sprint pane. Sprint capacity for each team member can be set based on available work hours, ensuring that the workload is balanced across the team.

```
Sprint Name: "Sprint 1"
Start Date: "2023-09-01"
End Date: "2023-09-14"
```

Kanban Board

The Kanban board aids in visualizing the workflow and ensures steady progress through development stages. Access the Kanban board via Boards > Boards. The work items appear as cards that can be moved across columns such as To Do, Doing, and Done. Administrators can customize these columns to reflect the exact workflow stages of the project. This visualization helps identify bottlenecks and provides an immediate overview of the project's status.

```
Column: "In Progress"
WIP Limit: "3"
```

Queries

Queries in Azure Boards allow for the creation of custom views to track specific sets of work items. Navigate to Boards > Queries to build queries. This feature is highly useful for generating reports, tracking progress, and identifying work items that meet certain criteria, such as all tasks assigned to a specific team member or all items tagged with a particular keyword.

```
Query Name: "Active Issues"
Filter: "State = Active"
Assigned to: "User: John Doe"
```

By utilizing Azure Boards, teams can ensure their agile planning and tracking practices are efficient, leading to improved productivity and successful project delivery. Each feature, from work items to Kanban boards, is designed to support the agile methodology, providing transparency and flexibility throughout the development lifecycle.

8.10 Implementing CI/CD Best Practices

Implementing Continuous Integration (CI) and Continuous Deployment (CD) effectively is critical for maintaining robust software development and delivery pipelines. This section outlines best practices that are essential for optimizing CI/CD workflows in Azure DevOps and ensuring the successful, efficient, and reliable delivery of applications.

To begin with, it is important to ensure that the base code is always in a deployable state. This means that the main branch in the version control system should be stable and capable of being deployed at any time. Developers should follow a branching strategy like GitFlow or trunk-based development to manage changes efficiently. Changes should be integrated into the main branch as frequently as possible, ideally multiple times a day, to avoid integration conflicts and to detect issues early.

```
# Create a feature branch
git checkout -b feature/new-feature

# Add and commit changes
git add .
git commit -m "Implemented new feature X"

# Push the feature branch to the repository
git push origin feature/new-feature

# Merge the feature branch back into the main branch
git checkout main
git pull origin main
git merge feature/new-feature

# Resolve any conflicts and push the merged main branch
git push origin main
```

Code quality is pivotal in CI/CD workflows. Automated code reviews, static code analysis, and linting should be integrated into the pipeline. Tools like SonarQube, ESLint, and StyleCop can be utilized to enforce coding standards and detect code smells early in the development cycle. These checks should be part of the build process to ensure that no substandard code is merged into the main branch.

```
# Example YAML snippet for Azure Pipelines
trigger:
- main

pool:
  vmImage: 'ubuntu-latest'

steps:
- script: |
    npm install eslint
    eslint . --ext .js
  displayName: 'Run ESLint Code Analysis'
```

Testing plays a crucial role in CI/CD. Both unit tests and integration tests should be automated and executed within the pipeline. Unit tests validate individual components, while integration tests ensure that the interactions between components work as expected. Tests should provide high coverage to maximize code verification. Incorporating threshold limits for code coverage can be beneficial. For instance, the build should fail if the coverage falls below a predefined percentage.

```
# Example YAML snippet for running tests
steps:
- script: |
    pip install -r requirements.txt
    pytest --cov=my_module tests/
  displayName: 'Run Unit Tests with Coverage Reporting'

- task: PublishTestResults@2
  inputs:
    testResultsFormat: 'JUnit'
    testResultsFiles: '**/test-results.xml'
    testRunTitle: 'Unit Tests'
```

Implementing continuous deployment goes hand in hand with continuous integration. Each successful build should ideally trigger an automated deployment to a staging environment. This ensures that the code is not only syntactically correct and tested but also that it works as expected in an environment similar to production. Using Infrastructure as Code (IaC) tools such as Azure Resource Manager (ARM) templates, Terraform, or Bicep ensures environment consistency and repeatability.

Secure practices should be adhered to throughout the CI/CD pipeline. Secrets and sensitive information such as API keys, passwords, and certificates should be stored securely using Azure Key Vault or Pipeline secrets. Avoid hardcoding these values in the source code or configuration files.

```
# Example YAML snippet for using secrets
steps:
- task: AzureKeyVault@1
  inputs:
    azureSubscription: 'MyAzureSubscription'
    KeyVaultName: 'MyKeyVault'
    SecretsFilter: '*'
    RunAsPreJob: true

- script: |
    echo "API_KEY: $(API_KEY)"
  displayName: 'Use Retrieve Secret API Key'
```

Monitoring and logging of the CI/CD pipeline should be enabled to gain insights into the build and deployment processes. Azure Monitor and Azure Log Analytics can be integrated to track pipeline performance, detect anomalies, and troubleshoot issues. Alerts can be configured to notify teams immediately if a pipeline fails, allowing for quick resolution and minimal disruption.

Regular reviews and audits of the CI/CD pipeline are essential for continuous improvement. Collecting feedback from the development and operation teams, analyzing build times, deployment success rates, and frequent failure points are vital metrics. This continuous feedback loop helps in identifying areas for optimization and ensures that the pipeline evolves to meet the changing needs of the project.

Applying these best practices will greatly enhance the efficiency, reliability, and security of your CI/CD pipelines in Azure DevOps. This integration allows teams to continuously deliver high-quality software at a faster pace, ultimately driving greater value and satisfaction for end-users.

8.11 Deploying Applications to Azure Kubernetes Service (AKS)

Azure Kubernetes Service (AKS) provides a robust environment for deploying and managing containerized applications with Kubernetes. It simplifies the process of building, delivering, and scaling containerized applications and microservices. This section details the steps involved in deploying applications to AKS, starting with the creation of an AKS cluster, configuring the necessary resources, and deploying containerized applications.

The first step in deploying to AKS is to create an AKS cluster. This involves setting up the Kubernetes control plane and the necessary nodes where the applications will run. The following Azure CLI command creates an AKS cluster:

```
az aks create --resource-group MyResourceGroup --name MyAKSCluster --node-count 3
    --enable-addons monitoring --generate-ssh-keys
```

This command creates an AKS cluster named MyAKSCluster in the resource group MyResourceGroup with three nodes and enables monitoring using Azure Monitor. The –generate-ssh-keys flag generates SSH keys for secure access to the nodes.

Once the AKS cluster is created, configure kubectl to connect to the cluster using the following command:

```
az aks get-credentials --resource-group MyResourceGroup --name MyAKSCluster
```

This command merges the cluster's configuration into the /.kube/config file, allowing kubectl to interact with the AKS cluster. To verify the connectivity, run:

```
kubectl get nodes
```

A successful connection will display a list of nodes in the cluster:

```
NAME                              STATUS   ROLES   AGE   VERSION
aks-nodepool1-12345678-vmss000000 Ready    agent   10m   v1.20.7
aks-nodepool1-12345678-vmss000001 Ready    agent   10m   v1.20.7
aks-nodepool1-12345678-vmss000002 Ready    agent   10m   v1.20.7
```

With the AKS cluster prepared, containerized applications can now be deployed. Containers are defined in Kubernetes using manifests, typically written in YAML format. For instance, a simple deployment of a web application using a Docker image might look like the following:

```
apiVersion: apps/v1
kind: Deployment
metadata:
  name: web-app
spec:
  replicas: 3
  selector:
    matchLabels:
      app: web-app
  template:
    metadata:
      labels:
        app: web-app
    spec:
      containers:
      - name: web-app
        image: mydockerhubusername/web-app:latest
        ports:
        - containerPort: 80
```

This deployment manifest specifies a Deployment that creates three replicas of the web-app container using the image mydockerhubusername/web-app:latest and exposes port 80.

Apply this configuration to the AKS cluster using:

```
kubectl apply -f web-app-deployment.yaml
```

The application is now deployed, but it needs to be accessible from outside the cluster. To achieve this, create a Service of type LoadBalancer:

```
apiVersion: v1
kind: Service
metadata:
  name: web-app-service
spec:
  selector:
    app: web-app
```

```
  ports:
    - protocol: TCP
      port: 80
      targetPort: 80
  type: LoadBalancer
```

Apply the service manifest using:

```
kubectl apply -f web-app-service.yaml
```

After the service is created, Kubernetes assigns an external IP address to the service for accessing the application. To check the external IP address, use:

```
kubectl get service web-app-service
```

The output will display the service details including the external IP:

```
NAME             TYPE           CLUSTER-IP    EXTERNAL-IP     PORT(S)        AGE
web-app-service  LoadBalancer   10.0.87.237   52.224.190.10   80:31554/TCP   5m
```

Navigate to the external IP in a web browser to access the deployed web application.

In scenarios requiring more complex configurations, such as managing secrets, config maps, or deploying Helm charts, AKS seamlessly integrates with various tools and services. For instance, using Helm, a package manager for Kubernetes, complex applications can be deployed easily. Install a Helm chart using:

```
helm install my-release stable/nginx-ingress
```

This command installs the NGINX ingress controller, enabling better traffic management for the deployed applications.

Through these steps, deploying applications to Azure Kubernetes Service (AKS) involves creating a cluster, configuring kubectl, defining deployment manifests, and setting up services to expose the applications. By leveraging the power of Kubernetes, AKS provides a flexible and scalable environment for managing modern containerized applications.

8.12 Monitoring and Feedback in Azure DevOps

Monitoring and feedback mechanisms are critical components of the DevOps lifecycle, ensuring that applications run smoothly, performance bottlenecks are identified, and any occurring issues are swiftly resolved. Azure DevOps provides a robust set of tools for monitoring applications and gathering actionable feedback. These tools facilitate real-time visibility into application performance, enabling proactive management and continuous improvement.

Azure Monitor is the primary service for monitoring in Azure. It collects and analyzes telemetry data from applications, enabling you to understand how your applications are performing and preemptively identify issues that affect their performance and availability. Azure Monitor encompasses several features:

- **Application Insights**: This is a feature of Azure Monitor designed for developers to monitor live applications. It automatically detects performance anomalies and includes powerful analytics tools to help diagnose issues and understand user interactions with your application. Application Insights can be integrated with various developer tools and services, including Azure DevOps.
- **Log Analytics**: This feature helps users collect and analyze data generated by resources in their cloud and on-premises environments. Logs can be queried using the Kusto Query Language (KQL) to identify trends, troubleshoot issues, and gather insights.
- **Azure Metrics Explorer**: This tool allows you to interactively work with the metrics data, creating rich visualizations, and providing a platform for detailed analysis of performance metrics.

Application Insights Integration with Azure DevOps begins with configuring Application Insights in your application. This setup allows the collection of detailed telemetry data such as request rates, response times, failure rates, and exception traces. To enable Application Insights in an ASP.NET application, for example, you can use the following code:

```
public void ConfigureServices(IServiceCollection services)
{
    services.AddApplicationInsightsTelemetry(Configuration["ApplicationInsights:
         InstrumentationKey"]);
```

```
}
```

After configuring Application Insights, the collected data can be visualized in the Azure DevOps dashboard. This integration allows for real-time telemetry data to be accessible within Azure DevOps, enabling teams to monitor application performance and quality directly from their DevOps environment.

Setting Up Alerts in Azure Monitor is another essential practice for efficient incident management. Alerts proactively notify teams about critical conditions. Follow these steps to set up an alert:

- Navigate to the Azure Monitor and click on Alerts.
- Select New alert rule.
- Define the resource on which you want to set the alert.
- Configure the condition, selecting the signal logic (e.g., CPU percentage, request rate).
- Set the action group. The action group determines what actions are taken when the alert is triggered (e.g., sending emails, invoking webhooks).
- Define the alert details, such as the severity and alert name.
- Create the alert.

```
{
  "name": "highCpuUsageAlert",
  "properties": {
    "description": "Alert for high CPU usage",
    "severity": 3,
    "enabled": true,
    "condition": {
      "allOf": [
        {
          "metricName": "Percentage CPU",
          "metricNamespace": "Microsoft.Compute/virtualMachines",
          "operator": "GreaterThan",
          "threshold": 80,
          "timeAggregation": "Average"
        }
      ]
    },
    "actions": [
      {
        "actionGroupId": "/subscriptions/{subscription-id}/resourceGroups/{resource-
            group}/providers/microsoft.insights/actiongroups/{action-group-name}"
      }
    ]
```

```
  }
}
```

Azure DevOps and Azure Monitor work synergistically to close the loop in the feedback cycle by supporting continuous monitoring, logging, alerting, and diagnostics. This integration facilitates identifying issues early, expediting resolution times, and ultimately enhancing the reliability and performance of applications.

Feedback Mechanisms in Azure DevOps are pivotal for fostering a continuous improvement culture. Azure DevOps provides features such as:

- **Work Items**: These are used to track features, user stories, bugs, and tasks. Work items can be linked to commits, branches, and pull requests, providing a comprehensive traceability from requirements to deployment.
- **Dashboards**: Customizable dashboards present a consolidated view of project health and are indispensable for real-time decision-making. Teams can create widgets to visualize key performance metrics, work item progress, and deployment statuses.
- **Analytics Services**: These services extend the reporting capabilities of Azure DevOps by enabling the creation of custom reports. It uses OData to expose data stored in Azure DevOps and can be utilized in tools like Power BI for advanced analysis.

By leveraging these tools, teams can gather targeted feedback from users and stakeholders, track the status of their development activities, and monitor the overall health of their projects comprehensively.

```
Example output after setting up a dashboard with monitoring widgets:

Widgets:
- Work Item Overview: Shows progress of active sprints.
- Deployment Status: Indicates latest commit deployments and statuses.
- Application Performance: Real-time graph of request rates and response times.
```

Enterprise-grade monitoring and feedback loops are vital for the operational success of software projects. Utilizing the full spectrum of Azure DevOps and Azure Monitor's capabilities ensures a seamless and efficient lifecycle process, proactively maintaining application integrity and continuously aligning with business objectives.

Chapter 9

Monitoring and Optimizing Azure

This chapter covers essential techniques and tools for monitoring and optimizing Azure environments. It includes an introduction to Azure Monitor, logging and metrics, and Application Insights. The chapter also addresses network monitoring with Azure Network Watcher, security monitoring with Azure Sentinel, and strategies for cost management and performance optimization. Additionally, it discusses autoscaling, leveraging Azure Advisor for best practices, and implementing effective alerting and notification systems.

9.1 Introduction to Monitoring in Azure

Monitoring in Azure is a critical component for managing and maintaining the health, performance, and reliability of your applications and infrastructure. It provides visibility into the operations of your systems, enabling proactive and reactive measures to ensure optimal performance and uptime.

Azure offers a comprehensive suite of monitoring tools and services designed to help you collect, analyze, and act on a wide range of telemetry data. This telemetry data is crucial for understanding the behavior of your systems, diagnosing issues, and making informed decisions to optimize performance and cost.

One of the foundational tools for monitoring in Azure is **Azure Monitor**. Azure Monitor provides a unified solution for collecting, analyzing, and responding to telemetry from your cloud and on-premises environments. It integrates with various Azure services to collect metrics, logs, and traces, and it offers robust analytics capabilities to derive insights and visualize data.

Azure Monitor includes several key components:

- **Metrics**: Quantitative measurements collected at regular intervals that provide insights into the performance and health of your resources.
- **Logs**: Detailed records of events and activities that occur within your systems, useful for troubleshooting and auditing purposes.
- **Alerts**: Notifications and automated actions triggered based on specific conditions within your metrics and logs, allowing you to respond proactively to issues.
- **Dashboards**: Customizable visual representations of your telemetry data, helping you monitor and understand the health and performance of your systems.

Metrics are vital for understanding the real-time performance of your services. They provide data points such as CPU usage, memory consumption, disk I/O, and network traffic. These metrics can be aggregated, filtered, and visualized to detect trends and identify anomalies.

Logs provide a more detailed view of system activities and events. These can include diagnostic logs, application logs, and security logs, among others. Collecting and analyzing logs helps you perform root cause analysis, track user activities, and ensure compliance with security policies.

Azure Monitor can automatically collect the necessary metrics and logs from most Azure resources. For instance, it can gather data from virtual machines, app services, databases, and storage accounts, among other resources. Additionally, it supports custom metrics and logs, allowing you to extend its capabilities to suit specific monitoring needs.

Alerts in Azure Monitor enhance your ability to react quickly to potential issues. Alerts can be configured based on thresholds or patterns in your telemetry data. When an alert condition is met, Azure Monitor can not only notify administrators but also trigger automated actions such as scaling operations, executing Azure Logic Apps, or invoking Azure Functions, enabling a seamless and responsive management strategy.

Dashboards are crucial for visualizing and making sense of the vast amounts of data collected by Azure Monitor. They offer interactive interfaces where you can pin specific metrics, logs, and other visual elements. These dashboards can be shared with team members, providing a central place for monitoring key performance indicators (KPIs) and operational status.

Another significant aspect of monitoring in Azure involves **Application Insights**. This feature of Azure Monitor focuses on the application layer, providing detailed telemetry for web applications and services. Application Insights collects performance data, user metrics, and diagnostic information across your applications, enabling in-depth analysis and troubleshooting.

The integration of Application Insights with Azure Monitor allows for end-to-end visibility into your application stack. From tracking request latencies and failure rates to analyzing user behavior and application dependencies, Application Insights provides a holistic view to optimize application performance and reliability.

For network monitoring, Azure provides tools such as **Azure Network Watcher**. This service offers capabilities to monitor, diagnose, and gain insights into your network performance and health. It supports flow logs, packet capture, and network topology visualization, providing a comprehensive view of your network infrastructure.

Security monitoring is another crucial aspect, addressed by **Azure Sentinel**. Azure Sentinel is a scalable, cloud-native security information and event management (SIEM) solution that collects, detects, and responds to security threats. It integrates with various data sources, including Azure services, on-premises systems, and third-party solutions, to provide a comprehensive security posture.

Efficient monitoring in Azure involves leveraging the full array of tools and services available to ensure that your applications and infrastructure are running at peak performance and are secure. By understanding and utilizing Azure Monitor, Application Insights, Network Watcher, and Azure Sentinel, you can build a robust monitoring strategy that supports your operational goals and compliance requirements, enabling a resilient and well-optimized Azure environment.

9.2 Getting Started with Azure Monitor

Azure Monitor provides comprehensive monitoring capabilities for applications, infrastructure, and networks within the Azure ecosystem. It serves as the foundational service for monitoring health, performance, and availability of Azure resources, by collecting, analyzing, and acting on telemetry data.

Azure Monitor's architecture is based on several key components: data collection, data analysis, and response mechanisms. Data collection is facilitated through diagnostic settings, Azure Monitor agents, and integration with other Azure services, such as Application Insights and Log Analytics. Data analysis is achieved through metrics and logs, while responses are managed through alerts, automated actions, and visualizations.

To effectively utilize Azure Monitor, begin by identifying the resources and metrics that are critical for your application and infrastructure. Following this, configure diagnostic settings for these resources to collect the necessary data. Azure Monitor can collect data from various sources, including:

- **Application Monitoring Data:** Captures application performance and behavior data using Application Insights.
- **Guest OS Monitoring Data:** Gathers performance data from operating systems using the Azure Monitor agent or Azure Diagnostics extension.
- **Resource Monitoring Data:** Collects data about the operation of Azure resources.
- **Subscription Monitoring Data:** Aggregates diagnostic logs and metrics from across a subscription using Activity Logs.
- **Azure Monitoring Data:** Acquires platform metrics related to Azure services.

Setting up monitoring involves configuring metrics and logs.

```
# Configure diagnostics settings for a resource
az monitor diagnostic-settings create \
  --resource /subscriptions/{subscription-id}/resourceGroups/{resource-group}/
      providers/{resource-provider}/{resource-name} \
  --workspace {log-analytics-workspace-id} \
  --name {diagnostic-setting-name} \
```

```
--metrics '[{"category": "AllMetrics", "enabled": true}]' \
--logs '[{"category": "Administrative", "enabled": true, "retentionPolicy": {"days":
    30, "enabled": true}}]'
```

This command configures a diagnostic setting for the specified resource, directing logs and metrics to a Log Analytics workspace. The metrics will be enabled for the category 'AllMetrics', and logs will be collected for the 'Administrative' category, with a retention policy of 30 days.

To configure and visualize metrics in the Azure portal:

- Navigate to Azure Monitor in the Azure portal.
- Under Insights, select Metrics.
- Choose the resource you wish to monitor.
- Select the metric namespace and metrics of interest.
- Create charts to visualize data trends.

Example of visualizing metrics in a chart:

```
# In the Azure Portal Metrics page:
# 1. Select a scope for your data (e.g., Virtual Machine)
# 2. Choose a metric namespace (e.g., "Virtual Machine Host")
# 3. Select a metric (e.g., "Percentage CPU")
# 4. Set the aggregation type (e.g., "Average")
# 5. Customize the timeframe and visualization type
# 6. Add the metric to a workbook for a consolidated view
```

Analyzing collected data involves using Azure Monitor logs, which are stored in Log Analytics workspaces. Use Azure Log Analytics' robust query language, Kusto Query Language (KQL), to query logs and analyze data effectively.

```
# Sample KQL query to analyze Virtual Machine's CPU usage trends over the last 7
    days
Perf
| where TimeGenerated > ago(7d)
| where CounterName == "% Processor Time"
| summarize avg(CounterValue) by bin(TimeGenerated, 1h)
| render timechart
```

This query retrieves the average CPU usage for each hour over the past 7 days and renders the results as a time chart.

Response actions are managed using alerts and automated responses. This includes setting up alert rules based on specific criteria and automating responses using Azure Logic Apps, Azure Automation, or integration with other systems.

```
# Create an alert rule for CPU usage going above a threshold
az monitor metrics alert create \
   --name HighCPUAlert \
   --resource-group {resource-group} \
   --scopes /subscriptions/{subscription-id}/resourceGroups/{resource-group}/
         providers/Microsoft.Compute/virtualMachines/{vm-name} \
   --condition "avg Percentage CPU > 80" \
   --description "Alert for high CPU usage" \
   --window-size 5m \
   --evaluation-frequency 1m \
   --action-group {action-group-id}
```

This command creates an alert rule that triggers when the average CPU usage of a Virtual Machine exceeds 80

By following these steps and utilizing Azure Monitor's rich feature set, you can establish a robust monitoring framework for proactive management of your Azure environment. This will provide crucial insights into the health and performance of your applications and infrastructure, enabling you to maintain optimal operations.

9.3 Azure Logs and Metrics

Understanding and effectively utilizing Azure's logging and metrics capabilities is essential for maintaining the health, performance, and security of any application running within the Azure ecosystem. Logs and metrics provide critical insights that can be harnessed for troubleshooting, optimization, and proactive monitoring.

Azure Monitor is the central hub for all monitoring data in Azure, including logs and metrics. Logs in Azure are structured and center around the activities that occur within resources, while metrics provide numerical values that describe some aspect of a system at a specific point in time.

Azure logs include activity logs and diagnostic logs. The activity logs contain information about operations performed on resources within your subscription, while the diagnostic logs provide insights about the internal operations of those resources.

```
# Enable Activity Log collection in a Log Analytics workspace
az monitor diagnostic-settings create \
  --name "activitylog-diagnostic" \
  --resource "/subscriptions/{subscription-id}" \
  --workspace "/subscriptions/{subscription-id}/resourcegroups/{resource-group}/
        providers/Microsoft.OperationalInsights/workspaces/{workspace-name}" \
```

```
--logs '[{"category": "Administrative", "enabled": true, "retentionPolicy": {"enabled":
      false, "days": 0}}, {"category": "Security", "enabled": true, "retentionPolicy":
      {"enabled": false, "days": 0}}, {"category": "ServiceHealth", "enabled": true, "
      retentionPolicy": {"enabled": false, "days": 0}}, {"category": "Alert", "enabled":
      true, "retentionPolicy": {"enabled": false, "days": 0}}, {"category": "
      Recommendation", "enabled": true, "retentionPolicy": {"enabled": false, "days":
      0}}]'
```

To analyze and query logs, Azure provides Kusto Query Language (KQL), a powerful tool for querying the Azure Log Analytics workspace. Here is an example of a KQL query to retrieve errors from a specific resource over the last 24 hours:

```
AzureDiagnostics
| where TimeGenerated > ago(24h)
| where ResourceId == "/subscriptions/{subscription-id}/resourcegroups/{resource-
    group}/providers/Microsoft.Compute/virtualMachines/{virtual-machine}"
| where Level == "Error"
| project TimeGenerated, ResourceId, OperationName, Level, Message
```

Metrics, on the other hand, provide quantitative performance data over time. Metrics in Azure are usually pre-defined and collected automatically. They consist of numerical data points reported at regular intervals. Metrics data can also be analyzed using Azure Monitor. For example, the following shows how to query CPU utilization metrics for a virtual machine:

```
# Retrieve CPU utilization metrics for a virtual machine
az monitor metrics list \
  --resource "/subscriptions/{subscription-id}/resourceGroups/{resource-group}/
      providers/Microsoft.Compute/virtualMachines/{virtual-machine}" \
  --metric "Percentage CPU" \
  --interval PT1H \
  --aggregation Average
```

The metrics API output can provide valuable insights. The following is an example of the metrics query output in JSON format:


```
{
 "cost": 0,
 "timespan": "2023-01-01T00:00:00Z/2023-01-01T01:00:00Z",
 "interval": "PT1H",
 "value": [
  {
   "id": "/subscriptions/{subscription-id}/resourceGroups/{resource-group}/providers/Microsoft.Compute/virtualMachines/{virtual-machine}/providers/Microsoft.Insights/metrics/Percentage CPU",
   "type": "Microsoft.Insights/metrics",
   "name": {
    "value": "Percentage CPU",
    "localizedValue": "Percentage CPU"
   },
   "timeseries": [
    {
     "data": [
      {
       "timeStamp": "2023-01-01T00:00:00Z",
       "average": 15.3
      },
      {
       "timeStamp": "2023-01-01T01:00:00Z",
       "average": 14.9
      }
     ]
    }
   ]
  }
 ]
}
```


Azure Monitor Metrics also provides the ability to create and manage alerts based on metrics values. Threshold-based alerts can be configured to notify stakeholders when a certain metric crosses a predefined limit. This can be particularly useful for proactive monitoring and avoiding downtime. The following example demonstrates how to create a metric alert rule for CPU usage:

```
# Create an alert rule for CPU usage
az monitor metrics alert create \
  --name "high-cpu-alert" \
  --resource-group "{resource-group}" \
  --scopes "/subscriptions/{subscription-id}/resourceGroups/{resource-group}/
      providers/Microsoft.Compute/virtualMachines/{virtual-machine}" \
  --condition "avg Percentage CPU > 80" \
  --description "Alert when CPU usage is greater than 80%" \
  --action "/subscriptions/{subscription-id}/resourceGroups/{resource-group}/
      providers/microsoft.insights/actionGroups/{action-group}"
```

Collecting and analyzing logs and metrics can provide deep visibility into the operational health and performance of your Azure resources. Best practices include structuring your logging and metrics strategy to cover all critical areas, such as availability, performance, security, and compliance.

Integrating logs and metrics with platforms like Azure Logic Apps, Power BI, or third-party tools can enhance the visualization and analysis capabilities, leading to better-informed decision-making.

9.4 Application Insights

Application Insights is a comprehensive application performance management (APM) service offered by Microsoft Azure. It is designed to help developers and IT professionals monitor and analyze the performance and usage of their applications in real-time. By leveraging Application Insights, teams can gain deep insights into their application's performance, detect anomalies, diagnose issues, and understand the end-user experience.

Application Insights provides a robust set of features, including telemetry data collection, powerful analytics, and diagnostics capabilities. This section delves into the core components, configuration, telemetry data, custom events, and metrics analysis using Application Insights.

Core Components of Application Insights

At its heart, Application Insights relies on a few core components to provide a seamless monitoring and diagnostics experience:

- **SDK (Software Development Kit)**: Application Insights SDK is integrated into the application code, which collects telemetry data such as request rates, response times, dependency rates, exceptions, and the performance of the application.

- **Instrumentation Key**: This is a unique key provided when creating an Application Insights resource in the Azure portal. It is used to associate the telemetry data collected by the SDK with your Application Insights resource.
- **Telemetry Data**: This encompasses a variety of data types including traces, events, metrics, performance counters, and exceptions. All these telemetry data points are collected and sent to the Application Insights service.
- **Azure Portal**: The Azure Portal provides a rich interface for analyzing the collected telemetry data. It includes powerful query and visualization tools, such as Metrics Explorer, Log Analytics, and Application Map.

Configuring Application Insights

The configuration of Application Insights involves setting up the SDK in your application and associating it with an Application Insights resource. Below are steps to configure Application Insights for an ASP.NET Core application:

1. **Create Application Insights Resource**: Navigate to the Azure Portal and create an Application Insights resource. Copy the instrumentation key provided.
2. **Install SDK**: Add the Application Insights SDK to your project. For example, in a .NET Core application, you can install the following NuGet package:

```
dotnet add package Microsoft.ApplicationInsights.AspNetCore
```

3. **Configure SDK**: Include the instrumentation key in your application settings. Then, modify the 'Startup.cs' file to add Application Insights services.

```
public class Startup
{
    public void ConfigureServices(IServiceCollection services)
    {
        services.AddApplicationInsightsTelemetry(Configuration["
            ApplicationInsights:InstrumentationKey"]);
    }
```

```
public void Configure(IApplicationBuilder app, IHostingEnvironment
    env)
{
    app.UseApplicationInsightsRequestTelemetry();
    app.UseApplicationInsightsExceptionTelemetry();
    // other middleware
}
}
```

After these steps, the application will start sending telemetry data to your Application Insights resource.

Telemetry Data and Custom Events

Application Insights automatically collects several types of telemetry data:

- **Request Telemetry**: Information about incoming HTTP requests, including URL, response time, and status code.
- **Dependency Telemetry**: Data about external calls made by the application to services such as databases, REST APIs, etc.
- **Exception Telemetry**: Details about any unhandled exceptions and stack traces that occur within the application.
- **Page View Telemetry**: Information about client-side page views for web applications.

Developers can also log custom events and metrics to provide more specific insights into the application's performance. For example:

```
var telemetryClient = new TelemetryClient();
telemetryClient.TrackEvent("UserLogin", new Dictionary<string, string>
{
    { "User", "JohnDoe" },
    { "Role", "Admin" }
});
```

This custom event can be queried and analyzed using the powerful analytics tools within Application Insights.

Analyzing Telemetry Data

The Azure Portal offers multiple tools to analyze the collected telemetry data:

- **Metrics Explorer**: Use this to create rich interactive dashboards, visualize key metrics over time, and set up charts that help in understanding performance trends.

- **Log Analytics**: Utilize Kusto Query Language (KQL) to create complex queries, extract insights, and diagnose issues from the collected telemetry data.
- **Application Map**: This provides a visual map of application components and their dependencies, highlighting performance bottlenecks and failure points.

Here is an example of a basic KQL query to retrieve failed requests:

```
requests
| where success == false
| order by timestamp desc
```

The results of this query can then be visualized or further analyzed to identify patterns and diagnose issues.

Application Insights is highly extensible and supports integration with other Azure services like Azure DevOps, Power BI, and Logic Apps, enhancing its capabilities for monitoring, alerting, and incident management.

Incorporating Application Insights into your monitoring strategy provides a robust framework to ensure application reliability, performance, and user satisfaction. This aligns with the broader goals of effective monitoring and optimization within Azure environments.

9.5 Network Monitoring with Azure Network Watcher

Azure Network Watcher is a powerful suite of tools designed specifically for monitoring, diagnosing, and gaining insights into the network performance and health of your Azure deployments. This service provides the necessary tools to capture and analyze network traffic, diagnose network issues, and visualize network topologies.

Azure Network Watcher offers several features that facilitate comprehensive network monitoring:

- **Topology**
- **Connection Monitor**
- **IP Flow Verify**

- **Next Hop**
- **Security Group View**
- **Packet Capture**
- **NSG Flow Logs**

Topology: The topology feature of Network Watcher allows you to visualize the network resources in your virtual network. It provides a graphical representation of all the network interfaces, network security groups, and other network resources. This visualization helps in understanding the overall layout and relationships between network components.

To retrieve the network topology, you can use the Azure CLI as follows:

```
az network watcher show-topology --location <region> --resource-group <resource-
    group-name>
```

The parameters specified include the location of your resources and the resource group that contains them. A successful command execution will produce a visual map of your network components.

```
{
  "id": "/subscriptions/.../topologies/default",
  "location": "eastus",
  "resourceId": "/subscriptions/.../resourceGroups/...",
  ...
}
```

Connection Monitor: Connection Monitor helps verify the reachability and latency between different points in your virtual network. It can monitor both cross-vNet and on-premises to Azure connectivity.

To set up a Connection Monitor using the Azure CLI:

```
az network watcher connection-monitor create --resource-group <resource-group-name>
    --name <monitor-name> --location <region> --source-resource <source-resource-
    id> --dest-resource <dest-resource-id> --dest-port <port-number>
```

The key parameters include the resource group, monitor name, region, source resource ID, destination resource ID, and destination port. Once created, Connection Monitor will start tracking connection status and latency.

IP Flow Verify: The IP Flow Verify tool helps diagnose connectivity issues by verifying whether a packet is allowed or denied based on the security group rules. This feature ensures traffic either reaches its intended destination or provides information on why it might be blocked.

To verify IP flow:

```
az network watcher test-ip-flow --resource-group <resource-group-name> --location <
    region> --direction <Inbound/Outbound> --protocol <Protocol> --local <Source
    details> --remote <Destination details>
```

Results indicate whether the traffic is allowed or denied along with the corresponding security rule applied.

Next Hop: The Next Hop feature helps determine the next hop in the network route for a packet to reach its destination, providing insights into effective route configurations.

To use Next Hop:

```
az network watcher show-next-hop --resource-group <resource-group-name> --network-
    interface <interface-name> --source-ip <source-ip> --dest-ip <destination-ip>
```

The information returned will include the next hop type and IP address, ensuring that packets take the intended routes.

Security Group View: This feature provides detailed insights into the security rules applied to network interfaces within a network security group, aiding in the efficient management of security configurations.

To get a view of the security group:

```
az network watcher show-security-group-view --resource-group <resource-group-name>
    --network-interface <interface-name>
```

The resulting output details the security rules applied to the specified network interface.

Packet Capture: Packet Capture allows you to capture network traffic for further analysis. It is useful for troubleshooting latency and detecting suspicious activities within the network.

To create a packet capture session:

```
az network watcher packet-capture create --resource-group <resource-group-name> --
    network-watcher-name <watcher-name> --vm <vm-name> --name <capture-
    name> --storage-account <storage-account> --filters <filters>
```

This command captures packets on the specified virtual machine and stores the data in your storage account for subsequent analysis.

NSG Flow Logs: NSG Flow Logs record information about the ingress and egress IP traffic through a Network Security Group. This helps in identifying traffic patterns and potential security threats.

To enable NSG Flow Logs:

```
az network watcher flow-log configure --nsg <nsg-name> --resource-group <resource-
    group-name> --enabled true --storage-account <storage-account-name> --
    retention <retention-days> --traffic-analytics true
```

This configuration logs traffic data and stores it in your storage account, optionally enabling traffic analytics for deeper insights.

The tools provided by Azure Network Watcher enable a comprehensive strategy for monitoring and diagnosing network issues within your Azure environment, ensuring that network performance remains optimal and security baselines are maintained. By leveraging these tools and their corresponding Azure CLI commands, administrators gain granular control and visibility over their network resources.

9.6 Security Monitoring with Azure Sentinel

Azure Sentinel is a comprehensive security information and event management (SIEM) solution that provides intelligent security analytics and threat intelligence across the enterprise. It enables the collection, detection, investigation, and response to security threats in real-time. By leveraging the power of machine learning and artificial intelligence, Azure Sentinel can analyze large volumes of data and help organizations identify potential security incidents before they result in damage.

Azure Sentinel integrates with many Microsoft and third-party security solutions, allowing for centralized security operations within a single pane of glass. This section will cover the essential components and functionalities of Azure Sentinel, including data connectors, analytics rules, workbooks, and playbooks.

Azure Sentinel's primary components include:

- **Data Connectors:** Data connectors facilitate the ingestion of data from various sources into Azure Sentinel. These sources can include Azure services like Azure Activity Logs, Office 365, and Microsoft Defender ATP, as well as non-Microsoft solutions through custom connectors or API integrations. Configuring data connectors ensures that Sentinel has access to all relevant security information.

- **Analytics Rules:** Analytics rules in Azure Sentinel are used to generate alerts based on specific criteria. These rules can be created using Kusto Query Language (KQL) to filter and correlate data from different sources. Once the criteria are met, an alert is generated, and security incidents can be investigated.

- **Workbooks:** Workbooks are customizable dashboards that provide visualizations and insights into the data collected by Azure Sentinel. They help security analysts monitor and analyze security events and trends, ensuring that they can respond swiftly to potential threats.

- **Playbooks:** Playbooks in Azure Sentinel are automated workflows built on Azure Logic Apps. They can be used to respond to alerts by taking predefined actions, such as sending notifications, creating tickets, or integrating with other security tools. Playbooks enhance the efficiency and consistency of incident response.

```
let suspicious_signins =
    SigninLogs
    | where ResultType != "0"
    | summarize count() by Location;
suspicious_signins
```

The above code snippet is an example of an analytics rule using KQL. This rule identifies sign-in attempts that were unsuccessful and summarizes the count of such attempts by location. The results of this query can be used to create an alert if the number of failed sign-ins from a particular location exceeds a specified threshold.

Once an alert is generated, Azure Sentinel facilitates the investigation process by providing detailed information about the incident. Analysts can drill down into the raw log data, view timeline events, and assess the potential impact. Sentinel allows the creation of incidents, which are collections of related alerts that provide a comprehensive view of a security event.

```
Alert: Unusual Sign-In Activity Detected
Timestamp: 2023-10-01T12:00:00Z
Source IP: 203.0.113.4
Location: United States
Failed Attempts: 15
```

The example above shows a potential output from an alert generated by the custom analytics rule. Analysts can use this information to investigate further, identify the cause of the failed sign-ins, and take required actions to mitigate potential security risks.

Workbooks in Azure Sentinel provide the means to create interactive reports and dashboards that visualize security data. Analysts can design workbooks to display trends, key metrics, and insights relevant to their needs. This visual representation aids in quickly identifying anomalies and assessing the overall security posture.

```
SigninLogs
| where ResultType == 0
| summarize success_count = count() by bin(TimeGenerated, 1h)
| render timechart
```

The query above visualizes the count of successful sign-ins over time, creating a timechart that helps analysts see patterns and identify periods of unusual sign-in activity.

Playbooks are an essential component for automating responses to security incidents. They are triggered by analytics alerts and can perform a variety of actions to address the detected threat. For example, a playbook might automatically block a suspicious IP address, notify the security team via email, or open a ticket in a third-party IT service management system.

```
# Azure Logic Apps code snippet to block IP address and send notification
import requests

# Block the IP address using Azure Firewall
def block_ip(ip_address):
    firewall_url = "https://management.azure.com/subscriptions/{subscription-id}/
        resourceGroups/{resource-group}/providers/Microsoft.Network/azureFirewalls
        /{firewall-name}/rules/{rule-name}?api-version=2020-11-01"
    headers = {"Authorization": "Bearer {access-token}"}
    payload = {
        "properties": {
            "ruleType": "NetworkRule",
            "description": "Block suspicious IP",
            "sourceAddresses": [ip_address],
            "destinationAddresses": ["*"],
            "destinationPorts": ["*"],
            "protocols": ["Any"]
        }
    }
    response = requests.put(firewall_url, json=payload, headers=headers)
    return response.status_code

# Send email notification
def send_notification(email, ip_address):
    email_service_url = "https://api.emailservice.com/send"
    payload = {
        "to": email,
```

```
        "subject": "Alert: Suspicious IP Blocked",
        "body": f"Suspicious IP {ip_address} has been blocked."
    }
    response = requests.post(email_service_url, json=payload)
    return response.status_code

# Main function to execute playbook actions
def main():
    ip_address = "203.0.113.4" # Example suspicious IP
    admin_email = "securityadmin@example.com"

    block_status = block_ip(ip_address)
    notify_status = send_notification(admin_email, ip_address)

    return block_status, notify_status

if __name__ == "__main__":
    main()
```

This example playbook automates actions to block a suspicious IP address using Azure Firewall and sends an email notification to the security administrator. By leveraging automation through playbooks, organizations can enhance their response times and streamline security operations.

Azure Sentinel also provides integration capabilities with other Microsoft security solutions such as Microsoft Defender, as well as with third-party solutions through REST APIs or custom connectors. This integration expands Sentinel's functionality and ensures comprehensive coverage of an organization's security landscape.

Through continuous monitoring, advanced analytics, and automated response capabilities, Azure Sentinel empowers organizations to proactively manage security threats and protect their assets effectively. Azure Sentinel represents a scalable, cloud-native SIEM solution that addresses the challenges of modern security monitoring and threat detection.

9.7 Performance Tuning and Optimization

Performance tuning and optimization in Azure involves a combination of proactive monitoring and reactive adjustments. This section delves into the methods and tools you can employ to ensure Azure services and applications run efficiently, minimizing both resource consumption and operational costs.

The cornerstone of performance tuning is the effective analysis of metrics and logs. Azure Monitor plays a crucial role by offering insights into resource utilization, response times, error rates, and other critical performance indicators. By understanding these metrics, you can pinpoint bottlenecks and inefficiencies within your Azure environment.

Azure Monitor allows you to set up dashboards, alerts, and automated actions based on predefined thresholds. For example, you might monitor CPU utilization for a virtual machine, disk I/O operations, or memory usage, and configure alerts that notify you or take corrective actions when metrics exceed typical operational values.

```
# Define the conditions under which the alert triggers
az monitor metrics alert create --name "HighCPUAlert" \
  --resource-group "yourResourceGroup" \
  --resource "/subscriptions/yourSubscriptionId/resourceGroups/yourResourceGroup/
      providers/Microsoft.Compute/virtualMachines/yourVM" \
  --condition "avg Percentage CPU > 80" \
  --description "Alert for high CPU usage"
```

When an alert is triggered, it's essential to perform a root cause analysis. Tools such as Azure Log Analytics, integrated into Azure Monitor, facilitate this by collecting and analyzing log data. Log Analytics can run queries to identify abnormal patterns and provide insights into the underlying issues. Querying large datasets efficiently is crucial, and Kusto Query Language (KQL) is the language used to perform these queries in Azure.

```
// Analyze average CPU utilization for the last 24 hours
Perf
| where TimeGenerated > ago(24h)
| where CounterName == "Percentage CPU"
| summarize avg(CounterValue) by Computer, bin(TimeGenerated, 1h)
| order by avg_CounterValue desc
```

Scaling is another critical component of performance optimization. Azure provides two primary scaling techniques: vertical scaling (scaling up) and horizontal scaling (scaling out). Vertical scaling involves adding more resources to a single instance, while horizontal scaling involves adding more instances to distribute the load.

For example, App Services can be scaled vertically by choosing higher-tier plans which provide more memory, CPU, and storage resources. Horizontal scaling is managed via the App Service Plan Scale-Out settings, allowing you to add additional instances based on specific rules or schedules.

```
# Scale up (vertical scaling) to a higher pricing tier
az appservice plan update --name "yourAppServicePlan" \
  --resource-group "yourResourceGroup" \
  --sku S1

# Scale out (horizontal scaling) to add more instances
```

```
az appservice plan update --name "yourAppServicePlan" \
  --resource-group "yourResourceGroup" \
  --number-of-workers 5
```

Autoscaling is particularly valuable for handling variable workloads. By defining autoscale rules, Azure can automatically adjust the number of instances based on CPU utilization, queue length, or other metrics. This ensures that applications can handle peak loads while minimizing costs during low-demand periods.

```
# Create an autoscale rule that adds instances when CPU > 75% for 5 minutes
az monitor autoscale rule create --resource-group "yourResourceGroup" \
  --autoscale-name "yourAutoscaleSettings" \
  --scale out 1 --condition "Percentage CPU > 75 avg 5m" \
  --scale in 1 --condition "Percentage CPU < 25 avg 5m" \
  --cooldown 10
```

High-performance storage solutions are also crucial to optimize application performance. Azure provides various storage options, from standard HDDs to high-performance SSDs. Choosing the right type of storage based on workload requirements can significantly impact performance. For example, Azure Premium Storage is optimized for IO-intensive workloads, offering low latency and high throughput.

Additionally, employing caching mechanisms like Azure Redis Cache can significantly reduce the load on databases by storing frequently accessed data in memory, thus providing faster access times.

```
# Create a new Azure Redis Cache instance
az redis create --name "yourRedisCache" \
  --resource-group "yourResourceGroup" \
  --location "eastus" \
  --sku "Premium" \
  --vm-size "P1"
```

Another essential part of performance tuning is database optimization. Tools like SQL Database Advisor provide recommendations for indexing, parameterization, and query performance. Additionally, using features like Read Scale-Out and geo-replication can improve read performance and provide high availability.

```
# Enable read scale-out on an Azure SQL database
az sql db replica create --resource-group "yourResourceGroup" \
  --server "yourSqlServer" \
  --name "yourDatabase" \
  --partner-server "yourSqlServer-secondary" \
  --partner-database "yourDatabase-secondary"
```

Effective use of these tools and strategies ensures that your Azure environment operates optimally, handling workload fluctuations and maximizing resource utilization. This ongoing process requires regular review and adjustment to accommodate changing application demands and technological advancements.

9.8 Autoscaling Applications in Azure

Autoscaling is a fundamental component in Azure that provides the ability to automatically adjust the computational resources allocated to your applications based on real-time demand, ensuring both cost efficiency and optimal performance. This section delves into the mechanisms of autoscaling within Azure and demonstrates how to effectively implement and manage these capabilities.

Azure's autoscaling is primarily achieved through two key services: **Virtual Machine Scale Sets (VMSS)** and **Azure App Service Autoscaling**. Each service offers distinct options and configurations to cater to different application types and requirements.

To illustrate how these services work, we will begin with an examination of Virtual Machine Scale Sets.

Virtual Machine Scale Sets (VMSS)

Virtual Machine Scale Sets enable you to create and manage a group of identical, load-balanced VMs. VMSS provides high availability and allows you to automatically increase or decrease the number of VMs in response to demand or a defined schedule.

Below is an example of how to create a sample VM scale set using the Azure CLI:

```
# Define variables
RESOURCE_GROUP=myResourceGroup
LOCATION=eastus
SCALESET_NAME=myScaleSet
IMAGE=UbuntuLTS

# Create a resource group
az group create --name $RESOURCE_GROUP --location $LOCATION

# Create a VM scale set
az vmss create --resource-group $RESOURCE_GROUP --name $SCALESET_NAME \
  --image $IMAGE --upgrade-policy-mode manual --custom-data cloud-init.txt \
  --admin-username azureuser --generate-ssh-keys
```

The above commands initialize a new resource group and create a VM scale set using the specified image and configuration.

Configuring Autoscale for a VM Scale Set

Once the VM scale set is created, configure autoscaling rules based on CPU usage. The following example demonstrates the process using the Azure CLI:

```
# Configure autoscale for the VM scale set
az monitor autoscale create --resource-group $RESOURCE_GROUP --name
    myAutoscaleSetting \
  --target-resource-id $(az vmss show --resource-group $RESOURCE_GROUP --name
     $SCALESET_NAME --query id --output tsv) \
  --min-count 2 --max-count 10 --count 2

# Add a rule to scale out if the average CPU usage is above 75% over a 5-minute
    period
az monitor autoscale rule create --resource-group $RESOURCE_GROUP --autoscale-
    name myAutoscaleSetting \
  --condition "Percentage CPU > 75 avg 5m" --scale out 1

# Add a rule to scale in if the average CPU usage is below 25% over a 10-minute
    period
az monitor autoscale rule create --resource-group $RESOURCE_GROUP --autoscale-
    name myAutoscaleSetting \
  --condition "Percentage CPU < 25 avg 10m" --scale in 1
```

In these commands, the autoscale configuration is set to a minimum of 2 VMs, a maximum of 10 VMs, and an initial instance count of 2. The autoscale rules ensure that the number of VMs is dynamically adjusted based on CPU usage.

Azure App Service Autoscaling

For web applications, mobile backends, and RESTful APIs, Azure App Service provides autoscale functionality without the need to manage virtual machines directly. Autoscaling in Azure App Service can be configured based on various metrics, such as HTTP requests, data throughput, or CPU load.

To configure autoscaling for an App Service, follow the same principles but use the Azure portal:

1. Navigate to the App Service in the Azure portal. 2. Select *Scale out (App Service plan)* under the *Settings* section. 3. Click *Add a rule* to define a new scaling rule.

The portal will offer options to set threshold values and determine the scaling actions.

For instance, you can define a rule as follows: - Increase the instance count by 1 if the average CPU usage exceeds 70- Decrease the instance count by 1 if the average CPU usage falls below 30

Policy-Based and Scheduled Autoscaling

Azure also supports scheduled autoscaling, which allows you to increase or decrease capacity at predetermined times. This approach is useful for handling known traffic patterns, such as peak times during business hours or specific promotional events.

Here's an example of how to configure scheduled autoscaling using Azure CLI for a VM scale set:

```
# Create a scheduled autoscale profile
az monitor autoscale profile create --resource-group $RESOURCE_GROUP --autoscale-
    name myAutoscaleSetting \
  --name OffPeakTimes --timezone "UTC" --start-time "00:00" --end-time "06:00" --
    recurrence week sat sun

# Scale down to 2 instances during off-peak hours
az monitor autoscale action create --resource-group $RESOURCE_GROUP --autoscale-
    name myAutoscaleSetting \
  --profile-name OffPeakTimes --scale-to 2
```

These commands configure a scaling profile named "OffPeakTimes" that reduces the scale set to 2 instances on Saturdays and Sundays between midnight and 6 AM UTC.

When configuring autoscaling, it is crucial to monitor the impact of scaling rules to ensure they align with actual workload patterns and performance requirements. Tools such as **Azure Monitor** and **Application Insights** can help track the utilization metrics and confirm that the autoscale actions are providing the desired results.

A thoughtful implementation of autoscaling not only optimizes costs by reducing the number of instances during low-demand periods but also ensures your applications are capable of handling increased load predictably and reliably.

9.9 Using Azure Advisor for Best Practices

Azure Advisor is an essential tool integrated into the Azure platform, designed to assist users in adhering to best practices when managing their Azure resources. By analyzing resource configurations and usage telemetry, Azure Advisor provides personalized recommendations in areas such as high availability, security, performance, and cost. Understanding how to leverage Azure Advisor can significantly enhance the efficiency and reliability of your cloud environment.

Azure Advisor offers actionable insights in five key categories: **Reliability**, **Security**, **Performance**, **Cost**, and **Operational Excellence**. Each recommendation includes specific actions users can take to optimize their resources. In this section, we will delve deeper into these categories, explore the types of recommendations provided, and demonstrate how to implement these suggestions effectively.

Reliability focuses on ensuring that your applications and services remain available and resilient. Recommendations might include enabling virtual machine backups, configuring disaster recovery, and deploying instances across multiple availability zones to avoid single points of failure. For example, Azure Advisor may suggest:

```
Enable backup for your virtual machines to ensure data resilience.
```

To implement the above recommendation, you would navigate to the "Backup" section in the Azure portal and configure the desired backup policy for each virtual machine.

Security involves protecting your resources against potential threats and vulnerabilities. Azure Advisor's recommendations for security can include enabling multi-factor authentication (MFA), configuring Network Security Groups (NSGs), and ensuring data encryption. Consider the following recommendation:

```
Configure Network Security Groups to restrict access to your virtual networks.
```

Applying this recommendation involves setting up NSGs to define and enforce rules that control incoming and outgoing network traffic to your resources.

Performance recommendations are aimed at improving the speed and responsiveness of your applications. These might involve resizing virtual machines, optimizing database queries, or implementing content delivery networks (CDNs) to reduce latency. For instance, a typical performance recommendation could be:

```
Consider scaling up your virtual machine to a higher SKU to handle increased
    workload.
```

To follow through, you can use the Azure portal's scaling options to upgrade your virtual machine instances to higher performance tiers suitable for your workload demands.

Cost recommendations help you achieve cost efficiency by identifying underutilized resources and suggesting ways to lower your expenses. This includes right-sizing virtual machines, deleting unused disks, and taking advantage of reserved instances. An example would be:

```
Right-size or delete underutilized virtual machines to save cost.
```

Implementing this recommendation involves reviewing resource usage metrics and adjusting the size or number of virtual machine instances to match your actual workload requirements more closely.

Operational Excellence is about ensuring that your cloud environment is well-governed and managed. Recommendations here might include setting up resource tagging, configuring resource locks, or establishing role-based access control (RBAC). An example recommendation might be:

```
Apply tags to your resources for better organization and management.
```

To act on this, you can use the tagging feature within the Azure portal to add metadata to your resources, which improves resource tracking and management.

```
Tag Name: Environment
Tag Value: Production
```

Utilizing the Azure portal, you can navigate to the desired resource, select the "Tags" feature, and apply relevant tags. This tagging process significantly enhances the operational management of resources, improving both discoverability and governance.

It is important to regularly review the Azure Advisor dashboard, which is accessible from the Azure portal. This dashboard aggregates recommendations and provides a consolidated view of your environment's health. Users can filter recommendations by category, resource type, or subscription, and each recommendation includes a detailed explanation with clear action steps.

```
Navigation Path: Azure Portal -> Advisor -> Recommendations
```

Additionally, you can use automation scripts to implement these recommendations efficiently. For example, to automate the right-sizing of virtual machines, you might write a script in PowerShell or Azure CLI. Below is an Azure CLI script that lists all virtual machines and then suggests resizing them based on predefined criteria:

```
# List all virtual machines in a subscription
az vm list --query "[].{Name:name, ResourceGroup:resourceGroup}" -o table

# Resize a specific virtual machine (example VM name and resource group)
az vm resize --resource-group MyResourceGroup --name MyVM --size
    Standard_DS3_v2
```

The output from the above command might look like the following, listing VM names and resource groups:

```
Name                    ResourceGroup
----------------------- -----------------
VM1                     MyResourceGroup
VM2                     MyResourceGroup2
```

Furthermore, integrating Azure Advisor with other Azure services can enhance the overall benefit. For example, combining insights from Azure Monitor and Azure Security Center can provide a more comprehensive view of both performance and security. Automating the implementation of recommendations using Azure Automation or integrating with Azure Logic Apps can streamline operational tasks and ensure continuous adherence to best practices.

By leveraging Azure Advisor, organizations can systematically and proactively address potential issues, optimize their resource configurations, and maintain an efficient, secure, and cost-effective Azure environment. The use of Azure Advisor recommendations aligns with maintaining the principles of good cloud governance and operational excellence within the ever-evolving landscape of cloud services.

9.10 Alerting and Notifications

Alerting and notifications are crucial components in the ecosystem of monitoring Azure environments. They enable real-time awareness of issues and facilitate prompt response to potential problems, thereby minimizing downtime and mitigating impact on system performance.

Azure offers a comprehensive alerting system integrated with Azure Monitor, Log Analytics, and other Azure services. This section delves into setting up alerts, configuring notification channels, and best practices for managing alerts effectively.

The first step in establishing an alerting system is to understand the different types of alerts available in Azure:

- **Metric Alerts** monitor specific metrics and trigger alerts based on predefined conditions.
- **Activity Log Alerts** respond to specific activities recorded in the Azure Activity Log.
- **Log Alerts** are generated from queries in Azure Log Analytics.
- **Service Health Alerts** notify users about service issues impacting Azure services.

- **Resource Health Alerts** track the health of individual Azure resources.

Creating a Metric Alert:

Consider a scenario where monitoring the CPU utilization of a virtual machine is necessary. Steps to create a metric alert are as follows:

```
# Define variables
$resourceGroupName = "MyResourceGroup"
$vmName = "MyVM"
$alertName = "HighCPUUtilizationAlert"

# Create a metric alert rule
az monitor metrics alert create `
  --resource-group $resourceGroupName `
  --name $alertName `
  --scopes /subscriptions/xxxxxx/resourceGroups/$resourceGroupName/providers/
      Microsoft.Compute/virtualMachines/$vmName `
  --condition "avg Percentage CPU > 80" `
  --description "Alert if CPU utilization exceeds 80%"
  --window-size 5m `
  --evaluation-frequency 1m `
  --severity 2 `
  --action-group "/subscriptions/xxxxxx/resourceGroups/$resourceGroupName/
      providers/microsoft.insights/actionGroups/MyActionGroup"
```

This command creates a metric alert that triggers if the CPU utilization exceeds 80% over a 5-minute window, evaluated every minute.

Configuring Action Groups:

Action Groups are collections of notification preferences and actions to use across multiple alerts. They can send email notifications, SMS messages, call webhook endpoints, or even invoke Azure Functions.

Creating an Action Group can be illustrated as follows:

```
# Define variables
$resourceGroupName = "MyResourceGroup"
$actionGroupName = "MyActionGroup"
$actionGroupShortName = "MyAG"

# Create an action group
az monitor action-group create `
  --resource-group $resourceGroupName `
  --name $actionGroupName `
  --short-name $actionGroupShortName `
  --action email MyEmailReceiver admin@example.com `
  --action sms MySmsReceiver +1234567890 `
  --action webhook MyWebhookReceiver https://example.com/webhook
```

Creating Log Alerts:

Log alerts are based on Log Analytics queries and can target data from various Azure resources. Here is an example of configuring a log alert to trigger when a specific error code appears in application logs:

```
# Define variables
$resourceGroupName = "MyResourceGroup"
$workspaceName = "MyLogAnalyticsWorkspace"
$alertRuleName = "ErrorCodeAlert"

# Define the query to monitor
$query = "AppEvents | where EventLevel == 'Error' and EventID == '500'"

# Create the log alert rule
az monitor scheduled-query create `
  --resource-group $resourceGroupName `
  --workspace-name $workspaceName `
  --name $alertRuleName `
  --description "Alert for error code 500 in application logs" `
  --query "$query" `
  --action "/subscriptions/xxxxxx/resourceGroups/$resourceGroupName/providers/
      microsoft.insights/actionGroups/MyActionGroup" `
  --severity 3 `
  --frequency "PT5M" `
  --time-window "PT5M"
```

Best Practices for Alert Management:

Effective alert management involves more than just setting up alerts. Follow these best practices to ensure a robust alerting system:

- **Prioritize Alerts:** Assign appropriate severity levels to alerts. For instance, critical system failures should have a high severity level, while informational alerts like backups completion can have lower severity.

- **Avoid Alert Fatigue:** Avoid setting too many alerts that could overwhelm the operators. Focus on actionable alerts that require immediate attention.

- **Review and Tune Regularly:** Periodically review alerts and their thresholds. Adjust based on the evolving patterns in the system's performance and behavior.

- **Use Dynamic Thresholds:** Instead of static thresholds, utilize dynamic thresholds that adapt based on historical metric data. This is particularly useful for environments with varying workloads.

- **Set Up Escalations:** Configure escalation matrices for critical alerts to ensure they are addressed promptly if the initial notifications are not acted upon.

- **Implement Automated Responses:** Where possible, set up automated responses, such as auto-scaling actions or restarting services, to handle alerts without manual intervention.

Implementing these best practices helps maintain a balance between being informed of potential issues and reducing noise from non-critical alerts. This enables efficient utilization of resources and ensures timely response to significant problems.


```
{
  "status": "Succeeded",
  "alertId": "/subscriptions/xxxxxx/resourceGroups/MyResourceGroup/providers/Microsoft.Insights/alerts/HighCPUUtilizationAlert"
}
```


9.11 Implementing Monitoring and Logging Best Practices

Effective monitoring and logging are critical components for maintaining and optimizing an Azure environment. By implementing best practices, organizations can ensure high availability, performance, and security of their applications and services hosted on Azure. This section discusses the key principles and practices to develop and sustain a robust monitoring and logging strategy.

Leverage Azure Monitor

Azure Monitor is a comprehensive solution for collecting, analyzing, and acting on telemetry from both Azure and on-premises environments. Following best practices to maximize its efficacy includes:

- **Centralized Log Management**: Azure Monitor should be the central repository for logs and metrics. Utilize Log Analytics workspaces to store and query data.
- **Data Collection Rules**: Configure data collection rules to ensure that only necessary data is ingested, reducing costs and enhancing performance.
- **Set Up Alerts**: Create alerts for critical conditions based on defined thresholds to proactively manage and resolve issues.
- **Dashboards and Views**: Develop custom dashboards and views within Azure Monitor to provide insights pertinent to different stakeholders.

Implement Structured Logging

Structured logging ensures that application logs are consistently formatted and easily searchable. Key practices include:

- **Consistent Formats**: Use JSON or other structured formats to log messages.
- **Contextual Information**: Include relevant contextual information such as request IDs, user IDs, and timestamps in log entries.
- **Log Levels**: Define and use consistent log levels (e.g., DEBUG, INFO, WARN, ERROR) across all applications to facilitate filtering and querying.

Enable Diagnostic Logging

Azure resources can emit diagnostic logs that provide insights into operations and errors. Best practices for diagnostic logging include:

- **Service-specific Logs**: Enable diagnostic logging for all key Azure services used, such as Azure App Service, Azure SQL Database, and Azure Storage.
- **Log Retention**: Set appropriate retention policies for diagnostic logs to balance storage costs and compliance requirements.
- **Log Streaming**: Stream diagnostic logs to centralized storage or monitoring solutions using Azure Event Hubs, Azure Storage, or third-party tools.

Utilize Application Insights

Application Insights, a feature of Azure Monitor, provides deep insights into application performance and user behavior. To effectively use Application Insights:

- **Instrumentation**: Instrument applications with the Application Insights SDK to collect telemetry data such as request rates, dependencies, exceptions, and trace logs.
- **Custom Events and Metrics**: Define and track custom events and metrics that are specific to the business and application functionality.

- **Performance Counters**: Monitor server and application performance counters to identify bottlenecks and resource constraints.
- **End-to-End Transactions**: Enable end-to-end transaction tracking to follow a request through multiple services and identify performance issues.

Security and Compliance

Monitoring and logging should also account for security and compliance considerations:

- **Secure Storage**: Ensure logs are stored securely and access is restricted based on the principle of least privilege.
- **Compliance**: Address regulatory compliance requirements, such as GDPR or HIPAA, by implementing appropriate logging and monitoring measures.
- **Audit Logs**: Enable and review audit logs regularly to detect unauthorized access or changes to resources.

Automated Monitoring Responses

Automate responses to common alerts to reduce manual intervention and response time:

- **Webhooks and Logic Apps**: Use webhooks or Azure Logic Apps to automate responses such as scaling out infrastructure or restarting services.
- **Self-healing Scripts**: Develop and deploy self-healing scripts that automatically resolve known issues detected through monitoring.
- **Notification Channels**: Configure multiple notification channels (e.g., email, SMS, push notifications) to ensure timely alerts to the right stakeholders.

Continuous Improvement

The monitoring and logging strategy should be revisited and improved regularly:

- **Review and Refine**: Regularly review monitoring data and logs to identify gaps and areas for improvement.
- **Feedback Loop**: Implement a feedback loop where lessons learned from incidents feed into refining monitoring rules and log collection strategies.
- **Training and Awareness**: Train teams on the importance of monitoring and logging best practices, and ensure they are aware of how to access and utilize monitoring data.

Adopting these monitoring and logging best practices in Azure will ensure efficient management, early detection of issues, and regulatory compliance. Implementing them rigorously will enhance the reliability, performance, and security of the Azure environment.

Chapter 10

Case Studies and Best Practices

This chapter presents real-world case studies and best practices for leveraging Azure effectively. It includes examples of migrating legacy applications, implementing CI/CD pipelines, and scaling web applications. The chapter discusses securing data with Azure Key Vault, cost management strategies, and ensuring security and compliance. Additionally, it covers high availability, disaster recovery, performance optimization, and DevOps practices, along with lessons learned from successful Azure implementations and future trends in the Azure ecosystem.

10.1 Introduction to Case Studies

Case studies provide a comprehensive way to understand the practical applications and best practices of using Microsoft Azure. These documented examples offer invaluable insights by illustrating how various organizations have successfully adopted Azure to solve specific challenges, streamline operations, and achieve business goals. By delving into these real-world examples, we can extract lessons that can be applied broadly across industries.

The effective use of Azure requires an understanding of its multitude of services, from cloud storage and virtual machines to sophisticated machine learning and artificial intelligence capabilities. However, it is equally important to appreciate how these services can be integrated and customized to meet particular needs. Through the case studies in this chapter, we will examine different scenarios where Azure's capabilities were leveraged to achieve desired outcomes.

These case studies will cover various domains and use cases. Some will demonstrate the migration of legacy applications to the cloud, highlighting the complexities and strategies involved in such transitions. Others will focus on the implementation of Continuous Integration and Continuous Deployment (CI/CD) pipelines using Azure DevOps, showcasing automation and operational efficiencies. Additionally, we will explore the scaling of web applications and the securing of data using Azure Key Vault.

Migration of Legacy Applications: Many organizations operate legacy systems that are critical to their operations but are inefficient or costly to maintain. Migrating these applications to Azure can provide enhanced flexibility, scalability, and cost savings. We will dissect a detailed case that follows the journey of a legacy application transitioning to Azure, examining the process, challenges encountered, and solutions deployed to overcome these challenges.

Implementation of CI/CD Pipelines: The adoption of CI/CD pipelines is gaining widespread importance as organizations strive for faster and more reliable deployment cycles. By automating the build, test, and deployment processes, Azure DevOps facilitates continuous integration and delivery. We will scrutinize a case study that demonstrates how implementing a CI/CD pipeline transformed an organization's software development lifecycle, contributing to higher efficiency and lower error rates.

Scaling Web Applications: Scalability is a key feature of cloud computing, enabling applications to handle varying loads efficiently. Azure App Services is a robust platform for deploying and scaling web applications. In our examination of this case study, we will explore how a web application was designed, deployed, and scaled using Azure, ensuring high availability and performance to meet user demands.

Securing Data with Azure Key Vault: Security remains a paramount concern in today's digital landscape. Azure Key Vault helps manage secrets, encryption keys, and certificates, thereby safeguarding sensitive data. A case study will illustrate how an organization utilized Azure Key Vault to enhance its data security posture, detailing the configurations and practices that led to compliance with industry regulations.

Furthermore, the best practices discussed in tandem with these case studies will focus on various aspects of effective Azure utilization. These encompass cost management strategies to optimize spending, security measures to protect data, high availability and disaster recovery plans to ensure business continuity, performance optimization techniques, and DevOps practices to streamline development workflows.

To better understand these practices, it is crucial to analyze real-world applications of Azure. This approach not only provides concrete examples but also highlights the flexibility and adaptability of Azure services across different scenarios. For professionals and organizations looking to harness the full potential of Azure, these case studies serve as both a guide and a source of inspiration.

The subsequent sections will delve deeply into these case studies, providing detailed narratives of how challenges were met and goals achieved with Azure. By exploring these examples, readers will acquire a nuanced understanding of the practical considerations and technical implementations that underpin successful Azure deployments. Each case study is chosen to exemplify common issues and creative solutions, thereby equipping the reader with both knowledge and actionable insights.

10.2 Case Study: Migrating a Legacy Application to Azure

The primary objective of migrating a legacy application to Azure is to leverage the benefits of cloud infrastructure, including scalability, reduced operational costs, and improved application performance. This section delineates the step-by-step process involved in the migration of a legacy application to Microsoft Azure, exemplified by a hypothetical e-commerce application named "ShopEase".

Assessment and Planning

Before initiating the migration, it is crucial to conduct a thorough assessment of the existing application. This involves identifying the dependencies, analyzing the current architecture, and understanding the performance requirements. Some tools like the Azure Migrate service can assist in this phase by providing insights and recommendations.

- **Inventory** - Catalog all components of the legacy system, including databases, application servers, web servers, and any third-party integrations.

- **Evaluation** - Assess each component for its compatibility with Azure services. Determine the required Azure resources like Virtual Machines (VMs), Azure App Services, Azure SQL Database, etc.
- **Cost Analysis** - Estimate the cost implications of running the application in Azure. Utilize tools like the Azure Pricing Calculator for this purpose.
- **Migration Strategy** - Define the approach: Rehost (Lift and Shift), Refactor, Rearchitect, Rebuild, or Replace.

Choosing the Migration Strategy

For ShopEase, the Lift and Shift strategy was chosen. This involves moving the application without modification to Azure's Infrastructure as a Service (IaaS).

Preparation

Before migration, the following preparatory steps are executed:

- **Set up an Azure Account** - Ensure that a subscription with sufficient resources is available.
- **Create Resource Groups** - For better management, resource groups such as 'ShopEase-Production' and 'ShopEase-Staging' are created.
- **Network Setup** - Set up a Virtual Network (VNet) to secure communications between Azure resources. A subnet 'ShopEase-Subnet' is also defined.
- **Backups** - Take a complete backup of databases and application files to handle any contingencies.

Migrating the Database

The database migration involves moving the existing on-premises SQL Server database to an Azure SQL Database.

```
-- Example of a database migration script
BACKUP DATABASE ShopEaseDB TO DISK = 'C:\backups\ShopEaseDB.bak'
GO
```

```
-- On Azure SQL Database
RESTORE DATABASE ShopEaseDB FROM DISK = 'https://<your_storage_account
    >.blob.core.windows.net/backups/ShopEaseDB.bak'
WITH MOVE 'ShopEaseDB' TO 'C:\Program Files\Microsoft SQL Server\MSSQL\
    Data\ShopEaseDB.mdf',
MOVE 'ShopEaseDB_log' TO 'C:\Program Files\Microsoft SQL Server\MSSQL\Data\
    ShopEaseDB_log.ldf'
GO
```

Tools like the Data Migration Assistant (DMA) can facilitate this by providing compatibility checks and generating scripts for schema and data migration.

Migrating the Application

The application migration involves moving the application files and configurations from the on-premises server to Azure VMs.

```
# Using AzCopy to transfer application files to Azure Storage
AzCopy /Source:C:\ShopEaseApp /Dest:https://<your_storage_account>.blob.core.
    windows.net/appfiles /DestKey:<storage_account_key> /S
```

After the files are transferred, an Azure VM running the same operating system as the on-premises server is configured. The application files are then deployed onto the VM.

- **VM Creation** - Create an Azure VM with necessary configurations (size, OS, network settings).
- **Software Installation** - Install required software (e.g., .NET Framework) and application dependencies.
- **Deployment** - Deploy the application files to the VM.
- **Configuration** - Update configuration files for any environment-specific settings (e.g., database connection strings).

Testing

Before making the Azure-hosted application live, thorough testing is conducted in the staging environment to ensure functionality.

- **Unit Tests** - Basic functionality of modules.
- **Integration Tests** - Interaction between different modules and services.
- **Performance Tests** - Application performance under anticipated load.

- **Security Tests** - Verification of security measures and compliance.

Validation and Optimization

After the migration, validation involves confirming that the application performs as expected in the Azure environment. Tools like Azure Monitor and Application Insights are employed for monitoring application health and performance.

Go-live and Monitoring

- **DNS Update** - Update DNS records to point to the new Azure-hosted application.
- **Monitoring Setup** - Utilize Azure Monitor to keep track of application health and performance metrics.
- **Optimize** - Continuously optimize the application based on performance data. For example, scaling VM sizes or using Azure App Services for specific components.

```
# Example of monitoring output
INFO: ShopEase app - CPU usage at 15%
INFO: ShopEase app - Memory usage at 45%
INFO: ShopEaseDB - Query response time within acceptable limits
```

This migration case study illustrates the complexities and detailed considerations necessary for successfully transitioning a legacy application to Azure, ensuring efficiency, scalability, and cost-effectiveness.

10.3 Case Study: Implementing a CI/CD Pipeline with Azure DevOps

In this section, we explore the implementation of a Continuous Integration (CI) and Continuous Deployment (CD) pipeline using Azure DevOps. This process involves several stages, from setting up the environment to deploying applications seamlessly. We will walk through each step meticulously, ensuring a comprehensive understanding.

Before diving into the details, we need to prepare an Azure DevOps organization and configure necessary permissions.

Step 1: Setting Up Azure DevOps

First, create an Azure DevOps organization if you do not have one. Navigate to the Azure DevOps portal and sign in using your Microsoft account. Click on *New organization*, name it, and select a region that is closest to your operations for optimal performance.

Next, within your organization, create a new project by clicking on *New Project*, providing a name, and setting visibility options according to your team's requirements. Once the project is created, configure necessary permissions to ensure all team members have appropriate access rights.

Step 2: Repository Setup

We must configure a version control repository where our application's code resides. Azure DevOps supports both Git and Team Foundation Version Control (TFVC), but Git is preferred for its widespread adoption and flexibility.

Create a new Git repository within your Azure DevOps project. Push your application's source code to this repository using the following Git commands:

```
git init
git remote add origin <repository-url>
git add .
git commit -m "Initial commit"
git push -u origin master
```

Step 3: Create a Build Pipeline

Navigate to *Pipelines* in your Azure DevOps project and select *New pipeline*. Connect your repository by choosing *Azure Repos Git*, select your repository, and configure the pipeline using the YAML or classic editor. For a Node.js application, a sample YAML pipeline configuration is as follows:

```
trigger:
- master

pool:
  vmImage: 'ubuntu-latest'

steps:
- task: UseNode@2
  inputs:
    version: '14.x'
- script: |
    npm install
    npm run build
  displayName: 'Install and Build'
- task: ArchiveFiles@2
  inputs:
    rootFolderOrFile: $(Build.BinariesDirectory)
```

```
    includeRootFolder: false
    archiveType: 'zip'
    archiveFile: $(Build.ArtifactStagingDirectory)/$(Build.BuildId).zip
    replaceExistingArchive: true
- publish: $(Build.ArtifactStagingDirectory)/$(Build.BuildId).zip
  artifactName: drop
```

This YAML configuration sets up a pipeline that triggers on every push to the *master* branch, installs Node.js dependencies, builds the application, archives the build artifacts, and publishes them for further use.

Step 4: Create a Release Pipeline

After a successful build, we need to deploy the application. Navigate to *Releases* under *Pipelines* and create a *New release pipeline*. Link it to the build pipeline artifacts created in the previous step by adding an *Artifact*.

Add a stage to the release pipeline representing the deployment environment (e.g., development, staging, production). Configure the deployment job within this stage. For deploying a web application to Azure App Service, use the Azure App Service deploy task:

```
- task: AzureRmWebAppDeployment@4
  inputs:
    ConnectedServiceName: 'AzureServiceConnection'
    WebAppName: 'my-web-app'
    DeployToSlotOrASE: false
    Package: '$(System.DefaultWorkingDirectory)/drop/$(Build.BuildId).zip'
```

This task requires an Azure service connection, which provides the necessary credentials to deploy resources to Azure. Set up this connection in the project settings under *Service connections* by providing your Azure subscription details.

Step 5: Configure CI/CD Triggers and Policies

Ensure your CI/CD pipeline operates seamlessly by configuring triggers and policies. Enable continuous deployment trigger on the release pipeline to initiate deployments upon the completion of a new build.

Set branch policies on the repository's *master* branch to enforce code review practices, such as requiring pull requests with mandatory approvals, ensuring quality before code merges. Define these policies under *Project Settings -> Repositories -> Policies*.

Step 6: Monitoring and Logging

Monitoring and logging are crucial for maintaining the health of your CI/CD processes. Azure DevOps provides built-in logs for build and release pipelines accessible under the *Logs* tab of any pipeline run.

Additionally, integrate Azure Monitor with your deployed resources to gain deeper insights into application performance and diagnostics. Configure Azure Monitor via the Azure portal for your App Service or other deployed resources to capture metrics and logs.

Step 7: Iterative Improvement

Finally, refining the CI/CD pipeline is an iterative process. Review pipeline logs, seek feedback from stakeholders, and continuously integrate improvements. Establish performance baselines and assess deployment frequencies.

Example improvements might include parallelizing jobs to reduce build time or integrating static code analysis tools to enhance code quality.

This detailed implementation walks through the setup of a robust CI/CD pipeline using Azure DevOps, demonstrating the automation of building, testing, and deploying applications efficiently. The integration of version control, automated builds, deployment strategies, and continuous monitoring ensures a streamlined and resilient development workflow.

10.4 Case Study: Scaling a Web Application with Azure App Services

To illustrate the practical implementations of scaling web applications on Azure, let's examine a comprehensive case study involving a hypothetical e-commerce application called ShopSmart. ShopSmart began as a small-scale online marketplace, but rapid growth necessitated a transition to a more scalable architecture. Here, we detail the steps taken to scale ShopSmart using Azure App Services, the challenges faced, the solutions implemented, and the outcomes of this scaling effort.

The initial version of ShopSmart was hosted on a single virtual machine (VM), which sufficed during its infancy. As user traffic surged, performance bottlenecks became apparent, leading to a degraded user experience. The primary challenge was to ensure that the application could handle increased load without sacrificing performance or reliability.

Azure App Services was chosen for its auto-scaling capabilities, integrated load balancing, and ease of management. The move to Azure App Services involved several key steps, which we will discuss in detail:

Step 1: Application and Architecture Analysis

The first step was a thorough analysis of the application architecture. ShopSmart's application stack comprised a .NET Core backend, an Angular frontend, and a SQL Server database. Understanding the dependencies, traffic patterns, and performance metrics was crucial. Profilers and monitoring tools were used to gather data on resource utilization and response times under various loads.

Step 2: Resource Provisioning

Based on the analysis, appropriate resource provisioning was planned. Azure App Services offer various pricing tiers such as Basic, Standard, and Premium. Each tier provides different levels of compute resources, storage, and scaling capabilities. Given the expected load, ShopSmart was initially deployed to the Standard S2 tier, which provided sufficient CPU cores and memory. This tier also supported auto-scaling and ensured high availability.

Step 3: Deploying to Azure App Services

Next, the application code was deployed to Azure App Services. The following example demonstrates the deployment of the .NET Core backend using Azure CLI:

```
az webapp up --name ShopSmartApp --resource-group ShopSmartResourceGroup --plan
    ShopSmartAppServicePlan --runtime "DOTNETCORE|3.1"
```

The command above creates and deploys the application to an Azure App Services plan named ShopSmartAppServicePlan. The –runtime "DOTNETCORE|3.1" parameter specifies the runtime stack required for the application.

Step 4: Configuring Auto-Scaling

Azure App Services provide out-of-the-box auto-scaling based on various metrics such as CPU usage, memory usage, or HTTP request count. Auto-scaling rules were defined to automatically scale out (add instances) or scale in (remove instances) based on shopSmart's traffic patterns. The rules were configured using the Azure Portal for simplicity:

1. Navigate to the App Service in the Azure Portal.
2. Select "Scale out (App Service plan)".
3. Add scaling rules like increasing instance count when average CPU usage exceeds 70% and decreasing when below 50

Step 5: Database Scaling

Scaling the web application also necessitated scaling the database. Azure SQL Database was used in an elastic pool configuration to handle varying loads efficiently. This allowed for seamless resource management across multiple databases, optimizing performance and cost. The following shows setting up an elastic pool:

```
az sql elastic-pool create --resource-group ShopSmartResourceGroup --server
    ShopSmartSqlServer --name ShopSmartPool --dtu 100 --database-dtu-max 20
```

Step 6: Implementing Azure CDN

To further enhance performance, particularly for static assets such as images and scripts, Azure Content Delivery Network (CDN) was integrated. Azure CDN helps by caching content at strategically distributed locations, reducing latency and bandwidth usage. The configuration would involve:

```
az cdn endpoint create --resource-group ShopSmartResourceGroup --profile-name
    ShopSmartCDNProfile --name ShopSmartCDNEndpoint --origin ShopSmartApp.
    azurewebsites.net
```

Step 7: Performance Monitoring and Diagnostics

Monitoring and diagnostics were set up using Azure Monitor and Application Insights. These tools provided real-time insights into application performance, user behavior, and any potential issues. Metrics such as response times, error rates, and dependencies were tracked, and alerts were configured for critical thresholds.

```
az monitor app-insights component create --app ShopSmartInsights --location eastus --
    resource-group ShopSmartResourceGroup --application-type web
```

Application Insights was then incorporated into the application code to collect telemetry data.

Challenges and Solutions

Several challenges emerged during the scaling process:

- **Session Management:** With multiple instances, managing user sessions became complex. Implementing Azure Redis Cache allowed for centralized session storage, ensuring seamless user experiences across different instances.
- **Latency:** Initial latency issues were mitigated through the use of Azure Traffic Manager, which provided geo-distribution and load balancing, directing users to the nearest available instance.

- **Cost Management:** Auto-scaling helped manage costs by scaling resources based on demand, ensuring that only necessary resources were utilized.

Outcomes

The scaling efforts yielded significant improvements. ShopSmart experienced reduced downtime, faster load times, and an enhanced ability to handle traffic spikes. Performance metrics indicated a 40

Continuous monitoring and periodic reviews ensured that the infrastructure remained efficient and cost-effective, adapting to evolving business needs and traffic patterns.

10.5 Case Study: Securing Data with Azure Key Vault

The Azure Key Vault plays an essential role in ensuring the security of sensitive data and secret management in the cloud. This case study explores a scenario where a financial services company needs to protect sensitive data such as API keys, passwords, certificates, and cryptographic keys within Microsoft Azure. We will delve into the steps taken to integrate Azure Key Vault into their workflow, exemplify key operations, and review best practices employed.

Consider a fictitious financial services company, FinCorp, that is migrating its data to Azure. An essential part of this migration is ensuring that sensitive information, such as database passwords and API keys, are securely stored and managed.

Step 1: Creating an Azure Key Vault

First, FinCorp begins by creating an Azure Key Vault. Using the Azure portal or Azure CLI, they create the vault in their resource group.

```
# Using Azure CLI to create a Key Vault
az keyvault create --name FinCorpKeyVault --resource-group FinCorpResourceGroup --
    location eastus
```

Upon execution, this command creates a Key Vault named FinCorpKeyVault in the specified resource group and location.

Step 2: Adding Secrets to the Key Vault

Next, FinCorp needs to store various secrets in their Key Vault. For example, they want to store a database connection string.

```
# Adding a database connection string to the Key Vault
az keyvault secret set --vault-name FinCorpKeyVault --name "DBConnectionString" --
    value "Server=tcp:fincorpdb.database.windows.net,1433;Database=fincorpdb;User
    ID=admin@fincorp;Password=your_password_here;"
```

The above command adds the database connection string which can be securely retrieved by the application.

Step 3: Managing Access with Access Policies

FinCorp needs to configure access policies to ensure only authorized applications and individuals can manage and retrieve secrets from the Key Vault.

```
# Assigning permissions to a user
az keyvault set-policy --name FinCorpKeyVault --upn user@example.com --secret-
    permissions get list set delete
```

This operation grants the specified user permissions to manage secrets in the Key Vault. FinCorp follows the principle of least privilege, ensuring only necessary permissions are granted.

Step 4: Integrating Key Vault with an Application

FinCorp's applications need access to the secrets stored in the Key Vault. They configure their applications to retrieve secrets using the Azure SDK.

```
from azure.keyvault.secrets import SecretClient
from azure.identity import DefaultAzureCredential

credential = DefaultAzureCredential()
key_vault_name = "FinCorpKeyVault"
KVUri = f"https://{key_vault_name}.vault.azure.net"

client = SecretClient(vault_url=KVUri, credential=credential)

retrieved_secret = client.get_secret("DBConnectionString")
print(f"Your DB Connection String is: {retrieved_secret.value}")
```

Using the Azure SDK, the application can securely retrieve the DBConnectionString from the Key Vault. The DefaultAzureCredential class attempts to authenticate using multiple methods, ensuring credentials are handled securely.

Step 5: Automatically Rotating Secrets

Security best practices recommend regular rotation of secrets. FinCorp configures an automation script to rotate their database passwords periodically.

```
import random
import string
from azure.identity import DefaultAzureCredential
from azure.keyvault.secrets import SecretClient

def generate_password(length):
    characters = string.ascii_letters + string.digits + string.punctuation
    return ''.join(random.choice(characters) for i in range(length))

vault_name = "FinCorpKeyVault"
secret_name = "DBConnectionString"
new_password = generate_password(20)

credential = DefaultAzureCredential()
client = SecretClient(vault_url=f"https://{vault_name}.vault.azure.net", credential=
    credential)

new_dsn = f"Server=tcp:fincorpdb.database.windows.net,1433;Database=fincorpdb;
    User ID=admin@fincorp;Password={new_password};"
client.set_secret(secret_name, new_dsn)

print(f"New password set for {secret_name}")
```

The script generates a new secure password and updates the secret in the Key Vault. It ensures the database credentials are never hard-coded or exposed.

Best Practices Implemented

FinCorp adopts several best practices to secure their data effectively:

- Enforcing least privilege access through Key Vault access policies.
- Utilizing Managed Identities for Azure resources to avoid managing credentials manually.
- Regularly rotating secrets to minimize the risk of compromised credentials.
- Leveraging Key Vault diagnostic settings to monitor and track access to the Key Vault.

Key Points of Learning

This case study demonstrates how Azure Key Vault can be effectively integrated into an organization's workflow to manage and secure sensitive information. FinCorp's adoption of robust access control, secure retrieval practices, and automation for secret management highlights the platform's capabilities in enhancing data security within Azure. With these steps, organizations can ensure their sensitive data remains protected against unauthorized access and potential security breaches.

10.6 Best Practices for Cost Management and Optimization

Effective cost management and optimization on Microsoft Azure are crucial for maintaining budgetary control while ensuring that the applications and services perform efficiently. This section will cover various strategies and best practices to manage and optimize costs, leveraging tools and services that Azure provides.

Azure offers several built-in features and tools aimed at cost management. One of the central tools is the Azure Cost Management and Billing service. This service provides comprehensive insights into consumption, spending patterns, and enables budget tracking and forecasting:

```
az costmanagement export create --name "CostManagementExport"
    --type "Usage"
    --timeframe "MonthToDate"
    --exportDataSettings "{'storageAccountId':
    'subscriptions/{subscriptionId}/resourceGroups/{resourceGroupName}
    /providers/Microsoft.Storage/storageAccounts/{storageName}'}"
```

Budgets and Alerts can be configured to ensure that spending does not exceed the predefined limits. Setting up alerts for nearing budget thresholds helps in proactive management:

```
az consumption budget create --amount 1000 --time-grain "Monthly" --name
    "MonthlyBudget" --resource-group "ResourceGroupName" --category "Cost"
    --start-date "2023-01-01T00:00:00Z" --end-date "2023-12-31T23:59:59Z"
```

Reserved Instances and Savings Plans: Azure Reserved Instances are a cost-saving tactic whereby a customer can reserve VM instances for a fixed period (one or three years). This results in substantial cost savings compared to pay-as-you-go pricing. Azure Savings Plans offer flexibility and savings across various services:

- Analyze your workloads to identify long-term requirements.
- Use the Cost Management Advisor to receive recommendations on potential savings by reserving instances.
- Regularly review and adjust your reserved instances to align with changing utilization.

Performance Tiers and Right-Sizing: It is vital to choose the appropriate performance tier for your workload. Overprovisioning results in unnecessary costs, while underprovisioning might affect performance.

- Utilize Azure's Performance Recommendations to ensure your instances are right-sized.
- Monitor performance and usage metrics to scale resources as needed.
- Consider implementing auto-scaling policies for dynamic workloads.

Azure Hybrid Benefit: This benefit allows you to use on-premises Windows Server and SQL Server licenses with Software Assurance to pay a reduced rate on Azure services. This is especially beneficial for enterprises with existing licenses.

Optimizing Storage Costs: Azure Storage offers several options to optimize costs based on access patterns.

- Use the right storage tier: Hot, Cool, or Archive.
- Manage Blob lifecycle policies to automate moving data between tiers.
- Implement data retention policies and regularly audit storage to delete obsolete data.

Cost Allocation and Monitoring:

- Create an appropriate tagging strategy to categorize resources effectively.
- Use resource groups to organize resources and track costs per group.
- Leverage Azure Cost Analysis to visualize and analyze cost data over time.

Example of setting up a cost allocation tag:

```
az resource tag --tags Dept=Finance Project=Migration --resource-id
  /subscriptions/{subscriptionId}/resourceGroups/{resourceGroupName}
```

Scaling and Automating Cost Controls:

Automation can significantly mitigate unexpected costs. Azure Policy and Azure Automation can enforce cost control and governance across your resources.

- Implement policies to enforce cost-saving configurations, such as mandatory usage of reserved instances.
- Use scripts to automate shutdown of non-critical VMs outside business hours:

```
$vmList = az vm list --query "[].{name:name, resourceGroup:resourceGroup}"
   --output tsv
foreach ($vm in $vmList) {
   az vm deallocate -g $vm.resourceGroup -n $vm.name
}
```

These practices, when systematically adopted, help organizations harness the full potential of Azure while keeping costs under control. By employing a combination of tools, policies, and proactive management, enterprises can achieve both efficiency and significant savings in their Azure environment.

10.7 Best Practices for Security and Compliance

The convergence of security protocols and compliance requirements is critical in the deployment and management of applications on Microsoft Azure. This section elaborates on distinct practices designed to fortify an organization's security posture while ensuring compliance with industry standards and regulations.

Azure offers a multi-layered approach to security, extending from infrastructure to application-level safeguards. Mastering these practices is indispensable for maintaining integrity, confidentiality, and availability within your cloud environments.

Identity and Access Management (IAM)

IAM is foundational to security on Azure. Proper identity management ensures that only authorized users have access to resources. Azure Active Directory (Azure AD) is a comprehensive identity as a service (IDaaS) offering that integrates into on-premises infrastructure and SaaS applications.

Consider implementing Multi-Factor Authentication (MFA) as part of your IAM strategy. This extra layer of security necessitates users to verify credentials through two or more methods: something they know (password), something they have (hardware tokens), or something they are (biometrics).

Furthermore, Role-Based Access Control (RBAC) permits granular access policies. With RBAC, you can assign specific permissions to users or groups, ensuring that they only have the level of access required for their role. To enable RBAC, you can use the Azure CLI as shown below:

```
# Assign the 'Reader' role to a user on a specific resource group
az role assignment create \
    --assignee user@domain.com \
    --role Reader \
    --resource-group MyResourceGroup
```

Data Encryption

Data encryption, both at rest and in transit, is paramount in protecting sensitive information. Azure offers various encryption mechanisms. Azure Storage Service Encryption (SSE) encrypts data at rest automatically using Microsoft-managed keys, customer-managed keys stored in Azure Key Vault, or customer-provided keys.

For data in transit, Azure enforces Transport Layer Security (TLS) to encrypt data traveling over the network. Additionally, consider enabling end-to-end encryption in your application layers.

To use Azure Key Vault for managing encryption keys:

```
# Create a Key Vault
az keyvault create --name MyKeyVault --resource-group MyResourceGroup --location
    eastus

# Add a key to the vault
az keyvault key create --vault-name MyKeyVault --name MyKey --protection software
```

Network Security

Establishing a secure network architecture is crucial. Azure provides several tools, such as Network Security Groups (NSGs), Azure Firewall, and Web Application Firewalls (WAFs). NSGs are essential for controlling inbound and outbound traffic to Azure resources.

To implement an NSG rule:

```
# Create a Network Security Group
az network nsg create --resource-group MyResourceGroup --name MyNSG

# Create an inbound rule to allow HTTP traffic
az network nsg rule create --resource-group MyResourceGroup --nsg-name MyNSG \
    --name AllowHTTP --protocol tcp --priority 1000 --destination-port-range 80 \
    --access allow
```

Using Virtual Network (VNet) peering, you can securely connect resources across different VNets. Azure Firewall can help monitor and control traffic, enforcing security rules across the entire deployment.

Securing Applications

Implementing secure development practices is fundamental. Adhere to the Secure Software Development Lifecycle (SSDL) which includes design reviews, threat modeling, code reviews, and security testing.

Utilize Azure Security Center for real-time threat protection and unified security management. Azure Security Center offers continuous assessment and recommendations for strengthening security postures.

To enable Azure Security Center:

```
# Enable Azure Security Center Standard Tier
az security pricing create --name default --tier standard
```

Compliance Management

To ensure compliance with standards such as GDPR, HIPAA, and ISO/IEC 27001, leverage Azure Policy to enforce compliance across your resources. Azure Policy allows you to create, assign, and manage policy definitions.

Example of creating an Azure Policy:

```
# Create a policy definition
az policy definition create --name 'audit-vm-managed-disks' \
    --display-name 'Audit VMs with managed disks' \
    --description 'Audit all VMs that do not use managed disks' \
    --rules '{
      "if": {
        "allOf": [
          {
            "field": "type",
            "equals": "Microsoft.Compute/virtualMachines"
          },
          {
            "field": "Microsoft.Compute/virtualMachines/storageProfile.osDisk.
                 managedDisk.id",
            "exists": "false"
          }
        ]
      },
      "then": {
```

```
        "effect": "audit"
    }
}'\
--mode Indexed
```

Lastly, the Azure Compliance Manager provides a dashboard to track your compliance status and offers recommendations for reaching compliance targets. Implementing these best practices comprehensively will enhance security and assure compliance, catering to the demands of both regulatory bodies and end-users.

10.8 Best Practices for High Availability and Disaster Recovery

High availability (HA) and disaster recovery (DR) are critical components of a robust cloud strategy. In this section, various best practices for ensuring that applications and services remain available and recoverable in the face of failures are discussed. Azure provides a suite of tools and services that facilitate the implementation of HA and DR.

High availability typically refers to the application's ability to operate continuously without failing for a designated period. Disaster recovery is the process of restoring application functionality after a catastrophic event. Both concepts are intertwined and critical for maintaining operational continuity.

1. Design for Failure

When architecting systems on Azure, it is essential to assume that failures will occur. Designing for failure involves creating resilient systems that can withstand and recover from unexpected events. This includes:

- Using multiple Availability Zones (AZs) to distribute resources across isolated data centers.
- Implementing redundant systems and failover mechanisms.
- Ensuring that application components are stateless or able to persist state reliably.

2. Implement Geo-Redundancy

Geo-redundancy involves replicating data and services across different geographic locations. This approach helps protect against regional outages. Azure provides geo-redundant storage (GRS) to ensure your data is preserved across multiple regions. Use:

```
az storage account create --name mystorageaccount --resource-group myresourcegroup --
    location westus --sku Standard_GRS
```

3. Utilize Azure Site Recovery (ASR)

Azure Site Recovery (ASR) orchestrates failover of on-premises and Azure-based applications to restore services during a disaster. ASR allows you to replicate workloads to a secondary location and maintain application consistency. Configuration example:

```
az site-recovery vault create --name myRecoveryVault --resource-group
    myResourceGroup --location eastus
az site-recovery fabric create --vault-name myRecoveryVault --resource-group
    myResourceGroup --name myFabric
```

4. Leverage Load Balancing

Utilize Azure Load Balancer or Azure Application Gateway to distribute network traffic across multiple instances of an application. This approach balances the load, enhances performance, and ensures high availability by rerouting traffic from unhealthy instances to healthy ones. Configuration example:

```
az network lb create --resource-group myResourceGroup --name myLoadBalancer --sku
    Standard --frontend-ip-name myFrontEnd --backend-pool-name myBackEnd
```

5. Implement Automated Backups

Regular, automated backups safeguard data integrity and facilitate recovery. Azure Backup provides scalable solutions for backing up and restoring data. Configuration example for VM backup:

```
az backup vault create --resource-group myResourceGroup --name myBackupVault --
    location eastus
az backup protection enable-for-vm --resource-group myResourceGroup --vault-name
    myBackupVault --vm myVM
```

6. Monitor and Alert

Continuous monitoring and setting up alerts are essential for proactive HA and DR strategies. Azure Monitor, combined with Azure Log Analytics, provides in-depth insights and customizable alerts to identify issues early. Example to create an alert:

```
az monitor metrics alert create --name 'CPU_Alert' --resource-group myResourceGroup
    --scopes myVM --condition "avg Percentage CPU > 80" --description 'Alert for
    high CPU utilization'
```

7. Conduct Regular DR Drills

Perform disaster recovery drills periodically to ensure the efficacy of your DR plan and update it based on findings. Azure allows you to perform non-disruptive testing through ASR, helping to validate the preparedness without affecting production workloads.

8. Utilize Automated Scaling

Auto-scaling ensures that your application can handle load fluctuations and remain available during spikes in demand. Azure Autoscale can be configured to scale out or in based on defined metrics. Configuration example:

```
az monitor autoscale create --resource-group myResourceGroup --name myAutoscale --
    min-count 1 --max-count 5 --count 2
az monitor autoscale rule create --resource-group myResourceGroup --autoscale-name
    myAutoscale --condition "Percentage CPU > 70" --scale out 1
```

9. Employ Network Security Practices

Secure your network to prevent breaches that can lead to downtime. Using services like Azure DDoS Protection, Network Security Groups (NSGs), and ensuring secure access with Azure Bastion significantly bolster network security, thus contributing to HA and DR.

10. Optimize Database Performance and Reliability

Use Azure SQL Database's built-in high availability options, such as zone redundant databases and failover groups. These features ensure resilience and minimal downtime for your databases. Example configuration for a failover group:

```
az sql failover-group create --name myFailoverGroup --resource-group
    myResourceGroup --server myPrimaryServer --partner-server mySecondaryServer
    --failover-policy Automatic
```

By integrating these best practices within your Azure environment, you can ensure high availability and effective disaster recovery, thereby maintaining the continuity and reliability of your services.

10.9 Best Practices for Scaling and Performance

Effective scaling and performance optimization are critical for applications hosted on Microsoft Azure to ensure reliability, responsiveness, and efficient resource utilization. This section delves into the fundamental best practices to achieve optimal scaling and performance, leveraging various Azure services and configurations.

Auto-scaling with Azure Virtual Machines

Utilizing Auto-scaling capabilities in Azure Virtual Machines (VMs) ensures that your application can handle varying load conditions by dynamically allocating resources. The configuration of auto-scaling policies involves setting thresholds for CPU usage, memory usage, and other performance metrics.

```
# Create a VM scale set
az vmss create --resource-group myResourceGroup --name myScaleSet --image
    UbuntuLTS --upgrade-policy-mode automatic --admin-username azureuser --
    generate-ssh-keys

# Update auto-scaling rules
az monitor autoscale create --resource-group myResourceGroup --resource myScaleSet --
    resource-type Microsoft.Compute/virtualMachineScaleSets --name autoscaleRule1
    --min-count 1 --max-count 10 --count 2

az monitor autoscale rule create --resource-group myResourceGroup --autoscale-name
    autoscaleRule1 --condition "Percentage CPU > 70 avg 5m" --scale out 1

az monitor autoscale rule create --resource-group myResourceGroup --autoscale-name
    autoscaleRule1 --condition "Percentage CPU < 30 avg 5m" --scale in 1
```

Leveraging Azure App Service Auto-Scaling

Azure App Services offers built-in auto-scaling that can respond to changes in demand without manual intervention. Configuring the auto-scaling rules can be performed through the Azure portal or using Azure Resource Manager (ARM) templates. Here is an example configuration:

```
{
  "resources": [
    {
      "type": "Microsoft.Insights/autoscalesettings",
      "apiVersion": "2015-04-01",
      "location": "[resourceGroup().location]",
      "name": "autoscale",
      "properties": {
        "profiles": [
          {
            "name": "defaultProfile",
            "capacity": {
              "minimum": "1",
              "maximum": "10",
              "default": "1"
            },
            "rules": [
              {
                "metricTrigger": {
                  "metricName": "CpuPercentage",
```

```
                "metricNamespace": "",
                "metricResourceUri": "[resourceId('Microsoft.Web/sites', variables('
                    appServiceName'))]",
                "timeGrain": "PT1M",
                "statistic": "Average",
                "timeWindow": "PT5M",
                "timeAggregation": "Average",
                "operator": "GreaterThan",
                "threshold": 70
              },
              "scaleAction": {
                "direction": "Increase",
                "type": "ChangeCount",
                "value": "1",
                "cooldown": "PT5M"
              }
            },
            {
              "metricTrigger": {
                "metricName": "CpuPercentage",
                "metricNamespace": "",
                "metricResourceUri": "[resourceId('Microsoft.Web/sites', variables('
                    appServiceName'))]",
                "timeGrain": "PT1M",
                "statistic": "Average",
                "timeWindow": "PT5M",
                "timeAggregation": "Average",
                "operator": "LessThan",
                "threshold": 30
              },
              "scaleAction": {
                "direction": "Decrease",
                "type": "ChangeCount",
                "value": "1",
                "cooldown": "PT5M"
              }
            }
          ]
        }
      ]
    }
  }
 ]
}
```

Azure Traffic Manager for Load Balancing

Azure Traffic Manager is a DNS-based traffic load balancer that enables you to distribute traffic optimally to services across global Azure regions while providing high availability and responsiveness. Configuring Traffic Manager involves creating Traffic Manager profiles and defining routing methods such as performance, priority, and geographical.

```
# Create a Traffic Manager profile
az network traffic-manager profile create --name myTrafficManagerProfile --resource-
    group myResourceGroup --routing-method Performance --unique-dns-name myapp

# Add endpoints to the Traffic Manager profile
```

```
az network traffic-manager endpoint create --resource-group myResourceGroup --profile-
    name myTrafficManagerProfile --name myEndpoint1 --type azureEndpoints --
    target-resource-id /subscriptions/{subscription-id}/resourceGroups/{resource-
    group}/providers/Microsoft.Web/sites/{app-service-name} --endpoint-status
    enabled

az network traffic-manager endpoint create --resource-group myResourceGroup --profile-
    name myTrafficManagerProfile --name myEndpoint2 --type azureEndpoints --
    target-resource-id /subscriptions/{subscription-id}/resourceGroups/{resource-
    group}/providers/Microsoft.Web/sites/{app-service-name} --endpoint-status
    enabled
```

Optimizing Database Performance with Azure SQL Database

Azure SQL Database includes built-in capabilities for performance tuning and scaling. Applying features such as query performance insights, index optimization, and elastic pools ensures that databases can handle varying workloads efficiently.

```
-- Query to identify long-running queries
SELECT TOP 10
    qt.text AS [SQLText],
    qs.execution_count,
    qs.total_worker_time AS [TotalCPU],
    qs.total_elapsed_time AS [TotalDuration],
    qs.total_logical_reads AS [TotalLogicalReads],
    qs.total_physical_reads AS [TotalPhysicalReads],
    qs.creation_time
FROM
    sys.dm_exec_query_stats AS qs
    CROSS APPLY sys.dm_exec_sql_text(qs.sql_handle) AS qt
ORDER BY
    qs.total_worker_time DESC;
```

```
# Create an Elastic Pool
az sql elastic-pool create --resource-group myResourceGroup --server myServer --name
    myElasticPool --dtu 50 --database-dtu-max 20 --database-dtu-min 0

# Add databases to the Elastic Pool
az sql db create --resource-group myResourceGroup --server myServer --name
    myDatabase1 --elastic-pool myElasticPool

az sql db create --resource-group myResourceGroup --server myServer --name
    myDatabase2 --elastic-pool myElasticPool
```

Using Caching for Performance Enhancement

Integrating a caching layer, such as Azure Cache for Redis, helps reduce latency and decrease the load on databases by storing frequently accessed data in-memory. Configuring caching involves creating a Redis cache instance and implementing caching logic within the application.

```
# Create a Redis Cache
az redis create --name myRedisCache --resource-group myResourceGroup --location
    eastus --sku Basic --vm-size C1
```

Example of using Azure Redis Cache in a .NET application:

```
using StackExchange.Redis;

ConnectionMultiplexer redis = ConnectionMultiplexer.Connect("myRedisCache.redis.
    cache.windows.net,password=myPassword,ssl=True,abortConnect=False");
IDatabase cache = redis.GetDatabase();

// Storing data in cache
cache.StringSet("key1", "value1");

// Retrieving data from cache
string value = cache.StringGet("key1");
```

Adhering to these best practices for scaling and performance ensures that your applications on Azure remain robust, responsive, and capable of handling peak loads efficiently. These approaches leverage Azure's comprehensive suite of services, providing a scalable and optimized environment for diverse application needs.

10.10 Best Practices for DevOps and Agile Development

DevOps and Agile development methodologies have become integral to modern application development and deployment strategies. Leveraging Azure services effectively within these methodologies requires adhering to certain best practices. This section delves into these practices to ensure efficient, scalable, and secure development processes.

Adopting **Infrastructure as Code (IaC)** is a pivotal best practice in DevOps. IaC involves managing and provisioning computing infrastructure through machine-readable definition files, rather than through physical hardware configuration or interactive configuration tools. Azure offers tools such as Azure Resource Manager (ARM) Templates, Terraform, and Pulumi to facilitate IaC. By defining infrastructure configurations in code, teams can ensure consistency across different environments, automate infrastructure provisioning, and improve traceability.

```
resource "azurerm_resource_group" "example" {
  name = "example-resources"
  location = "West US"
}

resource "azurerm_storage_account" "example" {
  name = "examplesa"
  resource_group_name = azurerm_resource_group.example.name
  location = azurerm_resource_group.example.location
```

```
  account_tier = "Standard"
  account_replication_type = "LRS"
}
```

Continuous Integration (CI) and Continuous Deployment (CD) form the backbone of modern DevOps practices. Azure DevOps Services provides comprehensive CI/CD capabilities that facilitate automated building, testing, and deploying applications. Integrating CI/CD pipelines into the development lifecycle ensures that code changes are consistently tested and deployed, reducing the chances of errors and enabling rapid delivery of features and fixes.

In a CI/CD pipeline, it is crucial to prioritize **Automated Testing**. Implementing extensive and comprehensive automated test suites, including unit tests, integration tests, and end-to-end tests, ensures that code changes do not introduce bugs or regressions. Tools such as Azure Pipelines can be configured to execute these tests automatically at each stage of the CI/CD process.

```
trigger:
- main

pool:
  vmImage: "ubuntu-latest"

jobs:
- job: Build_and_Test
  steps:
  - task: UsePythonVersion@0
    inputs:
      versionSpec: '3.x'
  - script: |
      pip install -r requirements.txt
      python -m unittest discover
    displayName: 'Run unit tests'
```

DevOps and Agile development emphasize the importance of **Monitoring and Feedback**. Continuous monitoring of applications and infrastructure is essential to understand performance, detect anomalies, and mitigate issues promptly. Azure Monitor and Application Insights provide extensive monitoring capabilities, enabling teams to gather telemetry data, set up alerts, and visualize performance metrics. Integrating monitoring data back into the CI/CD pipeline can provide actionable feedback, allowing teams to improve and optimize their applications iteratively.

Implementing **Canary Deployments** and **Blue-Green Deployments** are best practices for minimizing the risk associated with deploying new changes. In a canary deployment, a new version of an application is gradually rolled out to a subset of users before deploying it more widely. Whereas in a blue-green deployment, two identical production environments referred to as Blue and Green are maintained. The new version is deployed to the inactive environment and then traffic is switched to it. Azure App Service and Traffic Manager can be used to facilitate these deployment strategies, reducing downtime and ensuring a seamless user experience.

Configuration Management is another critical aspect. Ensuring that application configurations are managed properly can prevent configuration drift and make deployments more predictable. Azure provides several tools such as Azure Automation, Azure Policy, and Azure Blueprints to help manage configurations, enforce compliance, and deploy environments consistently.

```
Get-AzureRmAutomationAccount -ResourceGroupName "MyResourceGroup" -Name "
    MyAutomationAccount"

Start-AzureRmAutomationRunbook -AutomationAccountName "
    MyAutomationAccount" -Name "MyRunbookName"
```

Additionally, **Security and Compliance** should be integrated into every phase of the development and deployment lifecycle. DevSecOps extends the DevOps practices by embedding security practices into the CI/CD pipelines. Azure DevOps provides extensions such as Azure Security Center and OWASP ZAP for security assessments, vulnerability scanning, and compliance checks, ensuring that security is not an afterthought but a continuous process.

Collaboration and Communication are central to Agile development and DevOps. Utilizing tools such as Azure Boards for work item tracking, Azure Repos for source control, and integrating with communication platforms like Microsoft Teams can enable seamless collaboration across distributed teams, enhancing productivity and maintaining workflow transparency.

The practice of **Continuous Improvement** is fundamental to Agile methodologies. Teams should regularly conduct retrospectives, analyze performance metrics, and seek feedback to identify areas for improvement. Leveraging Azure DevOps analytics and reporting capabilities can help in capturing vital information to drive these improvement initiatives. Adhering to these best practices helps in fostering a robust, agile, and automated development and deployment pipeline, which is essential for delivering high-quality software applications on the Azure platform.

10.11 Lessons Learned from Real-world Azure Implementations

Implementing solutions on Microsoft Azure comes with its own set of challenges and opportunities. Numerous organizations have undertaken this journey, and their experiences provide valuable insights into making the most out of Azure's capabilities. This section delves into critical lessons learned from real-world implementations across various industries.

One of the primary lessons learned is the significance of thorough planning and assessment before migration. Migrating applications to Azure or developing new ones within the cloud environment requires comprehensive planning, which includes evaluating the existing infrastructure, identifying dependencies, and analyzing the cost implications. Planning should also involve a clear understanding of the scalability requirements and performance benchmarks.

Another key lesson is the fundamental importance of automation. Organizations that successfully leverage Azure often utilize automation extensively to manage resources efficiently. Tools such as Azure Resource Manager (ARM) templates, PowerShell scripts, and Azure CLI can automate resource deployment and management, significantly reducing the chances of human errors and ensuring consistent configurations.

```
# Create a resource group
az group create --name MyResourceGroup --location eastus
```

Equally important is the implementation of robust monitoring and logging mechanisms. Azure provides various tools like Azure Monitor, Application Insights, and Log Analytics, which are essential for maintaining visibility over the deployed infrastructure. These monitoring tools aid in detecting, diagnosing, and remedying issues promptly.

```
Output of Azure Monitor logs:
------------------------------------
Timestamp      Resource      Status
2023-02-15     VM1           Healthy
2023-02-15     DBServer1     Unresponsive
2023-02-15     WebApp1       Healthy
```

Security, often highlighted by many organizations, must be an integral part of the deployment strategy from the outset. Azure's comprehensive security features, including Azure Security Center, Azure Key Vault, and advanced threat protection mechanisms, should be leveraged to safeguard data and applications. Utilizing these tools can provide real-time security alerts and recommendations for mitigation.

A significant lesson in resource management is the necessity of cost optimization. Azure offers several cost management tools, such as Azure Cost Management + Billing, which can help track expenses and optimize resource usage. Practices such as using reserved instances, right-sizing virtual machines, and eliminating idle resources can lead to substantial cost savings without compromising performance.

Customizing and optimizing network configurations is another critical area of focus. Properly configured networks, using Virtual Networks (VNets), Network Security Groups (NSGs), and Azure Firewall, ensure secure and efficient communication between services. Misconfigurations can lead to bottlenecks or vulnerabilities that compromise performance and security.

High availability and disaster recovery are integral to the reliability of services hosted on Azure. Leveraging Azure's native capabilities, such as Availability Sets, Availability Zones, and Azure Site Recovery, ensures that applications remain resilient against failures. Implementing these strategies requires an understanding of how to design fault-tolerant applications and execute regular disaster recovery drills.

```
# Set up Azure Site Recovery
az recovery-services vault create --name MyRecoveryServicesVault --resource-group
    MyResourceGroup --location eastus
az recovery-services vault backup-properties set --vault-name MyRecoveryServicesVault
    --backup-storage-redundancy LocallyRedundant
```

Performance optimization emerges as a recurring theme in successful Azure implementations. Organizations stressed the importance of regular performance testing and tuning. Services like Azure Load Testing and tools for analyzing performance metrics can identify potential bottlenecks. Adjusting service plans and implementing caching strategies, such as using Azure Cache for Redis, can lead to significant performance gains.

Lastly, the adoption of DevOps practices has been a game-changer for many organizations utilizing Azure. Employing Azure DevOps for continuous integration and continuous deployment (CI/CD) has streamlined development workflows, improved code quality, and accelerated delivery cycles.

```
trigger:
- main

pool:
```

```
  vmImage: 'ubuntu-latest'

steps:
- task: UseDotNet@2
  inputs:
    packageType: 'sdk'
    version: '5.x'
- script: dotnet build --configuration Release
  displayName: 'Build project'
- task: AzureWebApp@1
  inputs:
    azureSubscription: 'AzureSubscription'
    appName: 'MyWebApp'
    package: '$(System.DefaultWorkingDirectory)/bin/Release/app.zip'
```

Real-world implementations reinforce that leveraging best practices and lessons learned from others can significantly ease the journey of adopting Azure technologies. The insights provided by these organizations serve as a blueprint for effective and efficient Azure deployments.

10.12 Future Trends and Innovations in Azure

Microsoft Azure continues to evolve rapidly, driven by advances in cloud computing technologies, artificial intelligence, and the increasing need for scalable and secure infrastructure. This section examines emerging trends and innovations that are likely to shape the future of Azure services, offering insights into how these developments can be leveraged for advanced cloud solutions.

Serverless Computing: One of the most significant trends in cloud computing is serverless architecture, where application developers can focus solely on code without managing the underlying infrastructure. Azure Functions and Azure Logic Apps are pivotal in this domain. Azure Functions allow for the execution of code in response to triggers, reducing the overhead of managing server resources. As serverless computing matures, we can expect further enhancements in terms of cold start reduction, advanced debugging, and wider language support.

```
import logging
import azure.functions as func

def main(req: func.HttpRequest) -> func.HttpResponse:
    logging.info('Python HTTP trigger function processed a request.')

    name = req.params.get('name')
    if not name:
        try:
```

```
            req_body = req.get_json()
        except ValueError:
            pass
        else:
            name = req_body.get('name')

    if name:
        return func.HttpResponse(f"Hello, {name}!")
    else:
        return func.HttpResponse(
             "Please pass a name on the query string or in the request body",
             status_code=400
        )
```

Artificial Intelligence and Machine Learning: Azure AI and Machine Learning services continue to expand, making it easier to integrate sophisticated models into applications. Future advancements will likely focus on enhancing the performance and capabilities of services like Azure Cognitive Services, Azure Machine Learning, and Bot Service. The trend towards AutoML (Automated Machine Learning) will further democratize AI by automating the time-consuming aspects of model development.

```
from azureml.core import Workspace, Dataset
from azureml.train.automl import AutoMLConfig
from azureml.core.experiment import Experiment

ws = Workspace.from_config()
# Access the dataset
dataset = Dataset.get_by_name(ws, name='my-dataset')
# Configure AutoML
automl_config = AutoMLConfig(
    task='classification',
    primary_metric='AUC_weighted',
    training_data=dataset,
    label_column_name='target_column',
    iterations=100)
# Create Experiment
experiment = Experiment(ws, "automl-classification")
# Submit Experiment
run = experiment.submit(automl_config)
```

Edge Computing: As IoT devices proliferate, the importance of edge computing grows. Azure IoT Edge enables the deployment of cloud workloads directly on IoT devices. This reduces latency and allows for real-time data processing closer to the data source. Future trends suggest improvements in the management and orchestration of edge devices, making them more autonomous and secure.

Quantum Computing: A groundbreaking area of research and development in Azure is quantum computing. Azure Quantum provides a cloud service enabling researchers and developers to explore quantum algorithms. As quantum computing matures, it is expected to revolutionize fields such as cryptography, material science, and complex system simulations.

```
from azure.quantum import Workspace
from azure.quantum.target.microsoft import MicrosoftEstimator

workspace = Workspace (
    resource_id = "/subscriptions/XXXXX/resourceGroups/XXXXX/providers/
        Microsoft.Quantum/workspaces/XXXXX",
    location = "XXXXX"
)

estimator = MicrosoftEstimator(
    workspace=workspace,
    target = "microsoft.estimator"
)

# Here, you would include the Q# code or specify the quantum simulator details
cost_estimate = estimator.estimate_cost(quantum_circuit)
print(f"Estimated cost: {cost_estimate}")
```

Hybrid and Multi-Cloud Environments: Enterprises are increasingly adopting hybrid and multi-cloud strategies to leverage the best features of different cloud providers. Azure Arc allows for extending Azure management and services to any location, including on-premises and other cloud platforms. Future innovations will likely enhance seamless integration, unified management, and advanced security features across diverse environments.

Enhanced Security Features: With the rise of cyber threats, Azure's security posture continues to strengthen. Innovations like Azure Confidential Computing provide secure enclaves for running sensitive workloads. Enhancements in AI-driven threat detection and response are expected, offering more robust and proactive security measures.

Sustainability Initiatives: Microsoft has committed to substantial sustainability goals, including making Azure data centers carbon-negative. Future trends in this area will encompass innovations in energy-efficient computing, use of renewable energy sources, and technologies that optimize resource usage for reducing the carbon footprint of cloud computing.

Integration with Emerging Technologies: Azure's future will likely see deeper integration with emerging technologies like blockchain, 5G, and advanced analytics. Azure Blockchain Service aids in constructing, managing, and growing blockchain networks in a unified manner, making it simpler to integrate distributed ledger technology with existing applications. The advent of 5G will enable more robust support for high-speed, low-latency applications across the Azure ecosystem.

Advanced Developer Tools and Services: Enhancements in Azure DevOps and the introduction of new developer tools will continue to empower software development teams. We anticipate more advanced CI/CD capabilities, improved developer experience, and deeper integration with other Microsoft services, such as GitHub, which will streamline the development lifecycle.

Future trends and innovations in Azure point towards a highly integrated and intelligent ecosystem, driven by advances in AI, automation, edge and quantum computing, security, and sustainability. Azure aims to provide versatile and resilient cloud solutions that cater to emerging technological needs and industry standards.

Made in the USA
Monee, IL
05 November 2026

67911512R00193